D0560693

PENGUIN PLAYS

PL 32

NEW ENGLISH DRAMATISTS

NEW
ENGLISH DRAMATISTS

THREE PLAYS
INTRODUCED AND EDITED BY
E. MARTIN BROWNE

EACH HIS OWN WILDERNESS
Doris Lessing

THE HAMLET OF STEPNEY GREEN
Bernard Kops

CHICKEN SOUP WITH BARLEY
Arnold Wesker

PENGUIN BOOKS

Penguin Books Ltd, Harmondsworth, Middlesex

AUSTRALIA: Penguin Books Pty Ltd, 762 Whitehorse Road,
Mitcham, Victoria

Made and printed in Great Britain
by Unwin Brothers Ltd,
Woking and London

CONTENTS

INTRODUCTION   7

EACH HIS OWN WILDERNESS   11
    Doris Lessing

THE HAMLET OF STEPNEY GREEN   97
    Bernard Kops

CHICKEN SOUP WITH BARLEY   173
    Arnold Wesker

INTRODUCTION

THIS is a book not only of promise but of significance in itself. The British Theatre has for too long been stuck in a rut, dug partly by those who insisted on everyone adhering to the commercially saleable, because familiar, form of the realistic three-act play, and more deeply by those who banned a considerable amount of what goes on in real life from being shown in the theatre. I do not only, or even chiefly, mean the Lord Chamberlain: he is a barometer of public opinion, and more often than not a useful one. I mean those who go to the theatre wanting to see only the class of life they know, and those who do not go but wish to make sure that this art, which at some times in history has been the means of bringing new ideas to birth, shall not do so in ours.

The result has been a theatre which has not been as much alive as its mechanical offspring the cinema, the radio, and television. But this book will prove that a new generation of dramatists has come into it whose work, whatever else there is to say against it, is alive, very much alive. No one can be bored by any of the plays in this collection.

Doris Lessing is the oldest of the three dramatists – she is 38. Born in Persia, she spent her childhood in Southern Rhodesia and came to England only in 1949. She brought with her her first novel, THE GRASS IS SINGING. This sold over 20,000 copies. Since then she has published eight books and become one of our leading writers. She has not worked in the theatre, but intends to continue writing plays; her first attempt at the medium, MR DOLINGER, was performed at the Oxford Playhouse early in 1958, and EACH HIS OWN WILDERNESS was given at the Royal Court Theatre, London, later in the same year.

The mention of these two theatres leads me to turn for a moment from the plays to the managements who put them on. There has been a general recognition of our lack of playwrights, and a general desire to give new playwrights a chance. Several of the repertory theatres, and Theatre Workshop at Stratford in the East End of London, have done useful work in staging new plays from time to time, as has the amateur Questors Theatre at Ealing. But the theatre which has devoted itself, as its main task, to the finding and production of a new race of dramatists is the Royal Court Theatre, Sloane Square, London. This was once the home of Granville-Barker, in the days when he produced many of G.B.S.'s finest plays. The English Stage Company was established there little more than two years ago under the direction of George Devine with the primary object of giving an opportunity to new dramatists; and it has done a large number of new plays both for short runs and on Sunday nights 'without décor'. It has succeeded remarkably well in creating a sense of freedom from the restrictions of the commercial theatre, and thanks to its early discovery of John Osborne, a hugely successful dramatist of the same generation as those represented in this book, it has been able to give continuing opportunities to many others. Such an enterprise has plenty of growing pains, but they serve to afford evidence, if that were needed, that it *is* growing.

To return to Miss Lessing's play, EACH HIS OWN WILDERNESS: like the others, it is full of turbulent life, the centre of which is a middle-aged Liberal, free-thinking, free-living woman. Myra Bolton ends by selling the house that is the one thing her son loves and relies on, so that she may be free and so that he may be free too: but he doesn't want that freedom. The most striking of many things that are remarkable about this play is that under the stress of our tumultuous age the young couple come in the end to want stability more than anything else:

> Never in the whole history of the world have people made a battle-cry out of being ordinary. Never. Supposing we all said to the politicians – we refuse to be heroic. We refuse to be brave. We are bored with all the noble gestures . . .; leave us alone, we'll say. Leave us alone to live . . .

And over against them in a conflict which rings true on both sides, stands Myra, still determined to take chances:

> I don't propose to keep my life clutched in my hand like small change . . .

The other two authors are both Jewish, and write about Jewish life. Bernard Kops was born in Stepney Green in 1926 of working-class parents and grew up in poverty. He had started early to write descriptions of what he saw about him: and by following a variety of occupations managed to make time for writing. For a while he worked in a fit-up company; he is the only one of the three who has had any experience of the stage. After his mother died in 1951, he went abroad, working as a docker and a labourer; returned to England penniless, sold his poems in the street, met his wife whom he married in Stepney Green; and created there THE HAMLET OF STEPNEY GREEN, his first play. It won him an Arts Council award of £500; was accepted for production in Germany, Holland, and

America as well as at the Oxford Playhouse. He now occupies the unique position of Resident Dramatist at the Bristol Old Vic, which is doing his new play THE DREAM OF PETER MANN during the 1958–9 season.

THE HAMLET OF STEPNEY GREEN is Jewish folk-drama, a play with songs in the manner popular in the last century. The traditions of the Jewish community are shown influencing the contemporary life which it lives in the full-blooded way characteristic of it. Kops is not afraid to exploit the supernatural elements in Jewish thought, to the great enlargement of his play; 'Hamlet's' father plays the principal part, and is specially effective when he is a ghost, in Acts II and III. The link between the crooner-son and Hamlet the Dane is rather tenuous: it is the author's link, not the character's, and its value lies in the measure of disengagement which it affords to a writer using material so close to his personal life. It also serves to give the play certain satiric overtones, which, added to its humour and depth of feeling, make it an attractive piece of work.

The third play in this volume is by Arnold Wesker. Born in 1932, he also comes from the East End of London. He worked as plumber's mate and kitchen porter until he finally acquired a trade, that of pastry-cook. In that capacity he worked for four years in kitchens in Norwich, London, and Paris. Then he went to the London School of Film Technique, where he wrote CHICKEN SOUP WITH BARLEY. It was first performed at the new Belgrade Theatre, Coventry, and then at the Royal Court, where it is to go into the repertory.

Again the vitality of the Jewish people fills the stage. There is a gallant woman of middle age, very different from Myra Bolton, but like her the centre of the play's action. It spans twenty years, and traces the disintegration of Sarah Kahn's husband; no details of the painful story are spared, but it is told with a sympathy which compels one to share it. The play has another aspect of peculiar interest; here is shown for the first time on a stage the disillusionment of British Communists by the development of Russian power-politics. Wesker's parents are Jewish-Hungarian and Russian, and the play doubtless reflects the tragic emotions of his own family. It is not sombre, however, but full of humour and warmth.

I hope that this collection may be the first of several in which these and other young British dramatists may be introduced to Penguin readers.

London, 1958

DORIS LESSING

Each His Own Wilderness

EACH HIS OWN WILDERNESS

First presented by The English Stage Society, at The Royal Court Theatre, London, on 23 March 1958, with the following cast:

TONY BOLTON	Colin Jeavons
MYRA BOLTON	Valerie Taylor
SANDY BOLES	Philip Bond
MIKE FERRIS	Vernon Smythe
PHILIP DURRANT	Ewen MacDuff
ROSEMARY	Sarah Preston
MILLY BOLES	Patricia Burke

Directed by John Dexter

SCENE

The hall of Myra Bolton's house in London

CHARACTERS OF THE PLAY

MYRA BOLTON *a middle-aged woman.*
TONY BOLTON *her son, aged 22.*
MILLY BOLES *a middle-aged woman, Myra's friend.*
SANDY BOLES *Milly's son, aged 22.*
MIKE FERRIS *an elderly Left Wing politician.*
PHILIP DURRANT *a middle-aged architect.*
ROSEMARY *a young girl engaged to Philip.*

ACT ONE

SCENE I

Before the curtain rises, an H-bomb explosion. CURTAIN UP *on the sound of blast. Silence. Machine-gun fire. The explosion again. These sounds come from tape-recording machine which has been left running.*

This is the hall of MYRA BOLTON'S *house in London, stairs ascending L back. Door L into living-room. Door R which is entrance from street. Window R looking into garden at front of the house.*

The essential furniture is a divan close to the foot of the stairs. A cupboard in the wall. A mirror. Odd chairs. A small radio.

Everything is extremely untidy: there are files, piles of newspapers, including the New Statesman, *posters lying about inscribed* BAN THE BOMB, WE WANT LIFE NOT DEATH, *etc. A typewriter on the floor. The radio is playing tea-room music behind the war-noises from the tape-recorder.*

After the second explosion TONY BOLTON *comes in R. He is in Army uniform and has this day finished his Army service. He is a dark, lightly built, rather graceful youth, attractive and aware of it, but uneasy and on the defensive in the same way and for the same reasons as an adolescent girl who makes herself attractive as a form of self-assertion but is afraid when the attention she draws is more than gently chivalrous. His concern for his appearance is also due to the longing for the forms of order common to people who have never known order. He is at bottom deeply uneasy, tense and anxious, fluctuating between the good manners of those who use manners as a defence, the abrupt rudeness of the very young, and a plaintive, almost querulous appeal.*

He stands looking at the disorder in the room, first ironically and then with irritation. As the music reaches a climax of bathos, he rushes to radio and turns it off.

TONY: What a mess. God, what a mess!

[*The sound of an H-bomb explosion gathering strength on the tape-*

*recorder. He turns to stare, appalled. Listens. Switches it off at ex-
plosion. There is a sudden complete silence.* TONY *breathes it in.
He passes his hands over his hair, his eyes. He opens his eyes. He
is staring at the window. Sunlight streams across the floor. He dives
at the window, draws the curtains, making a half-dark, goes to divan,
lets himself fall limp across it. A moment's complete silence.*

The telephone rings.]

[*querulously*] Oh, no, no, no. [*leaps up, goes to telephone*] Yes. It's
me, Tony. No, I'm not on leave. I don't know where my
mother is. I haven't seen her yet. Yes, Philip. I'll tell her. Who
did you say? Who's Rosemary? O.K. [*lets receiver fall back and
returns to divan, where he lies as before, eyes closed*].

[MYRA'S VOICE *upstairs, singing:* Boohoo, you've got me crying
for you.]

MYRA'S VOICE: Where are you, darling? [*continues singing*].

[*She comes into sight at head of the stairs. A good-looking woman of
about 45 or 50, and at the moment looking her age. She is wearing
bagged trousers and a sweat-shirt. She peers down into the half-lit hall
from the top of the stairs, and slowly comes down.*]

TONY [*languidly*]: Well, Mother, how are you?

MYRA: Tony! You might have let me know. [*She rushes at the window, pulls back the curtains, turns to look at him, the sunlight behind
her.*]

TONY [*shading his eyes*]: Do we have to have that glare?

MYRA: Have you got leave?

TONY [*without moving*]: I didn't imagine it was necessary to remind
you of the date my National Service finished.

MYRA: Oh, I see.

TONY: But, of course, if my coming is in any way inconvenient to
you, I'll go away again.

MYRA [*stares and then laughs*]: Oh, Tony . . . [*rushes across at him*].
Come on, get up out of that sofa.

[*He does not move. Then he languidly rises. She impulsively embraces
him. He allows himself to be embraced. Then he kisses her gracefully
on the cheek.*]

MYRA: Ohhh! What an iceberg! [*laughs, holding him by the arms*].
[*Suddenly he convulsively embraces her and at once pulls away.*]
Oh, darling, it is lovely to have you home. We must have a party
to celebrate.

TONY: Oh, *no*.

MYRA: What's the matter?

TONY: A party. I knew you'd say a party.

MYRA: Oh, very well [*examining him, suddenly irritated*]. For God's
sake get out of that ghastly uniform. It makes you look like a . . .

TONY: What?

MYRA: A soldier.

TONY: I've been one for two years.

MYRA: Isn't that long enough?

TONY: I think I'm rather sorry to part with it [*teasing her, but half-
serious*]. Rather nice, the army – being told what to do, everything
in its place, everything tidy . . .

MYRA: Tidy! It's lucky you weren't in Cyprus or Kenya or Suez –
keeping order [*laughing angrily*]. Keeping everything tidy.

TONY: Well?

MYRA: You don't believe in it. [*as he does not reply*] You might have
been killed for something you don't even believe in.

TONY: You're so delightfully old-fashioned. Getting killed for something you believe in is surely a bit of a luxury these days? Something your generation enjoyed. Now one just – gets killed. [*He has
intended this to sound calmly cynical, but in spite of himself it comes out
plaintive.*]

MYRA [*has an impulse to make a maternal protective gesture, suppresses it
at the last moment. Says quietly, but between her teeth*]: All the same,
get out of those clothes.

TONY [*angry, because he knows he has sounded like a child*]: All right –
but what do you suppose you look like?

MYRA [*cheerfully*]: Oh, the char, I know. But I've been cleaning the
stairs. If I'd known you were coming . . .

TONY: Oh, I know, you'd have changed your trousers.

MYRA: I might even have worn a dress.

TONY [*languidly charming*]: Really, Mother, when you look so charming when you try, do you have to look like that?

MYRA [*cheerfully impatient*]: Oh, don't be such a little – no one can look charming cleaning the stairs.

TONY [*unpleasantly*]: So you were cleaning the stairs. And who did you expect to find sitting here?

MYRA: Why, no one.

TONY: You came creeping down. Were you going to put your hands over my eyes and say: 'Peekaboo'? [*gives a young, aggressive, unhappy laugh*].

MYRA: It was dark. I couldn't see who it was. It might have been anybody.

TONY: Of course, anybody. Why don't you put your hands over my eyes now and say 'Peekaboo'? How do you know? – I might rather like it. Then you could bite my ear, or something like that [*gives the same laugh*].

MYRA [*quietly*]: Tony, you've just come home.

TONY: Well, and why did you come creeping down the stairs?

MYRA: I came down because the telephone was ringing earlier. I came to see. Did you take it?

TONY: So it was. Yes. I forgot.

MYRA [*cheerfully*]: You're a bloody boor, Tony.

TONY [*wincing*]: Do you have to swear?

MYRA: Well, now you're home I suppose I'll have to stop. [*in a refined voice*] There are times, dear, when you do rather irritate me.

TONY [*stiffly*]: I've already said that I'm quite prepared to go somewhere else if it's inconvenient for you to have me at such short notice.

[MYRA *watches him: she is on the defensive.*]

Well? Who is that you've got upstairs with you? Who is it this time?

MYRA: How do you know I've got anyone upstairs with me?

TONY: Who *is* it upstairs?

MYRA [*offhand*]: Sandy.

TONY: Sandy who?

MYRA: Don't be silly. Sandy Boles.

TONY [*staring*]: But he's my age.

MYRA: What of it?

TONY: He's my age. He's 22.

MYRA: I didn't ask to see his birth certificate when I engaged him.

TONY: Engaged him?

MYRA [*briskly*]: He's at a loose end. I wanted someone to help me. He's here for a while.

TONY [*slowly*]: He's staying here?

MYRA: Why not? This empty house . . . when you're not here it's so empty.

TONY: He's in my room?

MYRA: Yes. He can move out.

TONY: Thanks. [*They stare at each other like enemies.*]

MYRA: Well, what is it?

TONY: Perhaps you'd rather I moved out.

MYRA: Tony, mind your own bloody business. I've never interfered with anything you did.

TONY: No [*half-bitter, half-sad*]. No, you never did. You never had time.

MYRA [*hurt*]: That's unfair.

TONY: And where's dear Sandy's mamma?

MYRA: Milly is in Japan.

TONY: And what is dear Sandy's errant mamma doing in Japan?

MYRA: She's gone with a delegation of women.

TONY [*laughing*]: Oh I see. They are conveying the greetings of the British nation, with an apology because our Government uses their part of the world for H-bomb tests.

MYRA [*wistfully*]: Is it really so funny?

TONY [*not laughing*]: Hilarious. And why aren't you with them?

MYRA: Because I was expecting you.

TONY [*plaintively*]: But you'd forgotten I was coming.

MYRA [*irritated*]: I might have forgotten that you were expected home at four o'clock on Tuesday the 18th March, 1958, but I was expecting you. Otherwise, of course, I would have gone with Milly.

TONY: But Milly didn't deny herself the pleasure on Sandy's account. He could fend for himself.

MYRA: You talk as if . . . Sandy's 22. He's not a little boy who needs his mother to wipe his nose for him. He's a man.

TONY [*terribly hurt*]: That must be nice for you. I'm so glad.

MYRA [*between her teeth*]: My God, Tony. [*She moves angrily away.*]

TONY: Where are you going?

MYRA: I'm going to demonstrate about the hydrogen bomb outside Parliament with a lot of other women. [*as* TONY *laughs*] Yes, laugh, do.

TONY: Oh, I'm not laughing. I do really admire you, I suppose. But what use do you suppose it's going to be? What good is it?

MYRA [*who has responded to his tone like a little girl who has been praised*]: Oh, Tony, but of course it's some good. Surely you think so?

TONY: You've been demonstrating for good causes all your life. So many I've lost count. And I'm sure you have . . . And where are we now?

MYRA: How do you know things mightn't have been worse?

TONY: How could they possibly be worse? How could they?

[*He sounds so forlorn, almost tearful, that she impulsively comes to him where he sits on the arm of the sofa, and holds his head against her shoulder, laying her cheek against it.*]

One might almost think you were pleased to see me.

MYRA [*amazed*]: But of course I am.

[*He smiles, rather sadly.*]

Of course. [*Gaily, moving away from him*]. Tony, I must tell you about what I'm doing. You know we've got that big meeting the day after tomorrow.

TONY: Actually, not.

MYRA: We've advertised it in all the papers.

TONY: I never read newspapers.

MYRA: Oh. Well, it's tomorrow. And I've worked out a simply

marvellous ... wait, I'll show you. [*She is fiddling about near the tape-machine.*]

TONY: Do you have to? I thought you said you had to go to your demonstration?

MYRA: Yes, I must rush. I'll just do the end bit. It's a sort of symposium – you know, bits of idiotic speeches by politicians – like this ... [*switches on machine*].

POMPOUS VOICE: People who object to the hydrogen bomb are simply neurotic!

MYRA: And this –

PULPIT VOICE: The hydrogen bomb must be regarded by true Christians as part of God's plan for humanity.

MYRA: And then war effects, you know.

TONY: War effects?

MYRA: Listen [*puts on machine*].

[*Medley of war noises. Then machine-gun fire. Then the beginning of a scream – a conventional bomb falling.*]

TONY: For God's sake stop it.

MYRA [*stopping machine*]: What's the matter? You see, the thing is, people have no imagination. You've got to rub their noses in it [*starts machine again*].

[*The scream begins and gathers strength.* TONY *stands rigid, trembling. At the explosion he flings himself down on the divan, his arms over his ears.*]

[*taking needle off*] There. Not bad, is it? [*turning*] Where are you? Oh, there you are. Don't you think it's a good idea?

[TONY *sits limp on the divan, hand dangling, staring in front of him. He wipes sweat off his forehead slowly.*]

I'm really very pleased with it. [*She stands, looking out of the window, starts to hum.*] I must go and get dressed and go out. I do wish you young people would join in these demonstrations. Why don't you? – we're such a middle-aged lot. Why do you leave it all to us? [*hums*] Well, I'll finish the work on the tape tonight.

TONY: I forgot to tell you, there *was* a telephone message. From Philip. He says he wants you to put up Rosemary. Tonight.

MYRA: Who's Rosemary?

TONY: Didn't you know? He's getting married. To Rosemary.

[MYRA *slowly turns from the window. She looks as if she has been hit.*]

MYRA: Philip is getting married?

TONY: So he said.

MYRA: And he wants *me* to put her up?

TONY [*looking at her curiously*]: Why not? You're old friends, aren't you?

MYRA: Old friends?

TONY: Well, aren't you?

MYRA [*laughing bitterly*]: Of course. Old friends. As you know.

TONY [*examining her, surprised*]: But you surely don't mind. It's been years since . . .

MYRA: Since he threw me over – quite.

TONY: Threw you over? You're getting very emotional all of a sudden, aren't you – all these old-fashioned attitudes at the drop of a hat – I was under the impression that you parted because your fundamental psychological drives were not complementary! [*with another look at her stricken face*] Threw you over! I've never seen you like this.

MYRA [*dry and bitter*]: If you've lain in a man's arms every night for five years and he's thrown you over as if you were a tart he'd picked up in Brighton for the week-end, then the word friend has to be used with – a certain amount of irony, let's say. [*briskly*] We've been good friends ever since, yes.

[TONY *slowly rises, stands facing her.*]

TONY: Why do you talk like that to *me*?

MYRA [*noticing him*]: What's the matter now? Oh, I see. [*contemptuous*] You're not five years old. Why do you expect me to treat you as if you were five years old?

TONY: Perhaps I am five years old. But this is after all an extraordinary outburst of emotion. Dear Uncle Philip has been in and out of this house for years. Whenever he's in London he might just as well be living here. I can't remember a time when you and

Uncle Philip in animated conversation wasn't a permanent feature of the landscape.

MYRA [*drily*]: I am the woman Philip *talks* to, yes.

TONY: Why all this emotion, suddenly?

MYRA: He has not before asked me to put up his prospective wife.

TONY: For God's sake, why should you care? You've lain in men's arms since, haven't you? Well, isn't that how you want me to talk, like a big boy?

MYRA: I suppose you will grow up some day. [*goes to the foot of the stairs*] When's she coming?

TONY: Some time later this evening, he said. And he's coming, too. We're going to have a jolly family evening.

MYRA: You'll have to look after her until I get back. We must be perfectly charming to her.

TONY: I don't see why you should be if you don't feel like it.

MYRA: You don't see why?

TONY: No. I'm really interested. Why?

MYRA: Pride.

TONY [*laughing*]: Pride! You! [*He collapses on the divan laughing.*]

MYRA [*hurt*]: Oh, go to hell, you *bloody* little . . .

[*Her tone cuts his laughter. He sits stiffly in the corner of the divan. She makes an angry gesture and runs up the stairs. Before she is out of sight she is humming:* Boohoo, you've got me crying for you. TONY *strips off his uniform and puts on black trousers and a black sweater. He rolls up the uniform like dirty washing and stuffs it into the knapsack. He throws the knapsack into a cupboard. He stands unhappily smoothing back his hair with both hands. Then he goes to the looking-glass and stands smoothing his hair back and looking at his face. While he does this,* SANDY *very quietly comes down the stairs behind him. He is an amiable young man at ease in his world.*]

SANDY [*quietly*]: Hullo, Tony.

TONY [*still standing before the looking-glass. He stiffens, letting his hands drop. He slowly turns, with a cold smile*]: Hullo, Sandy.

SANDY [*at ease*]: I see you've disposed of the war paint already.

TONY: Yes.

SANDY: That's a very elegant sweater.

TONY [*responding*]: Yes, it's rather nice, isn't it . . . [*Disliking himself because he has responded, he stiffens up. He roughly rumples up his hair and hitches his shoulders uncomfortably in the sweater.*] Don't care what I wear.

SANDY: I'll move my things out of your room. Sorry, but we didn't expect you today.

TONY: Next time we will give you good warning.

SANDY: Cigarette?

TONY: That's a very smart cigarette case. No thanks.

SANDY: Mother brought it back from China last year. You remember she went?

TONY: Yes, I remember. Mother went, too. I suppose one does have to go to China for one's cigarette cases.

SANDY: I'm rather fond of it myself. [*pause*] Did you know I was helping Myra with her work?

TONY: As a matter of interest, what work are you doing?

SANDY: Formally, secretarial. But in practice – your mother has every talent in the world but one.

TONY: A sense of timing?

SANDY: You wouldn't exactly call her tidy.

TONY: Perhaps that's the same thing.

SANDY: She does need someone to sort things out for her.

TONY: Luckily she realizes it. In fact she makes a point of having someone around for that purpose.

[*As* SANDY *does not take this up –*]

Do you remember James?

SANDY: James? The boy with the golden gloves? Of course. Actually your mother told me she had him here for a time last year when he was out of a job.

TONY: He wasn't actually living here.

[SANDY *keeps his temper with an over-obvious effort.*]

James is working for Shepherds now and doing very nicely, thank you. You know, the new publishers.

SANDY [*lightly*]: Your mother has been pulling strings for me, too. I'm starting in with Mike Ferris next week.

TONY: *What?* I didn't know your politics were Left Wing.

SANDY: As much Left as anything, I suppose. But these labels are all rather *vieux jeu*, aren't they?

TONY: Oh, quite so – that's just the phrase I was looking for. Well, perhaps she can fix me up in Mike Ferris's office, too. After all, I don't find the political labels just a little *vieux jeu*.

SANDY: I was under the impression you were going to finish studying for your degree.

TONY: You were? Why?

SANDY: I imagined . . . well, I suppose I got the idea from Myra. I think she expects you to.

TONY: Really? I'm quite in the dark. Why should she?

SANDY: It was rather odd, your throwing it all up three weeks before the final exam. Training to be an architect is an expensive business, and then you threw it all up.

TONY: Mother said all that? She said all that to you? She's discussed it with *you*?

SANDY: No. But surely one is bound to think it? It's not everyone who can afford to spend four years studying and then throw it all up with three weeks to go.

TONY: Mother certainly couldn't afford it. And she quite rightly told me I would have to stand on my own feet from then on. Of course she didn't reproach me. One can scarcely imagine mother reproaching one for that sort of thing. Freedom of choice is everything. My mum is a great one for freedom. Odd, isn't it? [*He hums a bar or two of the* Internationale.] No, she merely said, in her inimitable way: 'Well, if you're determined to be illiterate, you'd better learn something useful. Like mending the electric lights.' So I took her at her word. I'm now a qualified electrician. Join the army and learn a trade.

SANDY [*whimsical again*]: I don't think she expects you to settle for being an electrician.

TONY: No? Why not? It was her suggestion. [*suspiciously*] What has she been saying to you?

SANDY: Nothing.

TONY: I expect she'll drop information about her plans for my future in her own good time. When she has a moment to spare from the H-bomb, perhaps.

[MYRA *appears at the head of the stairs. She looks beautiful, and one would hardly recognize her for the same woman. Her dress is elaborately smart.* TONY *looks at* SANDY, *winces as he sees his admiring face.* MYRA *descends, smiling with frank pleasure at the impression she is making.*]

TONY [*still looking at* SANDY]: We are repressing a desire to applaud.

MYRA: Oh, don't repress it. Please don't. [*reaching the foot of the stairs*] Where's my hat? [*rummaging about*] Where did I leave my hat?

TONY: What's your hat doing down here, anyway?

MYRA: Obviously I left it here when I took it off.

TONY: Why do you have to leave it in the hall?

SANDY: Darling, it's in the cupboard.

MYRA: Of course I did. [*She opens cupboard, seizes hat, throws out* TONY'S *army things.*] You can't leave your battle-gear in here. It's my china cupboard.

TONY: Why do you have to keep your hat and your china in a junk cupboard in the hall? Oh, Lord, Mother!

[MYRA *puts on her hat in front of the looking-glass. It is a very smart hat.*]

SANDY: Darling, you look beautiful.

TONY: For God's sake, you aren't going to wear that for a demonstration outside the House of Commons? Why don't you chain yourself to the railings and be done with it?

MYRA: Why not? I've been telling the committee that it is gravely underrated as a political weapon. It is time it was revived.

TONY [*furious*]: Christ, and you would, too.

MYRA [*furious*]: Yes, and it would be so unladylike, wouldn't it? How the hell did I come to have such a tenth-rate little snob for a son . . .? Oh, I'm sorry. Come on, give me a kiss.

[*She kisses him on the cheek. He suffers it.*]

I suppose you'll grow out of it. But if you only weren't so *glossy*.

TONY: Me, glossy!

MYRA [*in a fever of irritation*]: You're such a beautiful boy. [*to* SANDY, *half-laughing*] Isn't he a beautiful boy? [*almost growling*] Ohhh! Such a beautiful, glossy, well-groomed boy, and so neat in his habits.

TONY [*half-flattered, half-puzzled*]: Why are you so cross? You know quite well you look devastating and I'm bowled over. Do you want me to pay you compliments?

MYRA: Why not?

TONY: I thought that was what Sandy was here for.

[MYRA *and* TONY *glare at each other*, SANDY *turns away*.]

And now kiss Sandy too. On the cheek.

MYRA [*angrily*]: I was going to. Dear Sandy. [*She kisses* SANDY *soundly on both cheeks.*] And now I must run like the wind.

[*She makes a slow and impressive exit R, watched with affectionate admiration by* SANDY, *sardonically by* TONY.]

SANDY [*chuckling*]: Dear Myra. I've never known any woman with such a sense of gesture.

TONY [*coldly*]: Really? Gesture? She's sincere about this. She's sincere about war. It's no gesture.

SANDY [*chuckling*]: Of course she is. She's absolutely splendid. She's going to be at least an hour late. And she'll be ticked off by the committee again. Really so unjust, the work she puts into it. She was up till four this morning working out this tape-recording thing with me.

TONY: She was up till four? Really? [*gratefully*] You were both up till four.

SANDY: It's a magnificent job, it really is. Bits of speeches – she smuggled a tape recorder into the House. That took a bit of doing.

TONY: Illegal, of course.

SANDY: Oh, she's wonderful. Really wonderful propaganda. Asinine remarks from politicians, and war effects. She's worked in a terrific bit from Japan – you know, people dying as a result of the first atom bomb. And then children. That sort of thing.

TONY: Children.

SANDY: Children crying during a bombardment. Then machine guns and bomb noises. You really must hear it. [*going towards machine*] I'll put it on for you.

TONY [*violently*]: No.

SANDY: I think you'd be impressed. It's a splendid job.

TONY [*bitterly*]: I've no doubt it is. Splendid. [*goes to window*] But I rather doubt whether she's going to get near enough to the House of Commons even to get ticked off for being late. Because she's in animated conversation with Uncle Mike in the middle of the street – she's just missed being run over. Dear Mother.

SANDY: And who's Uncle Mike?

TONY: Why, Mike Ferris – your prospective sponsor for your life as a fighter for the people.

SANDY: Why Uncle?

TONY: I've had so many uncles. Well, Uncle Sandy? Oh, don't bother to get out your boxing gloves so as to defend Mum's honour. You don't want Mike to find us brawling, do you? Besides, in these matters at least, I am a pacifist. [*looks out of window*] Dear Mike. The very image of a politician. The old type of politician – the platform rather than the committee man. [*back at* SANDY] And which are you settling for, Uncle Sandy? Of course, you're the committee man. One must keep up with the times, mustn't one? Sandy Boles, M.P., backroom boy; Sandy Boles, centre of centre of the Labour Party. Yes, you're right, Sandy, it's the Labour Party for you – the road to ministerial position with the Tories is long and arduous and you haven't got the connexions. Oh yes, I can see you. Mr Sandy Boles, M.P. for Little Puddleditch, centre of centre. A sound man. Getting sounder and sounder as maturity sets in and you become certain that there are ever so many sides to every question . . .

SANDY [*extremely polite*]: Have a cigarette, Tony.

TONY: No thanks. He's coming in. [*He almost twists up with self-dislike.*] Why am I on to old Mike? I like him. I always have. He's the salt of the earth and all that. And I'm sure he's never said one thing and meant another in the whole of his life. Well, hardly ever. He'll never be Minister for anything. Not even an Under Secretary. Without people like him the whole show really would be a bloody circus. But he's so – bloody *innocent*. When he starts talking it makes me feel a thousand years old. Sometimes I think he's parodying the ordinary kind of political pomposity, and then, God help me, I see that he means every word. Every sweet silly word of it. Well … suppose after all the simple-minded do-gooders do turn up trumps. We'd look silly then, wouldn't we – Mr Sandy Boles, M.P.? Well, why shouldn't they? There's nothing left but simple-minded honesty – and faith.

SANDY [*blandly interested*]: Faith in what?

TONY [*after a long pause, allowing himself to straighten up*]: I don't know. Well? You can't possibly be prepared to go through all the slot-machines? You can't be.

SANDY: What's the alternative?

TONY: Oh, *Christ*! Seven years or so of establishing oneself as a *sound* young man. Marriage – for love, of course. Then divorce. Perhaps several divorces. Who are we to think ourselves better than our parents? Oh well. You'll be all right, Uncle Sandy. The glorious battle for socialism inside the Labour Party will save you from all that, won't it? Oh, *Christ*! Look at Mother's lot – fire-eating Socialists, every one of them, and here they are, all sorted out into neat little boxes.

SANDY: As a matter of interest, what label would you stick on the box Myra is in? Or my mother?

TONY [*after a pause, laughing*]: The dilettante daughters of the revolution?

SANDY: Come, come. Dilettantes don't work.

TONY [*impatiently*]: Oh, they're women who haven't succeeded in getting or staying married.

SANDY [*ironically*]: Well, well. Have a drink, Tony, do.

TONY: The only people I think I really admire are tramps. Something like that. I hitch-hiked from camp. There were two of us. The other chap was a man who threw up his job ten years ago and he has'nt worked since. Earns enough to keep eating. And drinking – he's a soak.

SANDY: *Sounds* all right.

TONY: We need a new form of – inner emigration. Drugs. Drink. Anything. I want to opt out. I don't want any part of it. [*at* SANDY's *raised eyebrows*] Well, what are you suggesting? That I'll settle down?

SANDY: Of course.

TONY: I'm in a bad mood! You sound like mother. I'll get over it, I suppose. Well, I suppose I will. All the same, what I think now is the truth, not the lies I'll be telling myself in five years' time when I've put down the first deposit on my future. If there is a future.

SANDY: My dear chap, you really had better get drunk.

TONY: Drinking bores me. [*He throws away his cigarette.*] And smoking. [*and now he is a querulous child again*] And women.

SANDY [*blandly*]: Women too?

TONY: What on earth do you talk to them about? All they're interested in is – Oh, hell! You can't possibly sit there and tell me you really like women.

SANDY: But I adore women.

TONY: That's what I mean. [*irritated*] Oh, hell! – the truth is I don't care for anything in the world except this house.

SANDY: Are you going to take it on your back with you when you go tramping?

TONY: Look out, here's Mike.

[MIKE FERRIS *enters from R. He is a man between 55 and 60, portly, kindly, with the dignity that comes from sincerity and a sound conscience. There is no conflict between his public face and his private face: there never has been. He went into politics thirty years ago out of a simple and earnest conviction, and he has never lost his simplicity and his earnestness.*]

[*languidly good-mannered*] My dear Mike, how nice to see you.

MIKE: Well, Tony, old chap. How nice to see you back in civilized clothes.

TONY [*still like a Society hostess*]: Do sit down, Mike. Can I get you a drink?

MIKE [*smiling, a little amused*]: No thanks. I just popped in to say hullo. Your mother said you were back, and I said I'd pop in to have a look at you. It really is so good to have you home again.

TONY [*deflating suddenly into awkward sincerity*]: Sit down, Mike. Don't rush off. You must have a drink.

MIKE: It's very kind of you. Just for a minute then. [*to* SANDY] And we are all looking forward very much to having you in the office. You're joining us at an interesting time, you know.

SANDY [*gracefully*]: I'm looking forward to it, too.

MIKE: Though when you think of the big issue, the hydrogen bomb business, nothing else seems to matter so much, does it? [*accepting a glass from* TONY] The more I think about it, the more I am convinced it is much more simple than we think. Simply a question of getting the Governments to agree, that's all.

TONY [*drily*]: That's all?

MIKE: Well, it really is hard to believe that people will be prepared to do things that will affect their own children, isn't it? I really can't believe, when it comes to the point, that common sense won't prevail.

TONY: You really believe that the men in power care about other people getting hurt?

MIKE: My dear boy – well, no. After a lifetime in politics – no. But everything's so critical – obviously we can get agreement if we try.

TONY: Are you suggesting that the voice of the people will prevail? Or, to coin another phrase, that the people are on the march?

MIKE: If the voice of the people doesn't prevail, what will? I really can't believe – I *can't* believe that after all we've done, all the glorious achievements of humanity, we are going to consent to blowing it all up.

TONY [*puzzled, more than derisive*]: You can't?

SANDY [*very smoothly, as it were testing a public voice*]: Quite obviously, the first step is to stop tests everywhere, and then we can proceed to a general discussion on disarmament.

TONY [*staring at him with disgust*]: Oh, hear, hear!

MIKE: If the tests are stopped we still have the Lord knows how many hydrogen bombs stored here and there, waiting for some madman to set them off. But I can't believe humanity will be so stupid.

TONY [*with fierce sincerity*]: Why can't you believe it?

MIKE: But, my dear boy, we do seem to get through somehow. We get through the most appalling messes.

TONY [*fiercely*]: No, I really do want to know. Why can't you believe it? This is what interests me. Mother can't believe it either. Speaking for myself, I can believe it only too readily.

SANDY [*whimsically*]: Oh, *I* can't believe it.

MIKE: I'm so glad to hear that, Sandy. Because, generally speaking, you young people ... well, well.

TONY: Why can't you and mother and the rest of you believe it? [*at* SANDY *derisively*] And *you*, of course, Sandy. [*To* MIKE] You seem to be constitutionally incapable of believing in the ultimate horrors. Why? You've lived through enough, haven't you? It gives me the creeps to listen to any of you when you're in one of your reminiscing moods – a record of murder and misery. Yet on you go, all jolly and optimistic that right will prevail.

MIKE [*with great sincerity*]: It's a question of getting agreement between men of good will everywhere.

TONY [*laughing incredulously*]: Good. Let's drink to that: the glorious achievements of humanity.

MIKE [*seriously*]: Yes. [*He lifts his glass to drink. Seeing* TONY'S *face, lowers it again.*] You're not looking too well, young Tony. And your mother's not looking too well either.

TONY: Mother's not looking well?

SANDY: Why, Myra's on top of her form.

MIKE: I thought she wasn't looking too well. [*wistfully*] She really does need someone to look after her.

TONY: I'm sorry you think I'm so inadequate.

MIKE: Yes. Well. But if you're going to start studying again –

TONY: But I'm not.

MIKE: You're not? What? But ... I see. [*He is very disturbed.*] But,

Tony, your mother . . . You do seem to have such a lot of problems, you young people. Of course one is rather bound to feel
insecure with that Government we've got.

TONY: We can always look forward to the blissful security we'll have
under the next Labour Government. [*as* MIKE *looks hurt*] There are
also the American Government and the Russian Government. And
how stand the Russians these days, Mike? In the right of it as usual?

MIKE: Tony, I do hope you're not getting at your mother over this
business – she's feeling very bad about it, you know. A lot of
people are. I am myself. It would be easy to say we were wrong.
But when it's a question of knowing you were both right and
wrong, and having to decide where you were wrong – I wish you
wouldn't get at Myra just now.

TONY [*irritated*]: Mike, I can't remember a time when the whole lot
of you weren't tortured by something happening thousands of
miles away. I don't see that anything's changed much.

MIKE: She's really so worried about everything.

TONY: Oh, I know she doesn't spare herself. But then she never has.

MIKE: No, she never has. And she has had rather a tough time of it.
It's odd how some people's lives – well, well. I often think of how
your mother used to be when your father was alive. They were so
happy. I loved being with them. They were such a happy couple.
And then he was killed that night.

TONY: It is the night Mother refers to in her inimitable way as the
Night the Bomb Fell.

MIKE: Yes. And your father was killed and you and your mother
were buried alive for hours. [TONY *winces, turns away to hide how
much he is affected.*] Yes. Perhaps you could persuade your mother
to go away with you for a holiday somewhere.

TONY [*wistfully*]: With me? mother? [*laughs*] With me?

MIKE: There's that cottage of mine in Essex. It's empty.

TONY: I shouldn't imagine that a cottage in Essex with me is mother's
idea of fun at all. [*at* SANDY] Do you fancy the idea of a holiday in
Essex, Uncle Sandy?

MIKE: Knowing that money is a bit short at the moment.

TONY: Yes, so I gather, but why?

MIKE [*evasively*]: Oh, one thing and another. For one thing she gave up her job to do this hydrogen bomb work and of course it's not paid. And . . . various things. I got the impression money was a bit short. And there's the cottage, empty.

TONY: It's very good of you. Thanks, Mike.

MIKE: The flat can wait. There's no problem about that.

TONY: The flat?

MIKE: I meant to tell Myra that it was all fixed up when I saw her in the street, but it slipped my mind.

TONY: What flat?

MIKE: As it happened, when Myra asked me if I could help, I could. It's an ill wind that blows nobody any good. Joan – my daughter, you know – is leaving her husband. I don't know why. I thought it was a rather good marriage. But it's broken up. Very sad. Well, well. And there's the flat. Just right for *you*.

TONY: For me? A flat?

MIKE: Didn't you know? Myra seemed to think you'd be wanting a place of your own when you came out of the Army.

TONY: I see. [*looks at* SANDY] I see.

[*He walks out of the room, R, slamming the door.*]

MIKE: What's wrong?

SANDY: He'll get over it.

MIKE: Myra thought he'd prefer to be by himself. She's always been very anxious about being the possessive mother, you know. She said *she* had to fight to leave home, and she doesn't want Tony to feel he should stay at home just because she's lonely.

SANDY [*chuckling*]: Myra's lonely? But she's never alone.

MIKE: Yes, well. [*with deliberate pleasantness*] It must be nice to hav you here.

SANDY [*whimsically*]: And nice for me.

MIKE: Yes, believe me, I'm glad. It's so nice to meet a young man who . . . there's my elder son. As far as I can make out he's a homosexual. Or if he's not, he might just as well be.

SANDY: I assure you, if it relieves your mind, that I'm not.

MIKE: Oh it does. And I'm pleased for both Myra and yourself that . . . not that I'm not jealous, I am.

SANDY: Mike, you really are wonderful.

MIKE: When I was young I had such a good time. I do believe that young people should have a good time. But they don't seem to. At least, none of my children seem to. They talk in the most sophisticated way, but when it comes to the point . . . And there's young Tony. Oh dear, he is in a mood. Well, that's one of the reasons Myra would like him to have his own flat. So he'd feel free. I think it would be better not to mention it again. So there's a perfectly good flat going begging.

SANDY: But he loves this house – or so he says. God knows why. It's such a mess. Besides, he *says* he wants to be a tramp.

MIKE [*seriously*]: He does, does he? Well, well. That's interesting.

SANDY: In order to escape the corruptions of modern life.

MIKE: Oh. I must tell Myra. She'll be delighted. Well, so I suppose you don't want a flat?

SANDY: I live at home with my mamma quite happily, thank you. I have the bottom half and she has the top half.

MIKE: That sounds reasonable. But you've never had the urge to leave home? To cast its dust off your feet?

SANDY: Good Lord, why should I? Besides, Mother's such a good cook. Almost as good as Myra.

MIKE: Don't you want to revolt against us? It was my first idea. And Myra's too. And she has been so looking forward to the moment when Tony would revolt against her.

SANDY: But how could one revolt against my mother or against Myra? They are both perfectly delightful. And besides, you've done all the revolting, haven't you? There's nothing left for us.

MIKE: Sure there must be something . . . a tramp. Good for him.

[TONY *comes in fast from R.*]

TONY: Mother and Philip are coming. Philip, but no Rosemary. [*to* MIKE] Do you know who Rosemary is?

MIKE: Rosemary? The only Rosemary I know is Rosemary Paine.

TONY: Who is Rosemary Paine?

MIKE: She used to be married to old Paddy – Secretary for – I forget now. She's interested in Housing. Yes. Nice woman. Very efficient.

TONY: Well, Philip is marrying her.

MIKE: Philip's marrying again, is he? Good for him.

TONY: We're in for such a jolly time. Mother, battling day and night – or at least, part of the night, with the Bomb. And Rosemary battling with Housing. And your mother, Sandy. Sandy, when's Milly coming back?

SANDY: Very soon now, I believe.

TONY: Milly will help mother to battle with the Bomb when she's not attending to racial prejudice and the Chinese peasantry. Oh, my God, they really are utterly intolerable. [*flinging himself down*] I simply cannot endure them. It's their utterly appalling vitality. They exhaust me.

SANDY: Perhaps it's time you took to the roads.

TONY: You don't seem to see the horrors of the situation. We're going to have this house full of Amazons. Three of them. My mother. Your mother, popping in and out with her hands full of pamphlets and files, as is her wont. And Rosemary.

[MYRA *and* PHILIP *come in R. They are laughing together, very gay and animated.* MYRA *is carrying her hat in her hand. As she enters she throws it on to a chair.* TONY *leaps up and bundles it into the cupboard.* PHILIP *is an attractive man of about 45.*]

MYRA: Did you say Rosemary? Has she come?

SANDY: No, she hasn't come yet; why aren't you outside the House of Commons, Myra?

TONY: Yes, why aren't you?

MYRA: Philip dropped in, we got talking, and I came back with him.

TONY: What do you mean, dropped in. You talk about the House of Commons as if it were the local.

PHILIP: I was driving past, and I saw Myra with the others, and I stopped to say hullo. Where's Rosemary? She said she'd get here under her own steam.

TONY: We are all sitting here waiting for Rosemary.

PHILIP: I do hope it's all right, her coming here.

MYRA [*gaily*]: Of course, where else should she come?

PHILIP [*a bit embarrassed*]: Well, I did try to fix her up somewhere else. Somewhere more central for shopping, I mean. [MYRA *smiles ironically at* PHILIP. *He responds unwillingly.*] Well, she says she can't get married without new clothes. [*turning away from* MYRA'S *irony*] Well, Mike – nice to see you again.

MIKE: Haven't seen you for some time, Philip. Haven't you time for politics any longer?

PHILIP: I'm up to my eyes with this new community centre we're building.

MIKE: Yes, I heard. So your firm got the contract? It's a big thing, isn't it?

MYRA [*delighted*]: Philip, darling, why didn't you tell me. I'm so glad.

PHILIP [*turning to her – they instantly make a close, absorbed pair*]: Do you remember those plans I was playing with that summer – when we were in Venice?

MYRA: But of course. They were beautiful. And you were in despair because you said you'd never see it built. [MYRA *and* PHILIP *are close together under the window.* MIKE, SANDY, TONY *stand separate, watching them.*]

MIKE [*trying to detach* PHILIP *from* MYRA]: We've been missing you on the committee, Philip.

PHILIP [*who has not heard* MIKE]: Myra, do you remember how I wanted that façade – remember, you said it wouldn't work?

MYRA [*laughing*]: Then I was wrong. Remember how we quarrelled about it? We quarrelled for three days?

PHILIP [*laughing*]: What, we only quarrelled for three days that time?

SANDY [*jealous and loud, with a step forward*]: I do so hope Rosemary is interested in architecture.

MYRA [*who has not heard*]: And what about the roof gardens – did you get your way about those too?

PHILIP: Yes, everything. Look, I'll show you the photographs.

[PHILIP *and* MYRA *stand side by side by the window, looking at the photographs. The door R slowly opens;* ROSEMARY *stands there. She*

*is a girl of 19 or 20, a slight creature with a sad little face. She wears
black trousers and a black sweater. In general style and type she is so
similar to* TONY *she might very well be his sister.*

SANDY, MIKE, *and* TONY *are watching the couple by the window.
No one notices her.*]

MYRA: This is going to take up a lot of your time, Philip. I do hope
you aren't going to drop out of politics altogether.

PHILIP: Myra darling, can't you see everyone's fed up with politics.
It's not the time.

MYRA: What do you mean, not the time . . .?

PHILIP: Not the old kind of politics. Surely you can see that? [ROSE-
MARY *takes a couple of steps forward.* TONY *sees her.*]

TONY [*to* ROSEMARY]: Can I do anything for you?

ROSEMARY: Well, yes.

TONY: My God, you aren't Rosemary?

ROSEMARY: Yes, I am. Who did you think I was?

TONY [*dramatically, to the* OTHERS]: Rosemary is here. [SANDY *and*
MIKE *turn, are stunned into silence. Simultaneously* PHILIP *and* MYRA
raise their voices. They do not hear TONY *nor see* ROSEMARY.]

MYRA: Oh, Philip, for God's sake, you're not going to change, are
you?

PHILIP: Well, why not?

MYRA: Philip, half the people I know, people who've spent all their
lives fighting and trying to change things, they've gone inside their
homes and shut their front doors and gone domestic and comfortable – and safe.

PHILIP: Well, what's wrong with that?

TONY [*shouting*]: Myra. Philip. Rosemary's here.

MYRA [*as she and* PHILIP *slowly turn*]: What's wrong with it? I never
believed I'd hear you say that – who's that?

[PHILIP *sees* ROSEMARY, *drops his arm from* MYRA, *moves away
from her.*]

ROSEMARY [*pathetically*]: Hullo, Philip.

CURTAIN

It is next morning. The place is in total disorder. The divan has been slept in and is tangled all over with clothes, sheets, newspapers, pillows.

TONY *is lying flat on the floor. He is wearing his black trousers and a pyjama jacket.*

ROSEMARY, *dressed as she was yesterday, in black trousers and sweater, comes half-way down the stairs.* TONY *does not move.*

ROSEMARY: What are you doing here?

TONY: This house has eight rooms in it and this is the only corner I can find to fit myself into – together with mother's hat, the china and the rest of the . . . [*indicates the files, papers, etc.*].

ROSEMARY: What's in the other rooms?

TONY: People. And Things. More Things than People. Extraordinary how much space the humanitarian conscience takes up. [*He again indicates the paraphernalia in the hall.*]

ROSEMARY: I'm sorry we've taken your room.

TONY [*eagerly*]: It's a pretty room, isn't it?

ROSEMARY: Yes. The sun has been in it since six this morning. Have you seen Philip?

TONY: I've slept in it for fifteen years.

ROSEMARY: Do you know where Philip is?

TONY: I expect he's talking to mother.

ROSEMARY: Oh. Well, they're very old friends, aren't they?

TONY: Inseparable. They started quarrelling this morning at seven o'clock.

ROSEMARY: What about? I thought Philip had gone for a walk?

TONY: They both went for a walk. Around and around the garden. Quarrelling.

ROSEMARY: But what about?

TONY: Politics.

ROSEMARY: Oh.

TONY: These people talk about politics with all the passionate intensity other people reserve for sex. Extraordinary.

ROSEMARY: I didn't know Philip was interested in politics.

TONY: Are you?

ROSEMARY: I've never thought about it. And you?

TONY [*after a pause*]: No.

ROSEMARY: I really must talk to Philip [*turning back upstairs*].

TONY: Don't go. Stay and talk to me.

ROSEMARY: What about?

TONY: Just talk.

ROSEMARY [*going back out of sight*]: Perhaps he's gone back to our room.

TONY [*looking round*]: Oh God what a *mess*! [*He leaps up, makes an ineffectual attempt to clear papers, etc. His eyes fall on the looking-glass; he goes over, is about to take it off the wall when* MYRA *comes into sight at the top of the stairs. She is wearing her old trousers and sweat-shirt, is unmade-up, and has a cigarette between her lips.*]

MYRA: What are you doing?

TONY [*into the mirror*]: Peekaboo.

MYRA: What are you doing?

TONY: What's this looking-glass doing here?

MYRA: Well, why not?

TONY [*pointing at place over divan*]: It's always hung there.

MYRA: Has it? Oh, do leave it alone, Tony.

TONY [*leaving it, returning to the divan*]: It's always hung here.

MYRA: Oh. Yes, I remember when you came back from school you always used to go all over the house to see if everything was in the same place. [*She laughs.*]

TONY [*anxious and querulous*]: Every time I go away, when I come back it's as if a bomb's exploded in it – why is everything in such a *mess*, Mother?

MYRA [*impatiently, as she begins to strip the divan and make it*]: Oh, I haven't time. I get bored with all these *things*. They just accumulate and pile up ... When I think I once swore I would never own *things*, I'd never accumulate possessions – and now I've lived in one house for fifteen years and I feel it's sitting all over me like a – toad!

TONY [*anxious, following her around*]: Mother, how can you say that – we've always lived here.

MYRA: Always! I would never have believed once that I'd live in one place for fifteen years – it's disgusting. I'll be so pleased to be rid of it.

TONY: Rid of it? You don't mean that?

MYRA: I do.

TONY: Mother, but what's disgusting is that it's such a *mess*. Lord, everything's in a mess. Even the front door lock is broken.

MYRA: Oh, what does it matter!

TONY: Oh, I'm sure *that* appeals to you: Walk right in, walk right in, ladies and gentlemen, the humanitarian conscience is always at home and waiting.

MYRA [*pushing him out of her way*]: Oh, Tony, when I do try and clear up . . . Why don't you put some clothes on? Or are you trying to get a glamorous tan?

TONY [*in disgust*]: Oh, Jesus! [*He drags his black sweater on over his pyjama coat.*] Well, how's the happy couple this morning?

MYRA: How should I know?

TONY: But you've been in animated conversation with Uncle Philip for hours.

MYRA [*grinning*]: I naturally didn't mention Rosemary – that would be in such bad taste.

TONY: You must have gathered through your antennae, so to speak, how things were going – no? Well, I'd like to know. They are sitting gazing into each other's eyes? Or perhaps they've gone back to bed. *My* bed. My well-warmed bed. First Sandy. Then Uncle Philip and Rosemary.

MYRA [*grimly amused*]: Philip asked me if I had another bed I could put into their room. So I did. Twin beds side by side like an advertisement in an American magazine. I felt so much better. [*She laughs.*]

TONY: I can't think why.

MYRA: Philip and I shared a three-foot bed for five years.

TONY: *Do you have to?*

MYRA: Yes, I do. *That he should bring her here.* God, men are the end. They really are the end.

TONY: Uncle Philip is probably not aware of your enduring passion for him.

MYRA: He's very well aware of it. *Ergo.*

TONY: *Ergo* what?

MYRA: Well, let's see what happens. [*She kicks* TONY'S *shoes out of the way.*]

[TONY, *irritated, jumps across, puts on his shoes, returns to the floor.*]

TONY: If you go on being so charming to that poor girl she might permanently lose her powers of speech.

MYRA [*genuinely upset*]: But, Tony, I was doing my best. I really was.

TONY: Last night at dinner you were like Beatrice Lillie impersonating – our dear queen.

MYRA: What do you want me to do – burst into tears?

TONY: Why not, if you feel like it? Why don't you ever?

MYRA: I do my crying in private. Do you imagine, after putting up such a good show with Philip all this time, I'm going to behave like a jilted 16-year-old? Obviously not.

TONY: Oh, obviously.

MYRA: What I can't stand is the damned dishonesty of it. Men are so dishonest.

TONY: I'm sure you're right. But why in this case?

MYRA [*impatiently*]: Oh, surely you can see? He doesn't want to marry her. But he hasn't got the guts to do it himself, so he brings her here. He never did have any guts. I was manoeuvred into a position where I had to break it off or lose my self-respect. And that's what he's doing with her. Bloody man.

TONY [*languidly*]: And why do you love such a despicable person?

MYRA: Oh – love. I never use the word.

TONY: I do.

MYRA: I wish you would.

TONY: When it means nothing?

MYRA [*laughs. But she is not far off tears*]: Oh, don't be so solemn. Can't you ever laugh? You're such a boring lot. The young are so boring. I've come to the conclusion I can't stand the company of anyone under the age of 35.

TONY: You mean you can't stand the company of the uncorrupted?

MYRA [*amused*]: Wh-at?

TONY: I've spent a good part of what are known as my formative years listening to the conversation of the mature. You set my teeth on edge. You're corrupt. You're sloppy and corrupt. I'm waiting for that moment when you put your foot down about something and say you've had enough. But you never do. All you do is watch things – with interest. If Philip murdered Rosemary, seduced Sandy and stole all your money, all you'd say would be: How interesting!

MYRA: He'd murder me, not Rosemary. Obviously.

TONY: Oh, obviously, obviously, obviously. That would be interesting, wouldn't it?

MYRA [*grimly amused*]: It's so hard for a man when his wife dies and leaves him unprotected!

TONY: I thought you liked his wife.

MYRA: I did. But alas, she's dead. Some men stay married because it protects them against the – necessity of marrying somebody else. Philip married her when she was 20, and after that they hardly saw each other. He was very fond of her – as the phrase goes. And so he should have been. She lived like a nun on a mountain peak, forgiving him his sins, and from time to time he returned to the *good* woman for a nice rest. But now she's dead. So there's Rosemary. The moment I heard Philip's wife was dead, I said to myself, 'Ah-ha,' I said, 'he's going to be in trouble with Rosemary before the year's out.'

TONY: I thought you'd never heard of Rosemary.

MYRA: Rosemary, Felicity, Harriet. What does it matter? Of course he doesn't want to marry her. So he brings her here, where she's thoroughly lost and humiliated. [*turning on him*] God, you are a cowardly hypocritical lot.

TONY [*languidly*]: Why me? You forget I haven't started using the word 'love' yet.

MYRA [*grimly*]: I've no doubt you soon will. But I'm not going to

41

cope with the sacrifices to your vanity – I'm not. You can manage them yourself.

TONY: Well, if you understand it all . . . if you understand it . . . [*He falls back on the floor.*] *You* understand it so that's enough.

MYRA: But I'm not blaming anyone for anything. It seems to me, as far as sex is concerned, or if you prefer it, love, the only thing to do is to shrug your shoulders [*she shrugs her shoulders*] and forgive everyone.

TONY: But you haven't forgiven Philip.

MYRA: No.

TONY: Do be nice to that poor girl. It's like seeing a poor little fly being hypnotized by a horrible brown spider.

MYRA: Poor little fly.

TONY: Can't you really see that she's terrified of you?

MYRA [*really surprised*]: Of me?

TONY: You've just explained to me why she should be.

MYRA: It's humiliating for both of us. But *frightened* – of *me*? [*She goes to the looking-glass and looks at herself.*] She's 20.

TONY: Then for God's sake why don't you at least make up your face? I really can't stand it, seeing you slop around the house half the day looking like that.

MYRA: When I'm cleaning the house I expect to be loved for myself.

TONY: Why do you have to clean it? [*as she does not reply, but begins to hum to herself*] Oh, all right, be a martyr. But I don't enjoy housework so don't expect me to slump about on my knees.

MYRA: I haven't asked you to. [*She has finished the divan and now bundles objects into the cupboard haphazard.*]

TONY: What interests me much more than the convolutions of your emotions and Uncle Philip's is Rosemary. Why does a girl of 20 want to marry a jaded old – uncle. The newspapers say it's the thing these days. One marries a man old enough to be your father. Why?

MYRA: I thought you didn't read the newspapers.

TONY: Why? Because he has *experience*? Is that it? [*in disgust*] Jesus!

MYRA: Philip has always been attractive to women.

TONY: Attractive! When I was doing my time in his office I was permanently amazed at the way all the women were ready to lie down and let him walk all over them. Why? Well, you did too, didn't you? So you can explain it to me.

MYRA: I dare say they are under the impression that older men are kinder than young ones.

TONY: *Kinder!* This morning I heard Rosemary say: 'Darling, don't you love me any more?' and he said: 'Darling, you're simply being hysterical.' [MYRA *turns away sharply*.] Well, did he tell you you were hysterical?

MYRA [*breaking down and crying for a few seconds before pulling herself together*]: Tony, have some pity on me sometimes.

TONY [*appalled*]: Pity? Me? But you're not crying, are you?

MYRA: No. [*She begins rubbing a cleaner over the boards around the carpet.*] No.

TONY: I should think not.

MYRA: If Philip's off to the office then I suppose we'll have to entertain Rosemary. Of course I can always rely on you. Thank God, there's Sandy.

TONY: Yes, thank God for Sandy. He can always be relied upon to cope with any social situation. Where is he?

MYRA: Working in my room, I suppose. We've got that big meeting tomorrow night.

TONY: So interesting how that boy's turned out. Who would have foreseen this idealism in Sandy? [MYRA *stands still, leaning on the cleaner*.] What's the matter?

MYRA: Giddy. No, leave me alone.

TONY: You're not still having the change of life, are you?

MYRA: No, dear. As you know, I've finished with it.

TONY: How should I know? [*muttering*] Change of life, change of life. Well, you haven't changed much.

MYRA: Tony, will you do me a small favour? Keep out of my way just for a couple of days.

TONY: I could move into Uncle Mike's flat.

MYRA: Oh, do anything you like.

TONY: If your sense of timing hadn't been wrong, and I had been coming home next week, what would I have found? Sandy back with Milly and a nice empty house and you all ready to entertain me.

MYRA: You know quite well you didn't let me know – just so as to catch me out.

TONY [*pathetically*]: Couldn't you really remember the date I was to finish?

MYRA: Oh, Tony, why should I? Any normal person would have let me know. It's been two years. You've been popping back and forth from camp for two years. It's a long time.

TONY: So you'd like me to move into that flat for a week?

MYRA: But you know I wouldn't. Why do you think I want to get rid of you? I thought you'd want to live by yourself.

TONY: But why?

MYRA: It's normal for a young man to want to live by himself, isn't it?

TONY: Then I'm obviously not normal.

MYRA: I was making it easy for you – that's all. I've told Mike you definitely don't want the flat.

TONY: Easy for me?

MYRA [*embarrassed*]: Well . . . in case you felt you ought to stay with me when you didn't want to.

TONY: Ought to? Why?

MYRA [*giving him a long incredulous look*]: Well, I don't know. [*pause*] I do wish Milly would come back.

TONY: Why?

MYRA: She's so kind.

TONY: Kind, kind! You've got Sandy, haven't you? Isn't Sandy kind?

MYRA: You're a lot of savages. The young are a lot of savages.

TONY: Then why – oh, don't tell me. Of course – he's good in bed. Is that it?

MYRA [*smoothly*]: Oh, he's very accomplished. Very. [*irritated*] He's *so* efficient. My dear, there are times when I feel I should be clapping.

TONY: Don't tell me that's not enough. Then *why*?

MYRA [*grinning*]: *Vieillesse oblige.*

TONY: That smooth-faced well-mannered little spiv. I should have thought that Sandy was everything you hated. He'll end up as Master of the Queen's Wardrobe. Or Personnel Manager for the Federation of Imperial Industries. Something needing *tact*. Tact. Tact. Tact. Well, it's no use your trying to be tactful, Mother. Who's been alerted to talk to me? Sandy? Is it dear Uncle Sandy? Or is it Uncle Philip?

MYRA [*grinning*]: Well, actually, it's Philip.

TONY [*grinning*]: What's the plot?

MYRA: You see, it's like this . . .

[PHILIP *and* ROSEMARY *come into view on the staircase.*]

ROSEMARY [*kissing him*]: Good-bye, darling.

PHILIP: Good-bye, darling.

ROSEMARY: Darling, you've forgotten your briefcase. [*They go back out of sight.*]

TONY [*grinning*]: He's forgotten his briefcase. Well, Mother?

MYRA: The idea was that he would handle you for me – I suggested he should take you back into his office. No, Tony, do wait a minute. It's your whole future at stake.

TONY: Yes, it's *my* future.

MYRA: It would take you six months to study for that examination.

TONY: A year, after my brain's gone to pot in the army.

MYRA: Ohhh – do stop being so sorry for yourself all the time.

PHILIP'S VOICE ABOVE: Good-bye, darling.

ROSEMARY'S VOICE: Good-bye, darling.

PHILIP'S VOICE: Good-bye.

TONY: Oh, *Christ*! It really is repulsive, you must admit. [*as* MYRA *shrugs*] All right, it's all very beautiful and holy. Mother – when I left Philip's office before, it was because I couldn't stand it.

MYRA: Couldn't stand what?

TONY: Seeing Uncle Philip and his admiring staff, his willing harem. [PHILIP *comes into sight at top of the stairs.*]

MYRA: Oh, you impossible bloody little *prig*. [*She stands at window, back turned, furious.*]

TONY [*talking up as* PHILIP *comes down*]: Uncle Philip, mother has left us alone for the interview.

PHILIP [*preoccupied*]: Yes. It's about this job. I expect she told you.

TONY: Thanks, I don't want it. Mother, interview over [*goes to divan, flings himself on it*].

MYRA [*coming fast across to* PHILIP]: Oh, Philip, can't you ... [PHILIP *shakes his head gently at her, smiles, offers her a cigarette. They smile and shrug.*]

TONY: Songs without words.

PHILIP: I must be getting along to the office. It's really very good of you to have Rosemary here, Myra.

MYRA [*laughing*]: I think so, too.

PHILIP [*embarrassed*]: Yes, well. [MYRA *laughs again. He suddenly leans forward and kisses her cheek. She kisses his.*]

MYRA [*amused*]: You know you can always count on me for anything.

PHILIP: Yes.

MYRA: Dear Philip.

PHILIP: I really must hurry.

MYRA: But I want to ask you something. It's about Max. You remember Max?

PHILIP: Well, of course. You mean the Max from the International Brigade?

MYRA: He's in trouble.

PHILIP: Who isn't?

MYRA: He's been blacklisted in America and he'd like a temporary job to tide him over.

PHILIP: But I don't need script-writers in my office. Well, what are his qualifications?

MYRA: He's an awfully nice person.

PHILIP [*laughing*]: All right, send him along.

MYRA: Philip, I suppose you wouldn't like to be one of the sponsors for a new protest we're getting up?

PHILIP [*cautiously*]: A protest against what?

MYRA: I'll explain.

[*The* TWO *of them are standing very close together by the window R, looking into each other's faces.* ROSEMARY *comes slowly down the stairs. She has been crying. They do not notice her.*]

PHILIP: Myra dear, I don't know how often I've told you that I don't believe in this – you can do more by quietly pulling strings than you ever can by mass protests and committees and that kind of thing.

MYRA: Since when have you told me! Yesterday. So now you believe in pulling strings. What's happened to you, Philip? What has happened? You used to be a Socialist.

PHILIP [*drily*]: I've discovered that I was a Socialist because I believed in liberty, freedom, democracy. [*laughs*] Well, Myra?

[ROSEMARY, *who has been waiting for* PHILIP *to see her, looks at* TONY. *He pats the divan beside him. She sits by him. They sit side by side, in the same listless pose, listening.*]

[*tenderly*] Myra dear, do you really imagine that any Government in the world cares about the protests of nice-minded humanitarians?

MYRA: They care about having pressure put on them. I've got a list as long as my two arms of people in prison, sentenced to death, deported, banned, prohibited, blacklisted . . .

PHILIP: Which side of the world this time? Ours or theirs?

MYRA: Ours.

PHILIP: And what about Dimitri?

MYRA: No. Oh, no . . . I thought he was out of prison.

PHILIP: I had a letter from Willi yesterday. He says Dimitri died in prison. Of course now he's officially rehabilitated and a hero of the people.

MYRA: Torture?

PHILIP: I suppose so. Probably. [*putting his arm round her*] Don't cry. What's the use? [*ironically*] Besides, he's died for socialism, hasn't he?

TONY: Don't let yourself be misled. They're talking about socialism in Russia, not Britain. It's tearing them apart, the way people are nasty to each other – in Russia.

MYRA: I can't stand your cynicism. I never could stand it.

PHILIP: You'd better stick to your Hydrogen Bomb. Stick to disarmament.

MYRA: You mean that we've got to accept the fact that in our time there's not going to be democracy, there's not going to be freedom, there's not going to be liberty?

PHILIP: Yes, of course. Who cares about liberty? The *people*? [*laughs bitterly*].

TONY [*to* ROSEMARY]: One half of this lot are bogged down emotionally in the thirties with the Spanish Civil War, and the other half came to a sticky end with Hungary. If you cut them open you'd find Spain or Hungary written in letters of blood on their soft hearts – but not Britain. Certainly not poor old Britain.

PHILIP [*with an eye on* TONY, *to* MYRA]: Why don't you recognize the fact that we've had it? We've served òur purpose.

MYRA: You mean we should leave it all to the youth? God help us, all they care about is ...

PHILIP: I'm late. See you later, Myra [*goes out hastily R*].

TONY [*to* MYRA]: Yes, why don't you recognize the fact that you've had it?

MYRA [*irritably, to* TONY *and* ROSEMARY]: If we stop do-gooding and just sit back with our feet up, are you going to take over? [*looking at their listless poses*] God, you are a petty, respectable little lot.

TONY [*facing her*]: Mother.

MYRA: Well?

TONY: I gather that at the moment your large heart is full of pity for the victims of *capitalist* witch-hunts.

MYRA: And why shouldn't it be? What are you trying to say?

TONY [*laughing*]: That's all.

MYRA: You could make out a case for the whole lot of us being so discredited, so morally discredited, that we should all take a unanimous decision to stay quiet for the rest of our lives. [*He does not reply.*] We should acknowledge our total failure and leave everything in your hands. In the hands of the glorious battling youth whose banners are unsmirched. If you had any banners, that is.

TONY [*shouting*]: You're so damned self-righteous.

MYRA: I don't feel self-righteous. Of course if we did retire gracefully from the field, you'd lose the benefit of our really rather unique experience.

TONY: Unique. All your lot have proved is that every political party lies and its members lie to themselves. Did that really need proving?

MYRA: What are you saying then? What is it that you want me to say?

TONY: I wonder how many people died in torture and misery and starvation during the years 1935 to 1939 while you stood on platforms smiling prettily and talking about democratic socialism.

MYRA: Yes, I know.

TONY: I wish I had a tape-recording of some of your speeches during that time. Well?

MYRA: What is it that you want me to say? Do you want me to give up – like Philip? Philip's going to become a nice kind-hearted business man giving money to good causes – Oh, God, *no.* [*remembering* ROSEMARY] Of course, he is a wonderful architect . . . Tony, I do wish you'd think about Philip's offer. You aren't really going to be an electrician, are you? [*humorously, to* ROSEMARY] Tony's going to be an electrician. He's quite determined to be. What do you think?

ROSEMARY [*fiercely*]: I think people ought to be what they want to be.

TONY: Hurray, Rosemary's on my side.

ROSEMARY: Mother wanted me to be a doctor, but I wanted to be a nurse.

TONY: Luckily Uncle Philip enjoys very good health for a man of his age. [*at* MYRA'S *angry look*] Well, he does, doesn't he?

ROSEMARY [*politely*]: Why do you want to be an electrician?

TONY: Perhaps I'll be a telephone engineer. Mother, did you know I could be a telephone engineer? Communications, that's the thing. Bringing people together. Mother, do you suppose if we talked to each other on the telephone it would be easier? We could go into different rooms and talk to each other – or play each other little items from your tape-recorder . . . [*imitates the sound of machine-gun fire*].

MYRA: Oh, damn you. What do you want? Is it that you want me to give up the H-Bomb work, is that it?

TONY: Well, of course not. Of course you should go on about the bomb. Or, as you usually refer to it – your bomb. Why, I might even help you with it.

MYRA: Then I don't know, I really don't.

TONY: The simple fight for survival – we're all in on that. But what for? Or don't you ask yourself any more? [*She shrugs impatiently.*] Why are you sitting there looking so tortured? You've got what you wanted, haven't you? Well? You've spent your life fighting for socialism. There it is, socialism. You said you wanted material progress for the masses. God knows there is *material* progress. Hundreds of millions of people progressing in leaps and bounds towards a materially-progressive heaven.

MYRA: Are you pleased about it or are you not?

TONY: Of course I'm pleased. Down with poverty. By the way, Mother, have you ever actually seen poverty? The real thing, I mean. I haven't. Well, have you? [*to* ROSEMARY] Have you, Rosemary?

ROSEMARY: My family aren't very well off.

TONY: Rosemary knows all about it. Hurray! In Britain people wear poverty like a medal around their necks – a sign of virtue. We aren't very well off! Mother, do you realize you've spent your whole life fighting to end something you know nothing about?

MYRA [*irritated to the point of tears*]: Would you please be kind enough to tell me what it is you want, then?

TONY: Do you know what it is you've created, you and your lot? What a vision it is! A house for every family. Just imagine – two hundred million families – or is it four hundred million families? To every family a front door. Behind every front door, a family. A house full of clean, well-fed people, and not one of them ever understands one word anyone else says. Everybody a kind of wilderness surrounded by barbed wire shouting across the defences into the other wildernesses and never getting an answer back. That's socialism. I suppose it's progress. Why not? To every man his wife and two children and a chicken in the pot on Sundays. A beautiful picture – I'd die for it. To every man his front door and his front door key. To each his own wilderness. [*He pauses for breath.*] Well?

MYRA: If you're going to put all that energy into dreaming dreams why don't you dream to some purpose?

TONY: Dreams, dreams, dreams – like your lot did? What are the words – don't say I've forgotten them, they've been stuffed down my throat all my life – liberty, democracy, brotherhood – and what's that other one? Ah, yes, comradeship, that's it. A world full of happy brothers and comrades.

MYRA: Does that really seem so silly?

TONY: Jesus, you aren't actually sitting there and telling me you still believe in – Jesus! [*to* ROSEMARY] Do you know, this lot still believe in it! What do you think?

ROSEMARY: I think I believe that people should be kind to each other.

TONY [*roaring with laughter*]: There, Mother, Rosemary's on your side – she believes people should be nice to each other.

[MYRA, *seeing* ROSEMARY *is hurt, puts out her hand to* ROSE-MARY'S *arm –* ROSEMARY *twitches away.*]

MYRA [*to* TONY]: So many people have died for it. Better people than you.

TONY: *Died* [*laughs*].

MYRA: Just imagine, during the last fifty years hundreds of thousands of people have died in torture and in loneliness, believing they were dying for the future – for *you* Tony.

TONY [*furious*]: Well, it doesn't mean anything to me. All your damned hierarchy of Socialist martyrs – what bloody right had they to die for me? Bullying, that's what it is. I'm not going to have your holy dead hung around my neck. [*to* ROSEMARY] Do you realize what it is they are saying? Because hundreds of thousands of Socialist martyrs took it upon themselves to die for a world full of happy brothers and comrades, we've got to fall into line. Well, what do you say?

ROSEMARY: I don't know – my parents weren't political.

TONY: Oh, aren't you lucky!

MYRA: Tony, please tell me – what is it that you want? You must want something?

TONY: To be left alone, that's all. And I don't want any more suffering – no more fighting and suffering and dying. What for? Oh, the great company of martyrs who went singing to the stake and the thumbscrews and the firing-squads for the sake of the noble dream of ever-fuller wage packets and a chicken in every pot. To each man his own front door – to each man his own – refrigerator! [*roars with laughter*].

[ROSEMARY *suddenly bursts into tears.* MYRA *tries to put her arms around her.* ROSEMARY *tears herself away and runs upstairs.*]

MYRA: Oh, Tony, do you have to.

TONY [*deflated and miserable*]: But I was talking to you. What does she have to cry for?

MYRA: I dare say the poor girl was upset by your happy picture of the world.

TONY: I didn't mean to make her cry. What shall I do?

MYRA: You could go upstairs and be nice to her.

TONY: Be nice to her. Say I'm sorry.

MYRA: Oh, do I have to tell you what to do? Go upstairs and put your arms around her.

TONY: I put my arms around her and then she'll feel fine.

MYRA: Really, is it such a hard thing to do – to go upstairs to that poor child and be warm and nice to her?

TONY: Yes, it is. Oh, very well, if you want me to. [*He stands as if waiting to be ordered.*]

MYRA [*shrugging*]: If *I* want you to.

TONY: Therapy for soul-trouble, a man's arms.

[*The door bell rings, R.*]

MYRA: Oh, *no.*

TONY: Perhaps it's Philip. Well, he can go and put his arms around her. [*Goes out R.* MYRA *lets herself slump on the divan, eyes closed.* TONY *comes back.*]

MYRA: Who is it? I'm not in.

TONY: I'll give you three guesses ... It's Milly.

MYRA [*jumping up, radiating joy*]: Milly, now?

TONY: You're surely not pleased? Now Sandy'll have to go back to his mum.

MYRA: Oh, don't be so stupid. [*goes fast towards R*] Where is Milly? [*to* TONY] Oh, get upstairs to that child, be a man for once in your life, can't you?

TONY: All right, I'm going [*goes obediently to stairs*].

MYRA: And could you please keep your jolly little tongue off Milly for a time? She's been traipsing back and forth across the world and she'll be tired.

TONY: Perhaps you'd like me to put my arms around her, too. Perhaps I should make love to Milly. Would it be good for her – soothing after her travels? Or good for me?

MYRA: Oh, Tony, don't take it out of Milly.

[*The door opens R and* MILLY *comes in. She is a large, firm-fleshed Yorkshire woman with a stubborn face and a practical manner. She wears her hair tight back in a firm chignon. Her voice is Yorkshire. She is beaming.*]

MILLY: Well, love, I'm back.

MYRA [*kissing her*]: Oh, Milly, I've never been so pleased to see anyone.

MILLY: Me, too. A delegation of twenty women for two weeks – not my idea of fun and games. I changed to an earlier plane and here I am.

MYRA: Milly, darling, you look marvellous. Tell me about Japan. Tell me about everything. Come and sit down and talk. We'll have a party. Yes, of course, that's what we must do. We'll have a party.

TONY [*disgusted, from the stairs*]: Oh, no, no, no, no, no.

CURTAIN

ACT TWO

SCENE I

The stage is semi-darkened. TONY *is lying on the divan, wearing his black cord trousers, but nothing on above the waist.*
The radio is playing an erotic tango.
TONY *is making machine-gun noises like a small boy. His movements are all tense and anxious. Throughout the first part of the scene, that is until he leaves* MILLY *and* MYRA *together, he is in that state of hysteria where one is compulsively acting a part, knows it, hates oneself for it, but can't stop.*
The door R held tight by a chair wedged under the handle. There is loud knocking on this door. TONY *runs across, opens with a flourish, shows his disappointment when he sees who it is.*
MYRA *enters dressed for the party and looking beautiful. She is carrying bottles for the party.*

MYRA: What's the matter, Tony?
  [*He replaces chair under the handle.*]
  Are you ill? What's wrong?
TONY: Now why should I be ill?
MYRA: Then why are you skulking in the dark, barricaded in?
TONY: This is now my bedroom.
MYRA: Oh, I see.
TONY: How many people have you got?
MYRA: About twenty, I suppose.
TONY: You blow up a party of twenty people at a couple of hours' notice?
MYRA: Some of the people who went to Japan with Milly came back this afternoon. What's that palm-court music for? What's this all about?
TONY: Milly. I'm going to seduce Milly.

54

MYRA [*irritated*]: Why can't you seduce Milly another time? I want her to help me cut sandwiches. [*She is on her way out L.*]

TONY [*in a Boyer voice*]: Darling, I love you.

MYRA [*irritated, but troubled*]: Tony, please stop it. I do wish you'd stop it.

TONY [*as before*]: Darling, I love you.

MYRA [*furious*]: Ohh ... I was probably wrong not to believe in corporal punishment for children.

[*She goes out L into living-room. There is a burst of music and laughter and talk from the party as she does so. As* TONY *is returning to divan, another knock on door, R.* TONY *opens it, admits* SANDY, *showing exaggerated disappointment when he sees who it is.*]

TONY: Oh, no [*wedges the chair back again*].

SANDY: What's wrong, are you ill?

TONY: Didn't you see the notice? I take it for granted that I'm invisible, that I'm simply something people walk through, but surely you saw the notice?

SANDY: What notice?

TONY: A large notice reading: No Admittance, use Tradesmen's Entrance.

SANDY: No.

TONY [*opening door to living-room, through a burst of music and talk*]: Mother, Mother!

MYRA'S VOICE: What?

TONY: Did you take down my notice?

MYRA'S VOICE: Oh, was that your notice?

TONY: I'm going to put it back.

MYRA'S VOICE: Oh, do anything you damned well like.

TONY [*shuts living-room door. Music, etc., stops*]: Everyone comes in, but simply everyone, as if my bedroom were – the hall. But not Milly, for whom I'm lying in wait.

SANDY [*blandly*]: And why are you lying in wait for my mother?

TONY [*in Boyer voice*]: I love her. The scene is set for seduction.

SANDY: Rather obviously so, perhaps. Why this cloistral gloom?

TONY [*instantly switching on more light*]: If you say so. You should know. [*in Boyer voice*] Darling, I love you. No, that doesn't sound right. [*trying again*] Darling, I love you. How's that?

SANDY: Is it true that Philip's looking for a personnel manager?

TONY [*stares. Gives his loud laugh*]: Yes. And I turned his kind offer down. It's all yours, Sandy.

SANDY: I thought I might discuss it with him. [*He proceeds L towards living-room.*]

TONY: And Mike's looking for you to see when you can start in with the Labour Party. The people wait, Sandy, they wait.

SANDY: Yes, I must discuss the whole thing with them both.

TONY: Darling, I love you. But it's no use. She'll simply go on cutting bread and butter. My body will be carried past her on a shutter and . . . I was born out of my time. Yes, I've suddenly understood what my tragedy is. I was born out of my time.

SANDY: Why don't you offer to help her cut the sandwiches? [*goes into living-room accompanied by a burst of music, etc.*]

TONY [*striking his forehead with his fist*]: Clown, I never thought of it. [*A knock on the door R. TONY opens it with a flourish, shows exaggerated delight as MILLY comes in. She is wearing a black sweater that leaves her shoulders bare. She drops her coat on a chair.*] Wait, I must hang up my notice [*goes out R*].

MILLY [*after him through the door*]: What notice?

TONY [*returning*]: There, we shall be undisturbed. [*Wedges the door again. Advances on her purposefully.*] But your shoulders, Milly, your shoulders, my eyes dazzle.

MILLY: What are you up to, young Tony?

TONY: I'm seducing you. [*kisses her shoulder*] There. Can I help you cut the sandwiches?

MILLY: What are you seducing me for?

TONY: Oh . . . to redress certain balances. [*pulls her towards him*] Besides, mother says I must.

MILLY [*amiably*]: Well, this is a surprise.

TONY: That's not what you should have said.

MILLY [*going calmly towards L*]: Perhaps another time. Where is my son?

TONY: You shouldn't ask that either.

MILLY: Is he coming home tonight or not? Because if not, one of the people I came back with on the plane could use his room.

TONY: You are a disgusting lot of women [*puts his arms around her from behind and bites her ear*].

MILLY: Mind, I don't want to have to do my hair again . . .

TONY: You should slap my face. Then I should slap yours. Then we should fall on the bed.

MILLY: But I haven't got time. And you don't know what you're doing, inviting a punch from me. My husband hit me the once [*shows him a large and efficient fist*].

TONY: Then I am afraid I am nonplussed. Doesn't that music do anything to you?

MILLY: What music? Oh – that. I've got so I never hear the radio or the telly [*is about to open door*].

TONY [*in Boyer voice*]: I love you.

[MILLY *does not turn.*]

I loo-ve you.

[MILLY *slowly turns, stands looking at him, hands on hips.* TONY *stares at her, derisive, rude, insulting.*]

MILLY [*quietly*]: What you're going to get from me, young Tony, is a damned good spanking.

[TONY *suddenly collapses into tired appeal, makes a helpless gesture.*]

MILLY [*in a different voice, warm and maternal*]: You take it easy, love. You just let up and take it a bit easier.

[MYRA *comes in from L. The* TWO WOMEN *stand side by side, looking at him.*]

MYRA [*irritated*]: Do put something on, Tony. You'll catch cold.

TONY [*instantly reverting to his previous aggressiveness*]: I know, and then you'll have to nurse me [*drags on his black sweater*].

MILLY [*easily*]: Eh, but he's a fine figure of a boy, that Tony.

MYRA: One sees such a lot of it. [*to* TONY] For God's sake, turn off that mush.

TONY [*turning off radio*]: I have failed. I have failed utterly.

MILLY: I want a large whisky. You'd better have one too, Myra.

TONY: And me too. Oh, I see. You want me to go away. Why can't I stay? I might learn something. [MYRA *and* MILLY *are arming themselves with stiff drinks.*] Mother, I thought you wanted Milly to help with the sandwiches. Why don't you both go and cut the sandwiches?

MYRA: I've finished the sandwiches.

TONY [*shrill and anxious*]: You'll be tight and giggly before the thing even starts. [*to* MYRA] Mother, you get giggly when you're tight. I really do hate to see women drink at all. [*to* MILLY, *as* MYRA *ignores him*] Do you, or do you not think I'm sexually attractive?

MILLY [*amiably but a trifle impatient*]: You're a knockout, love. [*to* MYRA] You've got to put me in the picture. What's this business with your Philip?

[TONY *regards them anxiously, as they settle down for a gossip.*]

MYRA: Oh, do run away, there's a good boy.

TONY: Well, I don't know, I don't really [*runs upstairs*].

[*The* TWO WOMEN *look at each other with raised eyebrows, sighing deeply.*]

MYRA: What am I going to do with him?

MILLY: Let me get some alcohol inside me if we are going to discuss the youth. Personally I think we should let the younger generation sink or swim without any further comment from us. [*takes a hearty swig*] They're only doing it to attract our attention.

MYRA: What's the good of sending one's son to a progressive school if he turns out like this? The idea was he'd be an integrated personality.

MILLY: Integrated with *what*?

MYRA: Ye-ees.

MILLY: Look what a public school did for Sandy.

MYRA: Hmmm. It did what it is supposed to do, surely.

MILLY: I walked out on Sandy's father because he was such a slick little go-getter, but one can't walk out on one's son.

MYRA: One doesn't even want to. Queer.

MILLY: Very, yes. [*There is a pause; they look at each other, eyeing each other ironically.*] He's not playing you up, is he?

MYRA: Sandy? But Sandy has such *beautiful* manners. [*She giggles.*]

MILLY [*giggling*]: I believe you. Well, give him the boot, I would. He's got what he wants, I suppose. [*At* MYRA'*s inquiring and rather hurt look.*] Never in his life did my Sandy do anything that wasn't calculated.

MYRA: What, never?

MILLY: My principle with Sandy is, wait until he's worked through some situation – he's always in a better position than he was when he started. Then you know what he was after from the start. [*at sight of* MYRA'*s face*] You're not going to shed any tears over my Sandy, are you? [*half-disgusted, half-admiring*] Wide boy ... Oh, I'm not saying he's not in love. But my Sandy'll always fall in love where it does him most good.

MYRA: An enviable talent.

MILLY: Not yours.

MYRA: Nor yours.

    [*They look at each other, grinning.*]

TOGETHER: Well, I don't know ...

    [*They roar with laughter. Pause.*]

MILLY: That Philip now.

MYRA [*drily*]: He's brought his lady-love to stay here.

MILLY [*drily*]: And he's going to marry her next week?

MYRA: So it would seem.

MILLY: Eh, but you're behaving nicely.

MYRA: There's such a satisfaction in behaving well. Not that one's more subtle forms of insult don't escape them entirely. [*She laughs shrilly, almost breaks down.*]

MILLY [*quiet and shrewd*]: Myra, love, you'd better take it easy.

MYRA: Yes. [*blowing her nose*] Yes. [*very gay*] What's happened to that man of yours? What's his name? Jack?

MILLY: Jack, yes. [*They look at each other and laugh.*]

MYRA: Well?

MILLY [*giggling*]: I walked out.

MYRA: What for this time?

MILLY: But it's always the same reason. Yes, come to think of it, it is.

Well, I was at his week-end cottage. I was going to marry him on the Monday week, as I recall . . . God knows what for. What's this thing we have about getting married?

MYRA [*grimly*]: I can't think.

MILLY: Yes, well.

MYRA: Oh well. [*They laugh.*]

MILLY: My man Jack. Yes. Well, I'd cleaned the cottage up all of Friday, just for the love of the thing. Cleaned it some more on the Saturday, cooked a dinner for ten people on Saturday night, and organized the vegetable garden Sunday. On Sunday afternoon Jack went off to play golf, and the little woman hung some new curtains in the living-room.

MYRA: You don't have to tell me. He came home at seven o'clock and wanted to know why your face wasn't made up.

MILLY: No, my man Jack didn't mind me in my working dirt. It wasn't that. He came home from his golf and gave me a nice kiss. Reward for hard work, as it were. Oddly enough, it always is.

MYRA [*grimly*]: Yes.

MILLY: Quite so. Well, then there were steps outside. My God, it was Mr Stent.

MYRA: Mr Stent?

MILLY: Assistant Manager. The shoes Jack will inherit.

MYRA: All right, I know. [*She groans.*]

MILLY: Suddenly Jack went into a tizzy. [*imitating a nervous flurried male voice*] 'Darling, that's Mr Stent. He can't see you like that. Do please change your dress.' [MYRA *giggles.*] I said to him: 'My man, your *property* is ready for display to anyone. But *I* have been cooking, cleaning, and digging for three days and I'm tired. Mr Stent will have to take me as I come.' Jack said – [*she imitates a nervous male voice*] – 'But darling, it will make such a bad impression.' [MYRA *is helpless with laughter.*] So I went up them stairs. I bathed. I changed. I made myself up like the Queen of Sheba. Then I went downstairs and cooked and served dinner for three. Then I entertained Mr Stent – oh, on his level, of course, keeping my tiny mind well in its place so as not to upset Mr Stent. Then I wished him a very good night. Then I wished Jack good-bye. Then I took my suitcase and walked out. I left the bill behind me. To charring eighteen hours at four shillings an hour. To buying and cooking and serving first-class dinner for ten, ten guineas. To planning and organizing vegetable garden, ten guineas. To making and hanging curtains, ten guineas. To acting as hostess to Mr Stent, five guineas. I didn't charge for my services in bed. Jack never did have a sense of humour. Besides, I didn't want to ruin him. And I asked him to make out the cheque for the Society for the protection of the Christian British Home.

MYRA: And did he?

MILLY: Oh yes, he did. He wrote me a letter saying why hadn't I let him know I was feeling like that. [*They both laugh.*]

MYRA: You have no discrimination.

MILLY: *I* haven't.

MYRA: Oh, all right.

MILLY: I suppose one has to make do with what there is.

MYRA: I was going to volunteer to go with those people to the testing area for the bomb. You know. Well, Tony was terribly upset. I was so happy. I was under the impression that he would mind if I got killed. Then he said: 'Mother, for God's sake have a sense of proportion.' Then I understood. It wouldn't have been respectable. That was what he minded. It wouldn't have been respectable [*laughs. Almost breaks down*].

MILLY: Myra, you must let up, you really must.

MYRA: Yes.

MILLY: Your Tony's got a heart, at least.

MYRA [*surprised*]: Tony has?

MILLY: Whereas my Sandy . . . When Sandy became a gentleman as a result of his expensive education, I was expecting him to drop me – Oh! very pleasantly of course. I was surprised when he opted to stay with me. I thought it was out of love and affection. One day I heard him saying to one of his posh friends – [*imitates* SANDY] – 'You must meet my mother, she's such a character.' Light dawned on me. I played up, you can imagine. I was a woman of the people with a heart of gold. Really, I made myself sick – revolting! I'll be an asset to him in the Labour Party, won't I? Meet my mum, a working woman with a heart of gold . . . Little – wide boy.

MYRA: Milly, Sandy's very fond of you.

MILLY: Hmmm, yes.

MYRA: Milly, why did you give him that kind of education then?

MILLY [*defensively*]: I was doing the best for him.

MYRA: Were you – well? I don't think he thinks so.

MILLY: What? What's he said to you?

MYRA: Milly, are you sure there's not a good part of you that likes Sandy the way he is?

MILLY: What's he said to you?

MYRA: He once said that you've equipped him to play the racket, and he has no choice but to play it.

MILLY: No choice. Ohhh! – so it's my fault, is it?

MYRA: Aren't our children our fault?

MILLY: No choice! [*throwing it off*] I wish you'd give him the boot before he drops you. I wish you would. It'd do him so much good.

MYRA [*with determination*]: Very well, I shall. Sandy, I shall say, Sandy, I no longer care for you.

MILLY: And do you?

MYRA [*grinning*]: It's so nice to have a man about the house.

MILLY [*grinning*]: Yeees.

MYRA: Well, it is. [*her face changes*] What am I going to do about Tony . . . Milly, what am I going to do? [*She almost breaks down.* MILLY *comes behind her, puts her arms around her.*]

MILLY: Myra, for God's sake, stop punishing yourself . . . We've lived our lives, haven't we? And we've neither of us given in to anything. We've both of us come through not too badly, considering everything. We're not going to come to a dead end in our sons?

MYRA: No.

MILLY: What's the use of living the way we have, what's the use of

us never settling for any of the little cosy corners or the little cages
or the second-rate men if we simply get tired now?

MYRA: Yes.

MILLY: Were you really going out with those people to the H-Bomb
tests?

MYRA: Yes.

MILLY: Because you knew the Government wouldn't let anyone get
near them anyway?

MYRA: No. I really wanted to – do something.

MILLY: You didn't mind getting killed?

MYRA: No.

MILLY: Myra, love, we all of us get depressed.

MYRA [*wrenching herself away from her*]: Depressed. That word annoys
me. Half the time we dope ourselves up with some stimulant –
men, our children, work. Then it fails and we see things straight,
and it's called being depressed. You know quite well that there's
only one question that everyone's asking – what are we alive for?
Why? Why shouldn't that damned bomb fall? Why not? Why
shouldn't the human race blow itself up? Is it such a loss? A little
dirty scum on the surface of the earth – that's what we are.

MILLY [*ironically*]: Scum, scum – that's all.

MYRA [*impatiently*]: All right – laugh me out of it – it's easy enough
[*laughs, irritably*].

MILLY: If I remind you in a month from now of things you are
saying tonight you'll laugh and say, 'Well, I was depressed then'.

MYRA: I dare say. Oh yes, I dare say. [*She is in a fever of irritation,
angry, laughing, stamping about the stage, deadly serious.*] I keep
dreaming, Milly. You know I keep having the same dream . . .

MILLY: Oh – dreams. So now we're going to turn into a pair of old
women plotting our dreams and looking for portents.

MYRA [*almost growling*]: Ohhh! – yes. But I do. Every time I get my
head on to a pillow, it's the same thing . . .

MILLY: Oh! Lord save us – get yourself tight and be done with it.

MYRA: No! Listen to me. Listen, Milly. [*She grabs* MILLY *to make her
listen.* MILLY *is ironical, sceptical, uncomfortable.*] The whole world is

full of great black machines. I am standing on the surface of the earth somewhere and everywhere about me on an enormous plain are great black machines. It is a world of cold white buildings and black motionless machines . . .

MILLY: Ho-ho – so we're against the machine now, are we; back to the Golden Age!

MYRA: . . . And I'm standing there, waiting. That's what it is, Milly, we're all waiting. No, listen . . . [*Now holds* MILLY *fast, making her listen. Slowly* MILLY *succumbs, becomes part of the dream with* MYRA.] We are standing, waiting. We lift our eyes and see the curve of the horizon . . . it's on fire, Milly. Not a real fire – the curve of the earth crackles with the cold white crackle of electricity. Then we understand – the earth is burning. They've set the bomb off somewhere and half of the earth is already gone. Everywhere in front of us the plain is disintegrating in a cold white crackle of fire. It will reach us in a minute. And we stand there thinking, thank God. Thank God it's all over. Thank God it's all over . . .

[*For a minute* MILLY *is held fast inside* MYRA'S *persuasiveness. She pulls away.*]

MILLY [*irritably*]: Oh! Myra . . . Well, I don't have to be asleep to see all that. I can see it when I'm awake.

MYRA [*grim and humorously desperate*]: Do you realize we've only got through half of our lives? We've got to get through another thirty or forty years of being alive – if we're unlucky.

MILLY [*with her hands over her ears*]: Shut up, shut up, Myra.

MYRA: I can't face it, Milly. I can't face another forty years of being alive.

MILLY [*uncovering her ears*]: Well, we'll both have to face it. We're both as strong as mules. [*gives* MYRA *a drink*] Now come clean, Myra. What's really eating you up? You've been talking around and around it . . . Philip's brought his girl here, Tony's in a bad mood, and it's all too much. That's all.

MYRA: That's all.

MILLY: Now listen to me. You had a good marriage with your husband. Then you and Philip were happy together for five years –

that's more than most people get in their lives. You and Philip are good friends now. There's old Mike hanging around waiting for your first moment of weakness so you'll give in and marry him. You've got Tony. You're not doing too badly.

MYRA: Oh, don't be so complacent . . . don't be so damned sensible . . . you know quite well that nothing you say to me now makes any sense at all.

MILLY [patiently]: Yes, love, I know.

MYRA: I wish you'd do something for me. I wish you'd talk to Tony. I can never say anything to him. He imagines I want to get rid of him. It's like this. I've got hold of some money – enough to finish his studying. Now he says he doesn't want to be an architect. So I'd like him to take it and go off for a couple of years – doing as he likes, wherever he likes. He'll never be free again. He'll be 40 before he knows it. I wish I'd had five hundred pounds at his age to spend as I liked, to find out about the world. Well, if you could talk to him perhaps he might listen.

MILLY: You've raised five hundred pounds by doing your own housework?

MYRA: No, no, of course not.

MILLY: Myra, what've you been up to – what've you done?

MYRA: But I can't talk to him, Milly. He thinks I want to get rid of him.

MILLY [holding her and forcing her to face her]: Myra, what have you done?

MYRA: I've sold the house.

MILLY: You haven't.

MYRA: Yes, I have. To raise money for Tony.

MILLY: But, Myra, what are you going to do?

MYRA [almost airily]: I have no idea.

MILLY: You're going to marry old Mike.

MYRA: Oh, no. Why, Milly, I didn't expect you to be so – careful. What does it matter? I do hate being tied down. I always did. Surely it's more important for Tony to be free than to fuss about some bricks and a roof . . . if it comes to the worst you'll always take me in.

MILLY: But what's Tony going to say? Have you told him?

MYRA: Why should he care? He's young.

MILLY: Why haven't you told him?

MYRA: Because I can't talk to him.

[TONY *comes down the stairs.*]

MILLY: Look out, he's coming.

[MYRA *hastily turns away to compose her face.*]

TONY: Finished your girlish confidences? Though why it has to be in my bedroom . . .

MILLY: Why don't you choose some other place to park yourself?

MYRA: Obviously the hall is the place most calculated to cause the maximum inconvenience to everybody.

TONY: I do hope you're going to make up your face, Mother.

[MYRA *goes into living-room without replying.*]

What's wrong with mother?

MILLY: She's tired. [*going towards living-room*] Come on, we've got to be gay if it kills us. Aren't you coming in at all?

TONY: No.

MILLY: You aren't interested to hear what's going on in Japan?

TONY: I'm sure the people in Japan feel like people everywhere else in the world – as if they've been handcuffed to a sleeping tiger.

MILLY: I want to talk to you sometime, young Tony.

TONY [*in Boyer voice*]: I want to talk to you, too. [MILLY *goes impatiently into living-room.*]

TONY [*collapsing on the divan*]: Thank God for the silence.

[*Almost at once he starts making machine-gun noises, pointing his arm all over the room. Stops. Imitates a bomb. More machine-gun noises.* ROSEMARY *comes in fast, from living-room. She is in a party dress and looking miserable.*]

TONY: Not in a party mood?

ROSEMARY: I can't stand listening to them talk. I can't. They talk about all kinds of horrors as if they were talking about the weather.

TONY [*laughing*]: They are.

ROSEMARY: I don't see how they can be so – matter-of-fact about everything.

TONY: Don't worry about them. They were just born thick-skinned. [ROSEMARY *sits, listlessly.* TONY *hesitates, then after a struggle with himself, sits beside her, puts his arm around her. She immediately snuggles against him and closes her eyes. There is a look on his face of incredulous but derisive pride.*] Feeling better?

ROSEMARY: Yes. Would your mother think it rude if I left here tonight?

TONY: Don't go – unless you want to. Don't just rush away.

ROSEMARY: It was all no good. It was a mistake.

TONY: Yes, I know. Never mind. [*There is a burst of laughter and music.*]

ROSEMARY [*wistfully*]: They have a good time, don't they?

TONY: They'd have a good time if the skies were falling. If the end of the world were announced for Friday, mother would say – 'Let's have a party'.

ROSEMARY [*fiercely*]: Yes, they're so childish.

TONY: Oh God, yes . . . Rosemary, I wish you'd tell me something.

ROSEMARY [*sitting up away from him*]: What – do you mean about politics – but I don't know about them.

TONY [*laughing*]: Yes, perhaps I do mean politics.

ROSEMARY: So *childish*. They talk as if they really believe what they do changes things. You know, 5,000 people listen to a speech and everything will be changed.

TONY [*laughing*]: Go on. Go on, Rosemary.

ROSEMARY: But it seems to me as if there are perhaps – six very important, very powerful men in the world – somewhere up there – we probably don't even know their names, and they make the decisions . . .

TONY: Go on.

ROSEMARY [*indicates living-room*]: In there they're talking about . . . I don't see how they can believe in it. If the 5,000 people killed themselves tomorrow in Trafalgar Square as a protest against – everything, the six powerful men up there wouldn't care, they wouldn't even notice. And it would be something in the news-papers for ordinary people.

TONY [*delighted, laughing*]: Go on, Rosemary, don't stop.

ROSEMARY: Just one of those important men can go mad or get drunk and – well, that's all. That's all.

TONY: Rosemary.

ROSEMARY: Yes. [*She lets herself fall back against him.* TONY *puts his arms around her, talks over her head.*]

TONY [*unconsciously rocking her*]: Rosemary, I've been thinking. What we need is something different. Something – very simple.

ROSEMARY [*eyes closed, against him*]: Yes.

TONY: Something very simple. I think I want to be a tramp. I've been thinking . . . the whole world is getting mass-produced and organized. But inside everybody's varnished and painted skin is a tramp. It's the inner emigration. Every morning in front of the bathroom mirror we polish our teeth and our hair and our skin, we set our faces to tick all day like metronomes against the image in the mirror until the lights go out at night. But inside, we've emigrated. We're tramps. Don't you see, Rosemary, we have to keep the tramp alive somehow. Would you like to be a tramp, Rosemary? [*Looks down at her face, but her eyes are closed. She is half-asleep.*] No, a tramp is solitary, a tramp is solitary . . . [*rocking her*] Shhh, Rosemary . . .

ROSEMARY [*sleepily*]: Yes . . .

[*The door L bursts open, letting in a shout of music and talk.* PHILIP *comes in fast,* SANDY *after him.*]

SANDY: So if you're really looking for someone perhaps you'd try me.

PHILIP [*briefly*]: Yes, of course.

SANDY: It's really awfully good of you. May I come into your office tomorrow and talk it over with you?

PHILIP [*curtly*]: Yes, do. [*to* ROSEMARY] Aren't you well?

ROSEMARY: Perfectly well, thank you. [*At her leisure she disengages herself from* TONY, *but remains sitting close beside him.*]

PHILIP: It's really very rude to run away like that. It's not polite to Myra.

ROSEMARY: I'm sure Myra will bear up.

[MYRA *comes in L, looking gay and beautiful.*]

MYRA: I can't have all the young people leaving my party. It leaves us all so dull.

SANDY [*laying his arm around her shoulders*]: Myra darling, how could any party be dull with you in it?

TONY: You should make up a Strontium-90 calypso and dance to it.

ROSEMARY: If you don't mind, Myra, I'd like to go to bed.

MYRA [*briefly*]: Of course I don't mind. [*to* TONY] I do think you might come in even if just for a few minutes.

TONY [*to* ROSEMARY]: Would you like to come out into the garden for a little? There's a moon tonight.

ROSEMARY [*with a defiantly guilty look at* PHILIP]: Yes, I'd love to ... just for a few minutes, and then I must go to bed.

[TONY *and* ROSEMARY *go out* R. PHILIP, *after a moment, walks angrily off after them.*]

SANDY [*gracefully amused*]: Lovers' quarrels.

MYRA: Oh, quite. Charming.

SANDY: How lucky we're more sensible.

MYRA [*gaily, flirting with him*]: Dear Sandy, you're always so sensible.

SANDY: Not so sensible as to be dull, I hope.

MYRA [*mocking and affectionate*]: Dull? You? Darling, never. [*kissing him*] Darling sensible Sandy.

SANDY: Dear Myra – so sad, isn't it?

MYRA: Sad? Sad – oh, I see [*bursts into laughter*].

SANDY [*uneasily*]: I love your laugh, darling.

MYRA: Oh, I love it too [*regards him mockingly*]. Well, go on.

SANDY: You're in a very odd mood.

MYRA: You're quite right, darling, it's quite time for us to call it a day.

SANDY [*disconcerted*]: Yes, well, of course.

MYRA: And you've been wonderful. [*imitating him*] Sandy, you're really so *wonderful*.

SANDY [*stiffly*]: I'm so glad we are both capable of being graceful about the end. Though of course you and I are much too close ever to part, darling.

MYRA: Oh, quite so. Exactly. [*kissing him mockingly*] There. [*laughing*] I've done it. Only by the skin of my teeth though. I must tell Milly. She'll be so pleased.

SANDY: Tell her what? You haven't been discussing *us* with mother? But I'm sure she would quite agree that I did the right thing in breaking it off.

MYRA [*astounded*]: *You* did the right thing . . . [*rocking with laughter*] Why of course, yes, you did, didn't you?

SANDY [*furious*]: Really, Myra, I do think your behaviour is in very bad taste.

[*He goes angrily out R as* PHILIP *comes in from the R.*]

PHILIP: And what's wrong with your young man?

MYRA: I might ask, what's wrong with your young woman?

[*He gives a short gruff laugh. They eye each other and both laugh.*]

PHILIP [*drily*]: Well, Myra?

MYRA: Well, Philip?

PHILIP [*with whimsical exasperation*]: Really, women, women.

MYRA: Tell me, do you find Rosemary's behaviour in bad taste?

PHILIP [*rather sentimentally*]: I suppose it is better that she should find out what I'm like before rather than after.

MYRA [*drily*]: It is *lucky*, isn't it? [*They eye each other, smiling, with an old and bitter emotion.*]

PHILIP [*on an impulse, dragged into saying it*]: It would be odd if we ended up with each other after all, wouldn't it?

MYRA [*tiredly*]: Rather odd, yes.

PHILIP [*with sentimental bitterness*]: You know me, Myra. I'm not much good . . . [*turns away, frowning – the frown is a nervous spasm of irritation against himself for the role he is playing*].

MYRA [*quickly*]: Don't do that, Philip, don't. I always did wish you wouldn't – it's so bloody insulting.

PHILIP [*gaily, but with self-dislike because he has not met her appeal*]: But, Myra, I'm proposing to you . . . I'm always proposing to you and you always turned me down.

MYRA [*ironically*]: Yes, you always were. But bigamy never did appeal to me much.

PHILIP [*half-serious, half playing at it and bitter with conflict*]: Well, old girl, what about it? Can you face all that over again?

MYRA [*against her will surrendering, smiling to him*]: What an awful prospect, all that over again . . .

[*They suddenly come together, cling together, almost kiss, passionately. But at the same moment with the same gesture of angry and bitter irritation, turn away from the embrace. They* BOTH *laugh, painfully.*]

PHILIP [*the mood of surrender is gone. They are both back in their roles. He speaks with whimsical bitterness*]: No woman ever made me as unhappy as you did. I wonder why . . .

[*She says nothing but watches him ironically.*]

MYRA: I wonder why, too.

PHILIP: I wish you'd tell me the truth now, Myra . . .

MYRA [*groaning and ironical*]: Ohhh – about my infidelities?

PHILIP [*suddenly painfully and eagerly intense*]: For instance, that American – you swore there was nothing – that he wasn't in your room that night?

MYRA [*almost groaning*]: Oh, Philip . . . do you suppose when we're both 70 you'll still be asking me . . . the one thing you can't afford to believe is that I always told you the truth.

PHILIP [*quickly*]: Oh come, come, you'll never change.

MYRA [*humorously groaning*]: Oh, Philip . . .

PHILIP [*gay, bitter, and guilty*]: After all, I can't say I don't know what I'm in for.

MYRA [*very dry*]: What you are saying is this: that you propose to marry me although you take your stand on the fact that I lied continuously to you for five years, that I was unfaithful to you for five years, and that you insist I will continue both to betray you and to lie about it.

PHILIP [*gay and guilty*]: Why, Myra dear, now that I'm older I'm more tolerant, that's all. Well, what do you say?

MYRA [*bitter, smiling*]: Obviously nothing.

PHILIP: What? [*quickly*] There you are – that's what always happens when I propose to you – you turn me down.

[*She smiles at him. He smiles back. It is very painful. A moment o, quiet.*]

[*almost groaning*] Oh, Lord . . .

MYRA [*groaning, painful but humorous*]: Ohhh . . . [*then, suddenly furious and loud*] I wish just once I could meet a man who didn't tell himself lies and expect me to believe them.

PHILIP [*shouting*]: You know quite well I can't stand the way you're always giving yourself away to everybody and everything. *I can't stand you, Myra.*

[*A moment's quiet. They look at each other, smiling bitterly.*]

[*whimsically*] When you've given up – when you've got grey hair and wrinkles, I'll take you on then.

MYRA: Shall I dye my hair and paint on wrinkles?

PHILIP: Yes.

MYRA: No one ever loved me as you did, no one. That's what I can't forgive you for – it wouldn't have mattered if you hadn't loved me. But you did. And you turned me down.

PHILIP [*groaning, turning away*]: Oh, let's leave it, let's leave it now.

MYRA: You turned me down because I loved you. You couldn't stand being loved.

PHILIP: Oh, Lord, it is absolutely *intolerable*!

MYRA [*between her teeth*]: Absolutely hopeless! [*They shrug, stand silent.*]

[MIKE *comes in from L.*]

MIKE: Why, here you are. Philip, where's your charming little Rosemary? Everybody's running away from the party. I thought I'd come and find you. [*comes up to* MYRA] What's wrong, dear? [*puts his arm around her*] Myra dear, you really do look bad, you know. You do really need someone to look after you.

MYRA [*letting her head lie on his shoulder*] Dear Mike. You are always so sweet.

MIKE [*to* PHILIP]: Myra needs someone to look after her.

PHILIP [*grimly*]: Perhaps she does. [*with a short laugh*] You two look rather well together.

MYRA [*smiling painfully to* MIKE]: He thinks we look well together. Philip does.

MIKE [*wistfully*]: You know what I think, dear.

MYRA [*to* PHILIP]: You like the sight of me and Mike together?

PHILIP [*embarrassed, hurt, and angry*]: Well, why not? If that's what you want.

MYRA [*to* MIKE]: You'd like to take me on?

MIKE [*carefully*]: I don't have to tell you what I've always wanted [*looks doubtfully from* MYRA *to* PHILIP].

MYRA: Can you *stand* me, Mike? Can you stand me?

   [PHILIP *turns away, frowning.*]

MIKE: Stand you, dear?

MYRA: It would be awful if you couldn't stand me.

MIKE: But, Myra dear, I've loved you for years. After all, I've never made any secret of it to anybody.

   [MYRA *smiles at him. In an impulse of joy* MIKE *embraces her. But because of her reaction the embrace ends in a brotherly hug.*]

MIKE [*hopefully*]: I'm so happy, dear.

MYRA: Dear Mike.

   [*She lays her head on his shoulder and looks at* PHILIP. PHILIP *turns away with a helpless and bitter gesture.* ROSEMARY *and* TONY *come in from garden R. They have been talking animatedly but at the sight of the three they stop still.*]

ROSEMARY [*awkward because of* PHILIP, *to* TONY]: I think I'll go to bed now.

TONY [*forgetting* ROSEMARY *at the sight of* MIKE *and* MYRA *who still have their arms around each other*]: Well, Mother? Well, Mike?

MIKE: There you are, my boy.

ROSEMARY [*defiantly, to* PHILIP]: I must really go to bed, I'm so tired.

PHILIP [*suddenly concerned to reclaim her*]: But, Rosemary, don't go yet. Stay down here and talk a little. Have a drink.

ROSEMARY [*unwillingly reclaimed*]: Well, just for a minute – no, I won't have a drink.

   [PHILIP *and* ROSEMARY *sit together on the stairs.* MYRA *and* MIKE *are standing together. His arm is still around her.*]

TONY [*looking from one couple to the other*]: Oh, no!

[MILLY *comes in from living-room.*]

MILLY: Do come and do your duty, Myra – I can't cope with all these people any longer by myself.

TONY [*fiercely to* MILLY]: Ever so interesting, sex, isn't it?

MILLY [*briskly*]: I've always found it so ... [*but she sees his face, turns to look first at* MYRA *and* MIKE *then at* PHILIP *and* ROSEMARY].

TONY [*shrilly*]: What astounds me is the way it so obviously is everyone's favourite occupation.

MILLY [*briskly*]: Never mind, love, you'll soon get into the way of it ... [*Looking at his face she suddenly understands he is about to crack. She lays a hand briefly on his shoulder, saying to* MIKE] Take Myra back to her guests, there's a dear.

MIKE: Of course, we're just going [*leads* MYRA *across to living-room door. They go out*].

[MILLY *locks the door, turns to* TONY.]

TONY [*pathetically*]: She's not starting something with Mike now, is she? Surely she isn't seriously going to ...

MILLY: And why not?

TONY [*almost beside himself, he runs to foot of stairs and confronts* ROSEMARY]: Rosemary, come and have a drink with me, come and talk.

ROSEMARY [*taking* PHILIP *with her upstairs*]: No thanks, Tony, I think Philip and I'll go to bed now.

[PHILIP *and* ROSEMARY *go out of sight upstairs.* MILLY *jams door on R with chair.*]

TONY: Oh *no*. [*whirling on* MILLY] Why? Half an hour ago she was ready to kick dear Uncle Philip downstairs.

MILLY: Bless you, dear.

TONY: It's going to be such a jolly night. Imagine it – Rosemary and Uncle Philip in one bed – *my* bed, but let that pass. Then there's mother. Will it be Sandy or Uncle Mike, do you suppose? Why not both?

MILLY [*calmly*]: You're not talking to me about your mother like that, young Tony.

TONY [*almost ecstatic with pain*]: Or they might have a little change

74

in the middle of the night. Mother and Uncle Philip – for old time's sake. And Sandy and Rosemary might have a good deal in common – who knows? Of course they *are* pretty near the same age, probably a handicap. Then there's you and me.

MILLY: Take it easy, Tony. Take it easy.

TONY: Three happy well-assorted couples . . . [*He roars with laughter.* MILLY, *seeing what is coming, moves towards him, stands waiting.*] Three couples, each couple in a nice tidy little room with the door locked. And in the morning we'll make polite conversation at breakfast. Of course, there is an odd man out – dear Uncle Mike. Well, he can lie on the mat outside mother's door. Why shouldn't we all ring each other up in the middle of the night and report progress. The grunts and groans of pleasurable love-making would be interrupted for the sake of a few minutes' militant conversation about the dangers of the hydrogen bomb. Then back to what everyone's really interested in. It's bloody funny, when you come to think about it . . . [*He breaks down, sobbing.* MILLY *catches him as he heels over on the divan, holds him against her, rocking him.*] I simply can't stand any of it. I can't stand it. I can't stand it.

CURTAIN

SCENE 2

The next morning, rather early.

The curtain rises on the room in disorder. MILLY *and* TONY *are lying on the untidy divan.* TONY *has his black trousers on, nothing above.* MILLY *is wearing a black lace petticoat. She is smoking and watching him with a calm maternal eye. The door L is wedged with the chair.*

TONY *makes the sound of machine-gun fire with his mouth, pointing an imaginary machine-gun over the ceiling, like a small boy.* MILLY *does not move.* TONY *does it again.*

MILLY: What's that in aid of?

TONY: I love that sound. That sound is me. I love it.

MILLY: Can't say I do.

TONY: What are you going to do when mother comes down those stairs? For God's sake put some clothes on.

MILLY: I like myself like this. Don't you?

TONY [examines her, drops his head on his arms]: I don't know. I don't know.

MILLY: I know. You don't. [She caresses the back of his neck, runs the side of her palm down his spine. He shrinks away from her.] No? [As he remains silent, she takes his head in her arms and cradles it.] Is this better? [rocks him, half-tender, half-derisive] Baby, baby, baby.

TONY [shutting his eyes]: Put on some clothes. Put some clothes on.

MILLY: You'd like me to put a veil over my face and keep my hair covered.

TONY: Yes.

MILLY: Well, I'm not going to. You'd better learn to like the female form. [rocking him] You wanted to take me into bed so as to annoy your mother. Here I am. But when it comes to the point you're scared she might know.

TONY: She'll come down the stairs, see us and say: 'Milly, where's my H-Bomb file?'

MILLY [laughing]: Child. You're a child.

TONY: Oh, I can hear her. She said, 'Milly, I'm worried about that son of mine. He's still a virgin. Do something about it, will you?' Then, dismissing this item on her agenda, she said: 'Where's my tape-recording of . . .' Oh, Christ . . . [He rolls away from her.]

MILLY [running the side of her palm down his spine]: Come here, young Tony.

TONY: If you're going to seduce me again then let's have some appropriate music [makes machine-gun noises again].

MILLY [calmly, moving away from him]: Young Tony, I'm going to give you some good advice, and if you've got any sense you'll take it.

TONY: Action. Action is what I want. Not words.

MILLY: You'll find yourself a nice friendly tart and put in a couple of weeks learning your job. Then perhaps you'll be fit for adult society.

TONY [*grinning*]: What? You're walking out on me? You've got other fish to fry? Is that it? I thought I'd found a nice friendly tart. [*She continues to regard him amiably.*] Well, why don't you hit me?

MILLY: What for?

TONY [*shrilly*]: I've insulted you.

MILLY: *You* insult *me*?

TONY: I expected you to hit me.

MILLY: Why do you want to be hit?

TONY [*collapsing on to the divan, face down*]: Oh, I don't know, I don't know, I don't know.

[MILLY *lays a hand on his shoulder. He flings it off.*]

[*shrilly*] I simply don't like women.

MILLY [*as she slowly puts on her black sweater*]: That's half of humanity disposed of.

TONY: All you're interested in is . . .

MILLY: I was under the impression that that night of love was your idea.

TONY: Love!

MILLY [*suddenly and for the first time hurt*]: You've made use of me, young Tony. You made use of me.

TONY [*guilty*]: Of course women are so much better than men.

MILLY [*grimly*]: Is that so?

TONY [*sentimental and shrill*]: You're so much stronger.

MILLY: That's very nice for you, isn't it?

TONY: But I mean it, you are.

MILLY: When I hear men saying that women are so much stronger than men, I feel like . . .

TONY: What?

MILLY: Reaching for my revolver.

TONY: I imagined it was a compliment.

MILLY: Did you now, love. I prefer the more obvious forms of contempt [*she slowly puts on her black skirt*]. If you really don't like sex why don't you leave us alone? Otherwise you're going to turn into one of those spiteful little men who spend their lives punishing women in bed ... Where's my brooch? [*She adjusts the sweater, which last night was open over her shoulders, tight to her throat with a brooch.*]

TONY: Now you look like a respectable *Hausfrau*.

MILLY: You might also put in some time asking yourself why you have to say you don't like women.

TONY [*slowly sits up on the divan, legs crossed*]: Women, women, women ... [*He meditatively and sensuously bites his own shoulder.*]
   [MILLY *stands watching satirically, hands on hips.*]

MILLY: You might find it all more satisfactory if you took a mirror into bed with you.

TONY: I have no idea at all what you're talking about.

MILLY: Oh, I believe you. You probably don't.

TONY [*shrilly*]: You lay all last night in my arms. You were perfectly sweet. And now ...

MILLY: What's the matter with you all, anyway? We've committed the basic and unforgivable crime of giving you birth – but we had no choice, after all ... Well, God damn the lot of you. [*going towards door R*] I'm going home. For the sake of appearances.

TONY: Oh, don't worry about my reputation, please.

MILLY [*amazed*]: Your reputation? [*scornful*] Your reputation. Why, do you consider yourself compromised? [*laughs*] I'm considering my Sandy.

TONY: Why? Your Sandy is such a man of the world.

MILLY: Not so far as I am concerned. I have preserved my Sandy's mental equilibrium by the practice of consummate hypocrisy. It is usually referred to as tact.

TONY: What a pity my mother thinks tact beneath her.

MILLY: It's always a mistake to treat you as if you were grown-ups. Always.

TONY [*jumping up*]: Milly, don't go. Don't go, Milly. [*He goes after her.*] You're not really going ... I'm sorry if I hurt you.

MILLY [*coming back, she stands with her hands on her hips, looking at him*]:

Young Tony, why don't you get out of here. For Christ's sake, *get out.*

TONY [*sharply*]: Mother told you to say that.

MILLY: The Lord help us. [*Goes to him, puts her hands on his shoulders from behind. He leans his head back against her and closes his eyes.*] You ought to get out, Tony. Bum around a bit. You can't stay here. Surely you can see that your mother's worried because you don't want any life of your own?

TONY: You mean, she wants a life of her own.

MILLY [*exasperated*]: Tony, you aren't ten years old.

TONY: What does she want? She wants to marry Uncle Mike? I don't believe it.

MILLY: Perhaps she thinks it would make you happy if she settled down.

TONY: With Uncle Mike? She's going to settle down with old Mike just to please me?

MILLY: But she's worried about you. You surely can see that she's bound to be worried about you?

TONY: With Aunty Mike [*laughs unpleasantly*].

MILLY: And besides, she's lonely.

TONY: Lonely? My battling mum? Why on earth? She's never alone. [*pause*] Then if she's lonely, why does she want to get rid of me?

MILLY [*dropping her hands, shrugs, and moves away*]: I give up. I simply give up. But you should get out. You're 22. You should be banging and crashing around South America or the Middle East, getting mixed up in all kinds of things, making a fool of yourself, having women . . .

TONY [*wincing*]: Oh Christ!

MILLY: You ought to be shouting your head off about everything, revolutionizing, upsetting all the equilibriums.

TONY: Equilibrium? What equilibrium? You don't really imagine that I should want to revolutionize after watching your lot at it all my life? Upsetting the equilibrium . . . that's just it! You're so childish . . . if there was, by any miracle, an equilibrium anywhere you'd put a bomb under it just for the sake of seeing everything rock. All I want is an equilibrium – just five minutes of stability. [*pause*] This house is the only thing in my life that has – stayed in one place. It's the only thing I can count on. Why should I want to leave it? [MILLY *slowly comes up behind him again, cradles him against her.*] I remember after our other house was blown up, that night mother and I were lying under the bricks waiting to be rescued, and my father was dead beside us, I remember thinking that there would never be another house. I remember thinking mother would get killed too, and I'd have to go to an orphanage. I remember lying there under the bricks with the bombs falling . . . after that we were in one furnished room after another for months and months. Then there was this house. I remember the first few weeks we were here I used to go secretly around looking at the walls, wondering if the cracks were going to appear soon. I couldn't believe a house could be something whole, without cracks. I love this house. I don't want ever to leave it. I'd like to – pull it over my ears like a pillow and never leave it.

MILLY: Tony, love, you can't build your life around a house.

TONY: Yes I can, yes I can . . . hold me, Milly.

MILLY [*rocking him*]: Tony, suppose you had to leave?

TONY [*eyes closed, blissfully, sleepily*]: Had to? Had to? Why? No. I'll stay here always. Hold me, Milly.

MILLY: Tony, love, listen to me, I must talk to you.

TONY: No, don't talk. Just hold me.

MILLY: Tony, Tony, Tony. But I have to talk to you . . .

[MYRA *comes down the stairs, wearing her old trousers, without make-up, smoking.*]

MYRA: Good morning.

MILLY [*without letting* TONY *go*]: Good morning, Myra.

TONY [*from* MILLY'S *arms*]: Slept well, Mother?

MYRA: Thank you, no. [*to* MILLY, *smiling*] You're a very early visitor.

MILLY [*grinning*]: Not too early, I hope.

[*She lets her arms fall away from* TONY. TONY *moves away in a*

drifting listless movement to the window, leans there, back turned.
MYRA *raises her eyebrows at* MILLY. MILLY *gives a massive good-natured shrug.*]

TONY: More songs without words. Yes, Mother, the operation is successfully concluded.

MILLY: Do you want me to tidy up this bed again?

MYRA: I don't know, I haven't thought. I don't know what's going on, if Philip and Rosemary have made it up or not. If she's going home, then Tony can have his room back.

TONY [*turning*]: I wish someone would explain this to me – last night Rosemary was through with Uncle Philip. She hated and despised him. If she comes down those stairs announcing that the marriage is on, are you two wise women going to let her marry him? You both know quite well that she'll be miserable. [*They both shrug.*] What? You aren't going to say that you don't believe in interfering with other people's lives?

MYRA: What do you think we should do? Take her aside and warn her against Philip? How can we?

TONY: Why not?

MYRA: You should do it.

TONY: Why me?

MYRA: You're her age. She'll trust you.

TONY: Oh – hell. [*aggressively, to his mother*] Where's Sandy? Surely he should do it? He's the boy for public and personal relations.

MILLY: Tony dear, that girl likes you.

TONY [*amazed*]: She likes *me*?

MILLY [*patting him*]: You've been kind to her.

TONY: Oh.

MILLY [*kissing him*]: Bless you, dear boy.

MYRA [*watching them, ironically*]: Oh well, I don't know. I'm feeling very old this morning. [*goes to the mirror and looks at it*] Oh, oh, oh.

TONY: Then for heaven's sake put some lipstick on at least. [*She winces.*] Sorry. Sorry, Mother. [*goes to her and says with rough gentleness*] Mother, if you knew how I hate it, the way you go slopping around like this, you'd do something about it. Please.

MYRA [*touched by his tone, turning to him*]: Really? You really care? Well, I'll try.

TONY: You look so beautiful when you try.

MYRA: Why, Tony, I shall burst into tears.

TONY: Mother, you surely aren't going to marry old Mike?

MYRA: It would seem so.

TONY: You don't want to, do you?

MYRA: Would you hate it if I did?

TONY: But, Mother, he's an old man.

MYRA [*touched to the point of tears*]: An old man ... but Tony, I'm not far off 50 ... [*laughing*] Oh, Tony, you are absurd. You're sweet. Well, of course I won't marry him if you don't like it.

TONY: Good God, how could I like it?

MYRA [*delighted*]: Well, that's easy, isn't it? [*She impulsively kisses him. He kisses her.*] Well, everything's all right, isn't it? [*Sits on the arm of a chair, humming* Boohoo, you've got me crying for you.]

MILLY [*reprovingly*]: Poor Mike.

MYRA [*blissfully*]: Oh, I'm so happy, what a relief. I've been awake all night thinking of my gloriously exciting future.

TONY [*suddenly furious*]: You're as irresponsible as a child.

MYRA [*blissfully*]: Yes, I know, I know.

TONY [*shouting*]: You just pick people up and drop them.

MYRA: How could I pick up Mike and drop him? I've known him for a thousand years.

MILLY [*drily*]: Last night you said you'd marry him. Or didn't you?

TONY: It was announced, no doubt, to all your guests.

MYRA: Yes, it was. Yes. But he'll understand. Mike has always been so sweet.

TONY: Sweet. And there's Sandy. He's always sweet too. Where *is* Sandy?

MYRA: Oh, Sandy – well, I don't know.

TONY: You mean he wasn't sharing your insomnia last night?

MYRA [*coldly*]: Obviously not. I believe he went home.

MILLY: Oh, did he now? [MILLY *looks at* MYRA. MYRA *looks at*

MILLY, *full of wild mischievous delight. She collapses in a chair, laughing.*]

MYRA: Oh, Milly, don't mind me – but this is one situation you can't walk out on.

[*As she laughs the door-bell rings, R.* TONY *looks out of window, turns to grin at* MILLY *and* MYRA. *Unwedges door.* SANDY *enters fast, goes straight to* MILLY.]

SANDY: Mother, you might have let me know that you had plans to stay out last night.

MILLY: I might have done. If I'd had plans.

SANDY: I was worried about you.

MILLY: I never worry about you. I know you can look after yourself.

SANDY: Where were you?

MILLY: Here.

SANDY [*relieved*]: Oh, you were with Myra. Oh . . . [*looks at* TONY *and stiffens*] I see.

[MYRA *laughs.* SANDY *turns on her, furious.*]

MYRA: Sandy dear, have you been worrying about *me* all this time and I never knew it?

SANDY [*furious*]: Really, Myra, I would never have believed it possible that you could behave in such sheer bad taste, really Myra . . .

[MYRA *laughs. Her attention is caught by* ROSEMARY *and* PHILIP *at the top of the stairs.* SANDY *turns, then* MILLY *and* TONY. *They all stand and watch as* ROSEMARY *and* PHILIP *slowly descend.*]

ROSEMARY [*half-way down the stairs, in command of the situation, bravely making a necessary announcement*]: Good morning. Philip and I have talked it over and we have decided that it would be very much more sensible *not* to get married. [*No one knows what to say.*]

TONY: I'm delighted there is one sensible person in this house.

[ROSEMARY *leaves* PHILIP *at the foot of the stairs and goes to stand by* TONY *at the window. The stage is now like this:* TONY *and* ROSEMARY *standing side by side, back to the window, watching.* PHILIP *at foot of the stairs.* SANDY *and* MILLY *together near the door, R.* MYRA *by herself at centre.*]

PHILIP: Well, Myra, I'm sorry all this has been foisted on you.

MYRA: Oh, don't mention it [*smiles ironically at him. Her smile brings him across to her*].

[THEY *are now close together, looking into each other's face.*]

SANDY [*from beside* MILLY]: Philip, perhaps I could go down to the office with you . . .

[*He is about to go over to* PHILIP: MILLY *grabs him by the arm and makes him stay by her. She keeps tight hold of him.*]

PHILIP [*to* MYRA, *in a low voice*]: So everyone's back where they started – except you? You're going to marry old Mike?

MYRA: No.

PHILIP: Well, old girl?

MYRA [*with grim humour*]: My hair isn't grey yet . . . I wouldn't forgive you, Philip. I wouldn't be the good woman sitting on the mountain-top forgiving you your sins.

PHILIP: Oh Lord, Myra, I'm tired . . . I really would like something – quiet. [*drily, tender, bitter*] Well, Myra?

MYRA: I've told you, I wouldn't forgive you. You cast me in the one role long enough – now you want me to be the quiet woman waiting to welcome you home? But I wouldn't forgive you. If I did it would be contempt. *I've* never despised you, Philip.

PHILIP [*half-groaning*]: Oh, Lord, it is utterly *intolerable*.

MYRA [*half-groaning, turning away*]: Oh God, yes . . .

SANDY: Philip, if you're going to the office, we could go together.

PHILIP [*impatiently*]: Yes.

MILLY [*holding* SANDY]: I was under the impression you came here for me – why are you so interested in Philip all of a sudden. [TONY *suddenly laughs.*] Oh, I see . . . I thought that was the job Philip had arranged for Tony.

SANDY: But I thought Tony had turned it down unconditionally.

TONY: He has, don't worry.

SANDY: I wouldn't have dreamed of approaching Philip unless I was sure Tony wasn't interested.

PHILIP: I'm late. I must go.

MILLY [*holding* SANDY *fast*]: You come home. You can arrange your career with Philip another day.

PHILIP: Where's my briefcase?

SANDY [*turning furiously on* MILLY]: Mother, if you didn't want me to get a decent job and do all the regular things why did you set me up for it?

MILLY: Oh – no one'll ever blame you for anything!

SANDY [*furious*]: Well, why did you? What am I doing wrong?

MILLY: Of course it's my fault. I'm your mother – that's what I'm for.

SANDY: And if Tony wants the job I'll stand down. What do you expect me to do? Be a tramp, like Tony?

MYRA [*absolutely delighted*]: Why, Tony darling, why didn't you tell me.

TONY: Oh, my God!

ROSEMARY [*holding* TONY]: Shhh, Tony.

MYRA: Why, darling Tony, that's wonderful, it would be so *good* for you.

PHILIP [*exasperated*]: Really, Myra, how can you be such a romantic.

TONY [*breaking from* ROSEMARY, *standing beside* PHILIP, *accusing her*]: Mother, why should it be *good* for me?

MYRA [*at the two of them*]: What have I done now? If you want to be a tramp, am I expected to lock you in the house?

TONY ⎫
⎬ [*together, shouting at her*]: Mother . . .
PHILIP ⎭ Myra, you're utterly intolerable!

MYRA [*gaily*]: What's wrong? Perhaps I'll be a tramp, too: why not?

TONY [*shouting at her*]: You are a tramp!

[MIKE *has entered*, R, *carrying a bunch of flowers.* PHILIP, TONY, *and* MYRA *have not seen him.*]

MILLY: Myra, you have a visitor.

[MYRA *turns*, PHILIP *and* TONY *fall back.*]

MIKE: Myra darling, I know it's appallingly early, but I had to come. [*He holds out the flowers. She does not take them.*] I've had some really lovely news, darling. Or, at least, I do hope you'll think so. I'm invited to China. For a series of lectures. And I spoke to the organizer this morning. If we're married, of course you'll come too. It would be a rather lovely honeymoon.

MYRA: I'm sorry, Mike.

MIKE: But, of course, if you feel you don't want to leave your committee work now I'll quite understand.

MYRA: Mike, I'm sorry. Last night I was just . . . [MIKE *stares at her, helpless.*] I'm so sorry. We'll just have to go on as we've always done. You must forgive me. You've forgiven me often enough, haven't you?

[MIKE *seems as if he's crumpling inwardly. He stares at her, around at the others, then blunders out, R, still holding the flowers.*]

TONY: Oh, *Mother!* [*He turns to watch out of window.*]

MYRA: Oh, that was bad, that was very bad.

MILLY: Yes, love, it was. Very bad.

PHILIP [*furious*]: Myra, you are utterly intolerable.

[MYRA *lays her head down on the back of her chair.*]

Intolerable. I'm very late. [*he is on his way out R, remembering* ROSEMARY] Good-bye, Rosemary. [*at door, back to* MYRA] I'll be seeing you, Myra. Look after yourself.

[ROSEMARY *has not responded to* PHILIP'*s good-bye. But she stands at the window, beside* TONY, *watching him go.*]

SANDY [*escaping from* MILLY]: I'll go with Philip. [*from door, hastily*] Good-bye, Myra. I'll be seeing you.

MYRA [*who has not lifted her head from the chair-back*]: Oh damn, damn, damn.

MILLY [*to* MYRA]: Charming. All quite charming. Oh well, look after yourself, love. And don't forget that tape-recording for the meeting. We'll need it. Meet you in the pub as usual [*goes out R*].

TONY [*turning from window*]: Mother, why did you do that?

MYRA: I thought you wanted me to.

TONY: Mother, he's standing in the garden, crying. He's standing there, crying. Did you have to do it like that? Oh, damn it all, Mother.

MYRA: I've broken with Mike. After twenty years.

TONY: Yes, and how did you do it? As if he were . . .

MYRA: And I've broken finally with Philip. That's all finished. And I've broken with Sandy. Well? Isn't that what you wanted?

TONY: I don't want you to do anything you don't . . . [MYRA *laughs*.] I don't want . . . All I want is to be here in this house, with you, Mother – and some sort of . . . dignity. I'm so tired of all the brave speeches and the epic battles and the gestures. Wouldn't it be enough if we were just peaceful together? This house is like a sounding-board.

MYRA: Yes, I was thinking we should move to a flat. This house is much too big.

TONY [*appalled*]: Mother, you can't be serious.

MYRA [*evasively*]: You don't think so? Why not?

TONY: Oh no, no, no.

MYRA: But it's so big. And I've got a bit of money. We could get ourselves a nice flat.

TONY: Money, yes. Where did you get it from?

MYRA [*proudly*]: Five hundred pounds. And more later.

TONY: Five hundred pounds. But where? We've never had all that money all at once.

MYRA: Oh, money from heaven. [*She moves away to escape his questioning, notices* ROSEMARY, *still bent by the window, back turned to them. She goes to* ROSEMARY *and puts her arm around her.*] Don't cry, Rosemary. [*She turns* ROSEMARY *round and smiles at her.*]

ROSEMARY [*rather bitterly, smiling back*]: I'm not crying.

TONY [*desperately anxious, pulling* MYRA *away from* ROSEMARY]: Mother, I want to know. You're not just going to get out of it like that.

MYRA: Tony, before you settle down to being an honest electrician, I wish you'd take that money and . . .

TONY: What? Sow a few wild oats?

MYRA: Oh . . . sow anything you damned well please.

TONY: Mother, I'm being serious. In about a month from now I'm going to get myself a job. As an electrician. It's what I want. Work for eight hours a day, regularly paid, three square meals a day and . . .

MYRA [*derisively*]: Security! [*to* ROSEMARY] All he wants is security.

ROSEMARY: But Myra, what's wrong with that?

MYRA [*shrugging contemptuously*]: Oh, I don't know ... I suppose you'll spend jolly evenings in the local coffee bar, join a skiffle group, become a scruffy little bohemian, one of the neo-conformists, enjoying all the postures of rebellion from safe positions of utter respectability.

TONY: That's it, exactly.

MYRA: 'And thus from no heights canst thou fall.'

TONY [*derisively, to* ROSEMARY]: Heights, she wants. [*derisively, at* MYRA] Heights, heights ... We'll leave you to skip about on the heights. Mother, why don't you leave people alone. Just leave us alone ... do you know what I'd really enjoy doing? I'd like to paint this house. To decorate it. I really would.

MYRA: You want to decorate the house? [*to* ROSEMARY, *blankly*] He's 22 and he wants to spend his time decorating the house.

ROSEMARY: I don't see what's wrong with it.

MYRA [*to* TONY]: Wait a bit, don't start painting the house yet.

TONY: But why should I wait? I'll go out this afternoon and choose colours. It'll be fun. [*suspiciously*] What's up? What are you up to?

MYRA: Oh, nothing. Nothing. Look, I've got an awful lot to do this morning. Will you help me? It's that tape-recording. Sandy said he'd help me but now he's gone.

TONY: Oh, *no*.

MYRA: But I promised it for the meeting tonight.

TONY: Meetings, meetings. Who cares what's said at meetings.

MYRA: Tony, if you're trying to stop my work for the committee I'm not going to.

TONY: All these people in and out. All the noise, the speeches, the *mess*.

MYRA: I'm not going to become a sort of monument to your desire for – whatever it is.

TONY: Dignity.

MYRA: If you call dignity sitting with your hands folded waiting to be blown up – well, I'm not going to be blackmailed into inertia.

Please help me. Are you an electrician or are you not? I want you to play that tape back and take out the bits that are simply dull.

TONY: Dull!

MYRA: Will you or won't you? If not I'll ring up . . .

TONY: Who? Uncle Mike?

MYRA: It seems at the moment there's no one I can ring up. At least, not with dignity. [*She suddenly bursts into tears, and turns away.*]

TONY [*appalled*]: Mother.

MYRA: Oh, leave me alone [*goes to window, stands with her back turned*].

[ROSEMARY *takes his arm, shakes her head. Indicates machine.*]

TONY: Oh, all right, I'll do it.

ROSEMARY: I'll help you.

[*The two crouch by the machine.* TONY *starts it going. After a few seconds of war noises, shuts it off.*]

TONY: Oh Lord, *no.*

MYRA [*still with back turned, her voice almost in control*]: You see, people have no imagination. That's the trouble.

TONY [*to her back*]: Can't you see that people can't bear to think about it? It's all too big for everyone. They simply can't bear to think about it. [*as* ROSEMARY *shakes her head at him*] Oh, all right.

MYRA: There's some new tape there if you want it.

TONY [*putting on the new tape; begins to run it*]: There, that's better.

ROSEMARY: What are you doing?

TONY: Playing a record of silence.

MYRA [*still with back turned*]: Tony, you said you'd help me.

TONY: A clean sheet. A new page. Rosemary, say something very simple, very quiet, very beautiful, something I'd like to hear when I play this thing back.

ROSEMARY [*in an urgent whisper*]: Tony, your mother is *crying.*

TONY: But what can I do? . . . Say something, Rosemary, do say something.

ROSEMARY: But what?

TONY: Surely there's something you need to say.

ROSEMARY: But what about?

TONY: Anything. What you feel about – life.

ROSEMARY: But I don't know.

TONY: Then – people.

ROSEMARY: Who?

TONY: Anybody.

ROSEMARY: Why?

TONY: Oh Lord. [*He switches off machine.*] All right, let's have bombs and blasts and gunfire. Oh *Lord*. For instance, you've just decided not to marry Philip. Well *you're* not going to cry, are you?

ROSEMARY: I've finished crying.

[MYRA *turns round from the window. She has controlled herself. Stands watching ironically.*]

TONY: Are you unhappy?

ROSEMARY: Yes.

TONY: But you wouldn't have been happy with him, would you?

ROSEMARY [*turning and seeing* MYRA]: Well . . .

MYRA: Go on.

ROSEMARY: I don't think I expected to be.

TONY: Then why did you say you'd marry him?

ROSEMARY: He said . . . people should be ready to take chances. He said people shouldn't be afraid.

TONY: And so you said you'd marry him?

[ROSEMARY *turns, gives* MYRA *another troubled but defiant look.* MYRA *nods at her to proceed.*]

ROSEMARY: Yes. Philip suddenly came into my life and made fun of everything I did. He said I wasn't alive at all. He made me read books.

TONY [*laughing*]: Books!

ROSEMARY: Yes, he said I might just as well be dead, the way I was living. He said when I came to die I wouldn't know I'd ever been alive . . .

TONY: And that's why you said you'd marry him?

ROSEMARY [*after another look at* MYRA, *who meets it with a grave ironical nod*]: Yes. He said there was only one thing people should be afraid of – of not growing. He said happiness didn't matter. People should grow, be everything, do a lot of things, and never be afraid of being unhappy . . .

TONY [*laughing derisively*]: Philip said all that, did he? Uncle Philip did? Well, look at him now, look at him now . . .

ROSEMARY [*suddenly furious, leaping up and away from him*]: Yes, he did. And I won't have you saying things about Philip, I won't have you . . . [*She begins to cry and* MYRA *comes up and puts her arms around her from behind.*]

MYRA: There, darling. It's all right.

TONY [*shouting*]: Oh yes, that's very much your cup of tea, isn't it, Mother? You like that, don't you? Suffering – the great cult of suffering. Strength through pain . . . that's your creed.

MYRA: Oh, shut up and stop bullying people.

TONY [*shouting*]: Well, I don't want any of it – I tell you, pain doesn't exist. I refuse to feel it . . .

MYRA [*to* ROSEMARY]: There . . . Listen – you don't regret having known Philip, do you?

ROSEMARY: Oh *no*.

MYRA: Then that's all. [*She makes* ROSEMARY *lift her face: she smiles into it.*] There, that's better. It's all not so serious – is it?

TONY: What are you doing now? Dancing on another emotional grave.

MYRA: Oh Tony . . . [*She leaves* ROSEMARY *and comes to* TONY.] I've got to tell you something. No, listen. I've been screwing up my courage to tell you.

TONY [*already half-knows*]: No – *what*?

MYRA [*after a pause, while she screws herself up to tell him*]: Tony . . . I've sold the house.

[*There is a long silence.*]

TONY [*very quiet, almost in a whisper*]: You've sold the house. Oh, my God, you've sold the house. [*grabbing at* ROSEMARY, *shaking her as if she were* MYRA] My God, she's sold the house!

ROSEMARY: But Tony, only yesterday you were talking about being a tramp.

TONY [*after a pause, as the word tramp strikes him*]: Tramp? A tramp?

... [*He is almost doubled up with pain.*] She's sold it. And do you know why? To raise five hundred pounds so that I can go and sow my wild oats. Oh God, God. So that I can go bumming off and having love affairs and revolutionizing ... [*He cackles with hysterical laughter.*]

ROSEMARY: Tony, don't do that. Stop it.

MYRA: Leave him. [*She slumps down in a chair, in the pose she had before, head down against the back of it.*]

TONY: My God, my mother's done that to me. She's done that to me. She's my mother and she might just as well have taken a knife and stabbed me with it. She's my mother and she knows so little about me that she doesn't suspect that there's one thing I love in this world, and it's this house ...

ROSEMARY: Tony, stop it, stop it, stop it.

TONY [*pulling himself away from* ROSEMARY, *shouting at* MYRA'S *head – she is sitting rocking back and forth with the pain of it*]: God, but you're destructive, destructive, destructive. There isn't anything you touch which doesn't go to pieces. You just go on from mess to mess ... you live in a mess of love affairs and committees and ... you live in a mess like a *pig*, Mother ... you're all over everything like a great crawling spider ...

ROSEMARY [*forcibly pulling him away*]: Tony, stop it at once.

TONY [*hunched up in* ROSEMARY'S *grasp*]: Sometimes when I hear her come down the stairs I feel every nerve in my body shrieking. I can't stand her, I simply can't stand her ... [*He collapses into chair, goes completely limp.* ROSEMARY *goes to* MYRA, *is too afraid of her clenched-up pose of pain to touch her, stands helplessly looking from one to the other.*]

TONY [*limply*]: Now we'll have to leave here and live in some – damned pretty little flat somewhere. I can't bear it, I can't bear it ... [*There is a silence.* MYRA *slowly straightens herself, stands up, walks slowly across the room.* ROSEMARY *watches her fearfully.*]

MYRA: If you hate me as much as that why do you put so much energy into getting me alone with you into this house. Well, why? For the pleasure of torturing me? Or of being tortured?

ROSEMARY: Oh Myra, he didn't mean it.

MYRA [*with a short laugh*]: Perhaps he does mean it. There's no law that says a son must like his mother, is there? [*after a pause*] And vice versa. [*She lights a cigarette. It can be seen her hand is trembling violently. Otherwise she is calm. Almost limp, with the same limpness as* TONY's.]

TONY [*looking at her, he begins to understand what he has done. Almost apologetically*]: I can't think why one of you doesn't say: There are millions of people in the world living in mud huts, and you make this fuss about moving from one comfortable home to another. Isn't that what I'm supposed to be feeling?

MYRA: Since you've said it, there's no need for me to.

TONY [*almost querulous*]: The other thing you could say is: Wait until you've got to my age and see if you've done any better. Well – if I haven't done any better I'd have the grace to kill myself.

MYRA: Luckily I don't take myself so seriously. Well, I'm going to leave you to it.

TONY [*desperately anxious*]: What do you mean, where are you going?

MYRA: I don't know.

TONY: You're not going?

MYRA: Why not? I don't propose to live with someone who can't stand me. Why should I . . . [*She makes a movement as if expanding, or about to take flight.*] It just occurs to me that for the first time in my life I'm free.

TONY: Mother, where are you going?

MYRA: It occurs to me that for the last twenty-two years my life has been governed by yours – by your needs. Oh, you may not think so – but the way I've lived, what I've done, my whole life has been governed by your needs. And what for . . . [*contemptuously*] What for – a little monster of egotism – that's what you are. A petty, envious, spiteful little egotist, concerned with nothing but yourself.

ROSEMARY [*almost in tears*]: Oh Myra, stop, stop.

MYRA [*ignoring her, to* TONY]: Well, I'm sure it's my fault. Obviously it is. If I've spent half my life bringing you up and you turn out – as you have – then it's my life that's a failure, isn't it? Well, it's not going to be a failure in future.

TONY: Mother, what are you going to do?

MYRA: There are a lot of things I've wanted to do for a long time, and I haven't done them. [*laughing*] Perhaps I'll take the money and go off; why not? Or perhaps I'll be a tramp. I could be, you know. I could walk out of this house with my needs in a small suitcase . . . and I shall. Or perhaps I'll go on that boat to the Pacific to the testing area – I wanted to do that and didn't, because of you.

TONY: Mother, you might get killed.

MYRA: Dear me, I might get killed. And what of it? I don't propose to keep my life clutched in my hand like small change . . .

TONY: Mother, you can't just walk off into – *nothing*.

MYRA: Nothing? I don't have to shelter under a heap of old bricks – like a frightened mouse. I'm going. I'll come back and collect what I need when I've decided what I'm going to do [*goes towards door, R*].

TONY [*angry and frightened*]: Mother.

[*She turns at the door. She is quite calm, but she is crying.*]

Mother, you're crying.

MYRA [*laughing*]: Why not? I'm nearly 50 – and it's true there's nothing much to show for it. Except that I've never been afraid to take chances and make mistakes. I've never wanted security and safety and the walls of respectability – you damned little petty-bourgeois. My God, the irony of it – that *we* should have given birth to a generation of little office boys and clerks and . . . little people who count their pensions before they're out of school . . . little petty bourgeois. Yes, I am crying. I've been alive for fifty years. Isn't that good enough cause for tears . . . [*she goes out R*].

TONY [*amazed, not believing it*]: But Rosemary, she's gone.

ROSEMARY: Yes.

TONY: But she'll come back.

ROSEMARY: No, I don't think so. [*She comes to him, puts her arm around him. They crouch down, side by side, arms around each other.*]

TONY: Rosemary, do you know that not one word of what she said made any sense to me at all ... slogans, slogans, slogans ...

ROSEMARY: What's the matter with being safe – and ordinary. What's wrong with being ordinary – and safe?

TONY: Rosemary, listen – never in the whole history of the world have people made a battle-cry out of being ordinary. Never. Supposing we all said to the politicians – we refuse to be heroic. We refuse to be brave. We are bored with all the noble gestures – what then, Rosemary?

ROSEMARY: Yes. Ordinary and safe.

TONY: Leave us alone, we'll say. Leave us alone to live. Just leave us alone ...

CURTAIN

BERNARD KOPS

The Hamlet of Stepney Green

A SAD COMEDY
WITH SOME SONGS

THE HAMLET OF STEPNEY GREEN

First presented by the Meadow Players Limited at the Playhouse, Oxford, on 19 May 1958, with the following cast:

THE CHILDREN	Marie Seaborne Linda Blackledge Janet Derry
HAVA SEGAL	Ruth Meyers
MR SEGAL	John Barrard
SAM LEVY	Harold Lang
DAVID LEVY	John Fraser
BESSIE LEVY	Dorothea Phillips
MR STONE	Joss Ackland
MRS STONE	Pat Keen
MR GREEN	Gilbert Vernon
MR BLACK	Christopher Hancock
MR WHITE	Robert Bernal
ACCORDIONIST	Leon Rosselson

Directed by Frank Hauser

The play was transferred to the Lyric Opera House, Hammersmith, on 15 July 1958. In this production the part of BESSIE LEVY was played by Thelma Ruby.

CHARACTERS OF THE PLAY

SAM LEVY: 65, *small and agile, a pickled-herring seller of Wentworth Street*
BESSIE LEVY: 52, *attractive, his wife. Plump and wears cheap jewellery*
DAVID LEVY: 22, *their son; tall and intelligent. Wants to be a crooner*
SOLLY SEGAL: 60, *retired. A friend of the family*
HAVA SEGAL: 18, *beautiful, and sure of herself. Has just returned from Israel*
MR STONE: *Fat and jovial; foolish and about fifty years old*
MRS STONE: *Fat and foolish; jovial and about fifty years old*
MR WHITE: *About 32, looks older. Insurance agent, over-positive and smug*
MR BLACK: 27, *well dressed. A tombstone salesman. Small and thin*
MR GREEN: 27, *well dressed. A tombstone salesman. Small and fat*
THREE CHILDREN: *Sing and dance*

ACT ONE

The action of the play is centred around the house of MR *and* MRS LEVY
Time: *The present.*
Place: *Stepney Green in the East End of London.*

*The setting is constant throughout and the stage is in two sections; one half
is part of the house, showing a cross section of the living-room and the
corridor. The living-room has the various pieces of furniture that one would
expect in a Jewish lower middle-class family, not too much bad taste is
apparent; the furnishing should be sparse and straightforward.*
The other half should be the garden of the LEVYS. *There are flowers in rich
profusion but this garden is surrounded by a great area of bomb damage;
it gives the hint of almost being an oasis; there is a fence around the garden,
and a gate leading off L: there should be a certain warmth about the set, as if
Van Gogh and Chagall had collaborated on this urban scene.*
*Curtain goes up revealing an empty stage. It is a very hot July afternoon;
nearby some* CHILDREN *are heard skipping and singing:*

CHILDREN [*off*]: On the hill there stands a lady, who she is I do not
know; all she wants is gold and silver, all she wants is a fine young
man.

> [*A ball comes over the fence and the* CHILDREN *run on stage after it;
> they explore the garden and sniff the flowers and then they begin to
> sing again.*]

On the hill there stands a lady, who she is I do not know –

> [*They are dancing round in a ring when they are interrupted by* HAVA
> *who comes into the garden from the house.*]

HAVA: Here, go on and buy some ice cream; play in the park. [*She
hands one of the children a sixpence; they just stare at her.*] Please run
away and play; Mr Levy isn't feeling too well.

> [*The* CHILDREN *run off and sing as they exit.*]

CHILDREN: All she wants is gold and silver, all she wants is a fine young man.

[*They exit.*]

HAVA: Don't we all. [*She sits down and reads a woman's magazine.*]

BESSIE [*off*]: I said no! ... N ... O ... NO, no, no, NO.

SAM [*off*]: I tell you yes: YE-YES. All my life I worked in the open air and you bet your life, I'm going to die there ... Come on, Mr Segal, push me into the garden.

BESSIE [*off*]: All right, I should worry! It's your funeral!

SAM [*off*]: You said it.

[*A small man is seen trying to push a bed into the garden from the back room;* HAVA *immediately gets up and helps* MR SEGAL, *her father, and both of them manage to push the bed into the centre of the garden;* MR SEGAL *is immaculately dressed and smokes a cigar.*]

MR SEGAL: Is this spot all right? Just here, Sam?

[*A frail old man levers himself up from his lying position in the bed; it is* SAM *and he wears pyjamas; he looks around.*]

SAM: This'll do fine. Just here. Thank you, Mr Segal. What a lovely day! What a lovely daughter you have! She's a credit to you; what's the matter, Hava? Why did you come back home? Didn't you like it out in Israel?

HAVA: It wasn't bad, but I was lonely; the life was different out there. I couldn't seem to settle down. England's where I belong. At least I've learned that much.

SAM: Still, you're looking very well. I was telling my Davey to go there; he wouldn't listen.

HAVA: I am looking forward to meeting your son David again. How is he, Mr Levy?

MR SEGAL: A lot of good that boy will be to you, anywhere in the world. Excuse me, Sam, but you must agree; he's good for nothing.

SAM: There I disagree with you, Mr Segal, he'll find his feet; he's going through a difficult phase, he's not so bad.

MR SEGAL: He's been going through this difficult phase for fifteen years; it's about time he settled down; it's your fault, you're not strict enough.

HAVA: I think David is a lovely boy; he's got such a wonderful voice, he'll go a long way.

MR SEGAL: The longer the way, the better. What a voice! Sam, she drives me mad talking about him. It wouldn't have been such a bad idea for your son and my daughter to – well – if he had a nice job with prospects, but a crooner? Hava, you've got a screw loose.

SAM: Hava, do you like my boy? Do you? Maybe you can help him. Help him to see sense; persuade him to give up his crazy ideas; does he like you?

HAVA: Like me? He never even sees me. He looks straight through me. The other day I passed him by near Brick Lane; he was just staring at the sky; I said 'Hello, Davey'. He didn't even bother to look my way! Oh well, what can you do?

SAM: It isn't natural. He's ambitious. I said: 'Look, Davey, all right I'll help you; go and study music, learn all about notes', but he refused.

HAVA: He's got a wonderful voice. He was always such a gentle boy.

SAM: If that is a wonderful voice then I'm Gregory Peck.

HAVA: He's got a lovely voice. He'll go a long way. You'll see.

SAM: What did you miss out there?

HAVA: I missed the cinemas and the dance halls; all my friends. I missed my own room and my own bed. I was homesick.

SAM: Are you going back?

HAVA: No. I don't think so; it's unwise to go back. I'm not fooling myself. I'm no pioneer.

SAM: I suppose you're right; anyway, everything turns out for the best. You'll meet a nice respectable boy, you'll settle down, get a nice flat and you'll get everything you want and deserve. You're attractive, you'll have no trouble.

HAVA: I hope so. Where's Davey now?

SAM: How should I know? Who knows where that boy is, even when he's here?

MR SEGAL: Forget about him! Do you know, Sam, she drives me mad, all day she's talking about him! What's he got, I wonder? What's he got that others ain't?

SAM: By the way it sounds, it seems he has a wonderful voice. What can you do with them?

HAVA: Here you go again! The younger generation! Good-bye, Daddy. [*She kisses* MR SEGAL.] I promised Miriam that I'd go over this afternoon. Don't come home too late. Good-bye, Mr Levy, take care of yourself. [*They shake hands.*] Good-bye. [*She exits.*]

SAM: What a nice girl! Do you know, Mr Segal, that for many years I thought about today. I wondered what it would be like when I died; I wondered what the weather would be like and if I would be nervous. It's funny, for years I've worried that I wouldn't have the chance to die naturally. I thought that it would be the A-Bomb or the H-Bomb or the Z-Bomb or bacteria, rockets, or gas, yet here I am on a fine summer's day going to die quietly in my garden; why, I never even retired, never even moved to Golders Green.

MR SEGAL: I know what you mean. Mr Miller was killed the other day by a van; he was worried about the world situation and was reading a newspaper as he crossed the road; you remember Mr Miller?

SAM: Not off-hand.

[*The* CHILDREN *have returned to the outside of the garden again; once more they start singing.*]

CHILDREN [*singing off*]: Julius Caesar, such a silly geezer, caught his head in a lemon squeezer.

MR SEGAL: I'll go and stop that noise; they should be ashamed of themselves. I tell you, Sam, the children of today –

[*He is about to go when* SAM *catches hold of his sleeve.*]

SAM: No, no, Mr Segal, let them sing; let them sing. Let everybody sing. Music makes the world go round. Mr Segal, you should never stop a child from singing. You should be ashamed of yourself, a man of your age. Tomorrow I'd give my right arm for the slightest sound from the tiniest throat.

MR SEGAL: What do you mean, Sam? You talk in riddles.

SAM: I mean that I shan't be here tomorrow. I won't have a right arm to give away. [*He is looking at his right arm and is shaking it.*]

It's all over, Mr Segal. Life slipped through my fingers and as it was slipping, that was life.

MR SEGAL: Of course. What do you mean?

SAM: I mean, life was no other time, no other place; it is here and now and gone. I came in at Odessa sixty-five years ago and today I'm going to die in Stepney Green, that's what I mean.

MR SEGAL: Don't be silly, Sam. You're not going to die, you're a bit delirious. If I died every time I thought like that I would have had forty or fifty coffins. Don't talk silly, you make me feel miserable.

SAM: I'm sorry. No, this is it, believe me. I've got more than a cold, I can tell you. I've been frightened recently; I've lain awake nearly all night and broke out into a terrible cold sweat when I realized that I was getting older and older and that I was getting nearer and nearer – to nothing! You can't run away from death, Mr Segal, there's no escaping it, it catches you in the end; my end is here and now, and now I'm resigned to it.

MR SEGAL: You've got a very vivid imagination, Sam; that's always been your trouble; now I know who your David takes after.

SAM: He takes after my grandfather's brother, according to what I heard about him, Manny Levy, got in with a bad crowd; but with a heart of gold. He ran away with an actress and everyone talked about it. [pause] Mr Segal, now I realize that I never lived; all my life I've been asleep. Been dead! My physical death will prove for ever that there was never anyone called Samuel Levy, pickled herring seller of Wentworth Street; two children and a widow; you'll read all about it in the *Jewish Chronicle* next week; they'll make up a little rhyme and then someone will come and sell my wife a stone.

MR SEGAL: Sam, what's come over you? You make me sad talking like this.

SAM: Don't upset yourself on my account. It hasn't been a bad life. Have the boys missed me in the market? Have any of them asked after me?

MR SEGAL: Yes. Moishe Newman told me to remind you that you still owe him thirty shillings.

SAM: Yes, I remember, for the chickens; tell Bessie, would you? She'll take care of everything. Thank God I've got myself insured, tomorrow she's got two hundred and fifty pounds coming to her.

MR SEGAL: Such money she can do without. What is going to matter if you die, anyway? Don't make me laugh; you're not going to die.

SAM: We're all going to die; you don't have to be a prophet to know that. I'm worried about my herring stall. I shall have to talk to Davey and make him see sense; he's got to get rid of these bright ideas; he's no longer a kid.

MR SEGAL: Why don't you try to rest now, Sam? Try and sleep.

SAM [*he sits right up in bed and leans forward*]: Try to sleep? Rest? Do me a favour. I've got a lot of rest coming to me, I can tell you. No – I must keep awake and take everything in; I want to be more observant today than I have ever been. Smoking cigars, eh. You bloody miser, how can you afford them on the old age pension? I always suspected that you had a tidy sum stuck away. Come on, own up, I'm a dying man.

MR SEGAL: My boy sends them to me from New York; he sends me fifty dollars a month, also; he's a good boy. I spoke to him on the telephone two months ago. He's got a proper Yank accent. He's married there to a girl.

SAM: I didn't think that he married a boy; what does he do for a living?

MR SEGAL: He travels; business, you know.

[SAM *nods.*]

I tell you, my children are as good as gold. Hava even came back to look after me when her mother died; she's just like a little mother, what would I have done without them?

SAM: Children, oy vay, don't talk to me about children. All your life you sweat your kishkers out to give them a good education and everything they want and what happens? Davey turns around and tells me that two and two don't add up to four, and Lottie joins the Communist Party. The Communist Party I can stand, but to add insult to injury she runs away with a goy; I've pushed it all inside me and I've swallowed it, so please don't talk about children.

MR SEGAL: Still, David isn't as bad as all that.

SAM: He was all right until he started going up west when he was 17; soon as his pimples went so do he, drifting from job to job, more out than in, getting a craze over one thing after another; but for years now he's been crooning and when he's not crooning he's listening to records of crooners; I wish he'd even go out sometimes but now he's got a new habit. He sits in the house every evening, mooching around and sighing. Who knows where it will end? Come on, give us a cigar, you stingy old sod.

[SAM *gets out of bed, to* MR SEGAL'S *horror. He walks over to* MR SEGAL *and* MR SEGAL *gravely hands him a cigar and lights it for him.* SAM *paces around the stage puffing at the cigar.* DAVID *comes on. He hovers in background. He is dressed in a well-made suit.*]

SAM: Beggars can't be choosers,
 So pass the word around,
 No matter what you do,
 You'll end up underground.

[MR SEGAL *tries to steer him back to bed but* SAM *refuses to go and walks around the stage looking at imaginary fruit and groceries.* DAVID *follows them, unseen. He sings.*]

DAVID [*sings*]: Silver trout are sleeping in heaps upon the slabs,
   With mackerel and lobsters and lethargic crabs.
   The dead are busy sleeping eternity away,
   They cannot go out shopping on this fair summer's day.

SEGAL }
SAM: } [*sing*]: Beggars can't be choosers, the executioner said,
   And if you beg for life, you're bound to lose your head.

DAVID [*sings*]: They do not smell the flowers that take the breath away
   Mimosa and Rose, Carnation and Lily;
   The dead are busy sleeping in the eternal dark,
   They do not go out shopping or walk in the park.

SEGAL }
SAM: } [*sing*]: Beggars can't be choosers, so pass the world away,
   No matter how you climb, you'll end up in the clay.

DAVID [*sings*]: They do not buy the warm bread, the wine and
watercress,
Or give a copper coin to a bronze accordionist.
The dead are busy sleeping eternity away,
They come not to the market, on this fair summer's
day.

SEGAL
SAM: } [*sing*]: Beggars can't be choosers, no matter what you're
worth,
The best of us, the worst of us,
Will burst beneath the earth.

[*They are both standing now arm in arm, breathless and happy.*
DAVID *retires to the background.*]

SAM: Yes, Mr Segal, in the market now there is a glut of cherries,
big, ripe, and red, red-currants and black-currants and golden
goosegogs as large as Chinese lanterns; grapes, figs, olives, dates,
melons, lemons. I tell you, Mr Segal, that's what I've missed.

MR SEGAL: What? Fruit?

SAM [*in the course of this speech music is playing.* SAM *almost breaks out
into song but never quite makes it. He speaks slowly*]: Oh, don't be
such a bloody fool, of course not. I mean going places and seeing
people. After all, that is all that there is in life, going places and
seeing people, different places, different people. I promised myself
a world trip before I died, to see for myself how people in other
countries lived. It never transpired. Working in the market makes
you curious; it does that for you ... You see the coloured labels
stuck upon the boxes, and you think of the man who packed those
boxes, and of the girl who stuck that label on. You think of the sun
beating down on the wharves and the boat being loaded by sweat-
ing men, gently swaying in the golden waves; but – it's too late for
the holiday you planned and you never left the market where you
stand.

MR SEGAL: A vivid imagination, Sam, that's your trouble.

SAM: Beggars can't be choosers, Mr Segal, and my only regret is not
travelling, not having seen California and the Caucasus, Haifa and
Helsinki. I never even saw Odessa again; not that I ever saw it

really. I came on an onion boat to Tilbury when I was 14. Boxes
and boxes of onions on that boat, all with labels stuck on saying
ONIONS, MADE IN RUSSIA. I was also made in Russia, so I came
to Tilbury, and then I came here and I have been here ever since.

BOTH [*sing slowly*]: Beggars can't be choosers,
                    So pass the word around,
                         You do not need a passport when you travel to
                            the ground.

   [*The mood changes and* SAM *seems very tired again.*]

SAM: Would you please help me back into bed, Mr Segal?

   [MR SEGAL *does so and* SAM *settles down.* DAVID *comes forward. He
   speaks very slowly as if every word were a jewel to be weighed and
   valued.*]

SAM: Where have you been all day, Davey boy?

DAVID: Whitechapel Art Gallery and the Public Library next door,
   that is to say if one should call them that. The Art Gallery contained no art and the Public Library contained no public, just one
   or two down-and-outs reading the long newspapers in the racks.

   [MR SEGAL *whispers to* DAVID.]

MR SEGAL: David, listen to me, try and be a good boy for a change,
   your father is dying.

DAVID: So are we all, all the time.

SAM: Stop whispering, Mr Segal. It's not good manners.

DAVID: Anyway, he looks perfectly all right to me.

SAM: Mr Segal, do me a favour, leave me here with my boy for a
   moment; I want to talk to him.

   [MR SEGAL *is looking over the wall and is shouting at the children
   who have been making a little noise.*]

MR SEGAL: Go on – do us a favour – play somewhere else, little
   ruffians. [*He goes off in their direction.*]

CHILDREN [*off*]: Silly Solly Segal – nose like an eagle – eyes like two
   jelly-fish – teeth like a weasel . . . [*Their voices disappear in the
   distance.*]

   [DAVID *walks round the stage: he stretches his arms exuberantly but
   he is nervous.*]

SAM: Na Davey, what can I say to you? All these years I wanted you
to work in the market with me, then I told myself – 'Don't worry,
Sam, he's looking for something better' – well – what are you going
to do? No more pie in the sky. You've got to support your mother
now.

DAVID: Oh, what can I do?

SAM: You'll have to work.

DAVID: Why should I work when I've got my health and strength?
The thought of having to spend the rest of my life looking at the
heads of herrings and the heads of hungry people makes me sick.

SAM: What do you think crooners see? Stop dreaming and settle
down.

DAVID [*swings around the stage*]: I want to be a crooner – I want to be
a king – to be looked at – to be looked up to. I want people to
nudge each other as they pass and say 'Look! there goes David
Levy – the most famous – fabulous crooner in the world'. I want
to hear my voice blaring from the record shops as I whizz by in my
Jaguar – I want to switch on the radio – any time – and any day
and hear my voice on records.

SAM: Why, Davey? Why have you got these crazy ideas? Who do
you take after?

DAVID: I feel good when I'm singing.

SAM: But I'm going to die – who'll look after you?

DAVID: Don't worry about me – I'll be all right, and don't keep on
saying you're dying. Whatever happens, though – I won't work
down the lane – I refuse – I won't – I'll . . .

SAM: It's not natural – already you're 22 – other boys grow out
of these mad ideas already. Other people have only joy from
their children – I have a pain in my heart – just my luck. You have
no trade – no profession – you're not interested in politics and you
drift from job to job – All this has got to stop – I'm a dying man –
don't argue.

DAVID: I'm fed up round here. I'm bored. Nothing happens except
to other people in the papers. It was bad enough before we got
television – now it's worse – everyone sleeps all the time – no one's

got any life – now if they gave me a chance on the tele I'd wake them all up – I'd stun them – I'd be the greatest thing – don't ya see – I want to make people happy – I'VE GOT TO MAKE them listen – they'd love me.

SAM: And they call me delirious. What do you want? Look! Tell me – between you and me – I told you the facts of life, didn't I? – Well, you owe me something in exchange – I helped to make you – well, don't make any more nonsense – tell me.

DAVID: You made me all right – you made me what I am. Aren't you proud of me? I know you are deep down – What do you want me to do? – be honest.

SAM: To settle down – take over the business – marry a nice girl.

DAVID: What, and then have a complicated son like me? Something's wrong and you know it. You haven't really been a success because you don't really want me to end up in the market like you – come on, own up.

SAM: Naturally – I expect you to improve – big business man with a wonderful education.

DAVID: You admit, then, you don't want me to have the same life as yourself?

[SAM *cannot reply*.]

It didn't turn out too well, so surely you don't want me to fail – do you? [SAM *cannot reply*.] Well, do you? See – you don't know what to say.

SAM: All I can say is that I don't know where you come from.

DAVID: Singing makes me feel safe – it'll give me a place in the world.

SAM: What a complicated boy I have to turn out!

DAVID: When I croon I feel free.

SAM: Davey – all this nonsense has got to stop.

DAVID: Pipe down – you're dying, remember – we've been through this so many times.

SAM: What a way to treat a father; especially on his death-bed. [*He almost cries.*]

DAVID: Sorry, Dad – but you've been on this death-bed so many times before – don't blackmail me – anyway – why do you want to bequeath me the things you hated – and I know you hated – you told me you hated – as often as you said you were going to kick the bucket – tell me that?

SAM: I shall die a very confused man – now I don't know what I mean.

DAVID: Say that again and anyway even if you were dying how do you do – I'm dying also – dying to be famous and express myself – you'll be all right – It's me I'm worried about – but just give me a chance – Give me time and I'll make you proud of me – So long – I'll be seeing you. I've got some mirror exercises to do. See you soon.

SAM: I wonder.

[DAVID *goes off.* SAM *laughs ironically.* HAVA *enters from the garden and* BESSIE *enters from the house.*]

BESSIE: Sam, Sam. What's the matter with you? Have you been lecturing my Davey again? You'll upset him.

[*Her hair is dyed blonde; she is trying to look ten years younger, and uses cosmetics profusely.*]

SAM: Bessie, please believe me; I tell you I'm very ill, please believe me.

BESSIE: If you say so who am I to argue. You were very ill last year and the year before that and the year before that; it's funny but every time it becomes July, you become ill as regular as clockwork. Just when everyone starts to think about holidays, he gets ill. What's the matter? Why don't you say that you don't want to take me to the seaside? And if you're so ill why won't you let me call for a doctor?

SAM: Oh, leave me alone, what do you care? You'll be able to play on your little spirit board and talk to me next week.

BESSIE: Look, Sammy, please be a good boy; it's so hot and I'm expecting Mr and Mrs Stone to tea.

SAM: How is the new Jewish Spiritualist Synagogue doing? Are you playing to full houses? Who ever heard of it? Yiddisher Spiritualism! Is there anyone there? Is it you up there Moisher: send me down a dozen pairs of nylons and five pounds of smoked salmon; I should like to see you all tapping the table for a change, instead of each other.

BESSIE: You disgust me, you old fool; and if you're going to die, please do it before tea-time because I've got a sponge-cake in the oven. [*She exits into the house.*]

[*HAVA comes forward.*]

SAM [*does not see her*]: Eh? Sammy? So this is what you made of your life; well, maybe it's just as well; think how difficult it would be to part for ever if you loved each other.

HAVA: Don't worry, Mr Levy, try and go to sleep.

SAM: Who's that? [*He sits up.*] Oh, it's you, Hava. Looking for your Dad?

HAVA: No, I just looked in. Miriam wasn't in.

SAM: Oh, God, life was a mistake; it shouldn't have been given to us, we didn't deserve it. The cockroaches deserve life more than human beings.

HAVA: Don't you love each other any more?

SAM: No, no more.

HAVA: Did you ever love each other?

SAM: Yes; I tell you this as a warning. I was on a steamer going to Southend for the day; she was sitting on the top deck in a white calico dress and her lovely black eyes smiled down at me, oh, so expressive. Two years later we got married, and moved to this house and after Davey was born we went shopping and bought twin beds. What went wrong? I shall never know! There is too much in life, too much to learn, not enough time. Too many problems to be solved. It's too late, now.

[*DAVID comes back into the garden; his mood has changed.*]

HAVA: Look, there's David.

[*DAVID ignores her completely as if she doesn't exist. SAM continues talking.*]

SAM: I used to think that the top of my head would blow off trying to answer these questions; then one day I thought that I'd grow a new head where these problems would seem like simple sums, nice pieces of cake that you could digest and get rid of easily. Hello, Davey, you met Hava, didn't you?

DAVID: I'm sorry, Dad, but a person can't help being himself. Oh? Yes, I've seen her around. [*He ignores her.*]

SAM: Hava, come here, you've met my boy, Davey, haven't you?

HAVA: Well, we never quite –

[HAVA *offers* DAVID *her hand and he shakes it limply and then continues ignoring her. She just does not exist in* DAVID'S *eyes.*

SAM *pulls* DAVID *close and ruffles his hair.* HAVA *walks around the garden sometimes looking at them and sometimes looking at and sniffing the flowers.*]

Don't mind me.

SAM: We shouldn't argue, you and I. I've always loved you. You were all I really ever lived for; part of that lovely dream that slipped through my fingers. I'm sure you'll find yourself, one day, and when you do remember me and all the others who never got anywhere.

[DAVID *is sad.*]

Come on, Davey, pull yourself together; liven up, sing. Say all those crazy things I used to chastise you for saying. Spout all the things you read from books and heard from your strange friends. I want to change everything. I want something new to happen. I want to lose all sense of order, so that I'll be prepared for my new existence if there is one! Everyone where I'm going may be like you; I want my son to vouch for me in the unaccustomed darkness. Come on, Davey, '*Hurrah, hurrah*'; come on, darling, spout poetry, sing, shout, come on, Davey. [*He claps his hands and so does* HAVA. SAM *has got out of bed again.*]

DAVID [*shouting*]: Listen, everyone; listen, folks. This is David Levy speaking, your master of ceremonies, your own prince of song, a prisoner of seasons, a disciple of dust. I fell out of the sky and a name fell upon me, and I was called Levy and now for a time I answer to that. My old man is going to die and so are we all before your very eyes.

HAVA: Come on, Davey, sing. I like hearing your voice.

SAM: Come on, Davey, sing.

DAVID: No! Not now. I want to speak. Tonight, friends, I'm going to launch my father into space.

SAM: Halleluia, I'm a bum; Halleluia, bum again; halleluia, give us a handout to revive us again.

[*There is a general commotion in the neighbourhood; irate voices are heard and the* CHILDREN *have come on the stage and are standing around happy and delighted.*]

DAVID: This is David Levy speaking to you; I'm consigning my father to you, oh mighty dead, he is a king if ever there was one, first because he is my father, and then he is king of the herrings; to you, oh mighty dead, to you, all you billions and billions of dead who have passed this way over the earth, since it shot off from the sun, accept my father, a humble novice in this game of chance, in this maze of existence, look after him for my sake.

[MR SEGAL *enters.*]

SEGAL: What on earth are you doing? Sam, get back into bed at once, do you want to catch your death of cold?

HAVA: Daddy, please; don't interfere.

SAM: I'll die from what I choose. I'll die from playing blind man's buff if I feel like it; it's a free country; come on, kiddies, come and play with me.

SEGAL [*to* HAVA]: You shouldn't have let him, anyway what are you doing now? [*He sees* DAVID.] Don't you get mixed up with him, that's all I ask. Haven't I been a good father? Don't the things that I tell you count?

HAVA: Oh, Daddy, shut up, shush . . .

[*The* CHILDREN *are reluctantly approaching* SAM, *who is beckoning them.*]

SAM: Go on, sing and dance, show me how to do it.

[*The* CHILDREN *join hands nervously.*]

What games shall we play? What songs do you know?

[*The* CHILDREN *move around in a circle.*]

CHILDREN: There were three crows sat on a stone.

Fal, la, la, la, lal, de.
Two flew away and then there was one.
Fal, la, la, la, lal, de.
The other crow finding himself alone,
Fal, la, la, la, lal, de.
He flew away and then there was none,
Fal, la, la, la, lal, de.

[*They continue dancing around like this and* SAM *and* HAVA *join in with them. They become quieter and dance on like this whilst* DAVID *looks at them and sings simultaneously.*]

DAVID: Sky, sky, the children cry,
Where do we go to when we die?
What are we doing in this dream?
Sky, sky, the children scream,
Sky, sky, the children scream,
Life is nothing but a dream,
A game of dancing in a ring,
Sky, sky, the children sing.
Sky, sky, the children sing,
Who'll be beggar? Who'll be king?
Let's dance for joy, let's sing and leap,
And comfort everyone who weeps.
Sky, sky, the children weep,
Why are we falling fast asleep?
We'll play this game until we die.
Sky, sky, the children cry.

CHILDREN: He flew away and then there was none;
Fal, la, la, la, lal, de.

[*The* CHILDREN *clap and* SAM *is encouraging them.* SEGAL *is still trying to get him back into bed, without success.*]

HAVA [*to* DAVID]: That was very nice, you can really sing.

DAVID: Who are you? Oh, yes! Thanks. [*He smiles and moves away, disinterested, before she can reply.*]

HAVA: My – I'm – Hava . . . You've got a lovely – voi . . . Oh, dear, what a life!

SAM: Come on, now, ring-a-ring-a-roses. [*He and* DAVID *now form a circle with the* CHILDREN.]

[HAVA *stands sadly near her father, watching.*]

Ring-a-ring-a-roses, a pocket full of posies,

Usher, usher, we . . . all fall . . . DOWN.

[*They all fall on the grass, and* DAVID *and the* CHILDREN *manage to get up, but* SAM *can't manage it.*]

DAVID: Come on, Dad, come back to bed.

[SAM *pushes him away with a silent gesture of his hands, crawls over to a rose-bush. He plucks enough and then he staggers to his feet; he stoops and gives a flower to each child, one to* DAVID, *which he puts into his lapel, and one to* HAVA.]

SAM: Go on now, kiddies, hide-and-seek, now we are playing hide-and-seek; run away and hide; run away, quickly get away, hide-and-seek. [*He is shouting at them and the* CHILDREN *quickly run from the garden.*]

[DAVID *and* HAVA *help* SAM *back into the bed.* SAM *settles back and is calm again.*]

Now, seriously, let's face facts, what's going to happen to you, Davey?

SEGAL: What do you mean? God forbid if anything happens to you, he'll take over the stall; he's bound to.

DAVID: Here we go again. Oh well, I know – I've had it – I'm caught – What do you want of me? Bang go my dreams, my lovely dreams, my prospects.

SEGAL: Now he's beginning to see sense. By the way, Davey, have you met my daughter . . . ?

DAVID: Yes. We met.

SAM: Mr Segal, would you mind not interfering in my business; you've done so long enough.

[SEGAL *is offended and sits back and reads a newspaper, and through the next scene he is very interested, though every time* DAVID *or* SAM *looks his way he quickly reverts to the paper.*]

HAVA: Well, I'll go and see if Miriam is home yet. Good-bye, Mr Levy. Good-bye, Davey. Don't worry, everything will be all right.

SAM: Good-bye, darling . . . What a lovely g . . .

DAVID: Oh? Oh, good-bye . . . I'm sure it will.

[HAVA *kisses her father on the cheek and goes sadly off.*]

SAM: You are covered, Davey boy, I hope you realize that; I've got a special endowment for you. When I die you will get two hundred pounds. Well? You don't seem very eager, don't you want the money?

DAVID: I don't want that sort of money. Anyway, what can you do with two hundred pounds?

SAM: You can build up the business into a really posh layout; or you can take a world trip before you begin.

DAVID: Don't make me laugh, a world trip? You're living in the past. All I could do is buy a motor-scooter or eight new suits.

[*The stage is slowly getting darker, slightly.*]

Look, Dad, no one thinks for one moment that you're going to die. Nobody takes you seriously; everybody believes that you'll outlive the lot of us.

SAM: Believe it or not, I want to tell you something and I want you to make me one promise. Listen, Davey; today boys and girls go out with each other, they press against each other in doorways, under the moon, they experience a thrill and they call it love. They get married on the strength of this feeling and they still call it love. All right for a time, this new experience waking up in the morning and finding a warm, naked girl beside you in bed; but all the time the gilt is wearing off the gingerbread; soon the only time they meet is in bed and they meet there less and less. About this time the child usually comes and the woman has something to keep her occupied and the man drinks and returns to his dreams. It is too late. Time passes; they decide to make the most of a bad job. Don't settle for second best like your mother and I did. Marry a girl who shares your interests, so that when the love of passion cools down, the love of admiration and real friendship flares up and compensates; and then you have deep ties that can never be broken, not by anything. Do you understand what I mean?

DAVID: Of course.

SAM: Then promise me you'll try your best.

DAVID: Oh, Dad, why do you think . . .? Oh, never mind – I'll try.

SAM: Will you stay here when I'm dead?

DAVID: I don't know – I suppose so.

SAM: Good boy, but are you sure? I mean, be careful of your mother – She'll kill you with her love for you.

DAVID: Make up your mind – now I decide to stay you start getting cold feet.

SAM: I've got more than cold feet I've got the screaming willies and the heeby-jeebies multiplied together. There's a great wail leaving my soul as if my body was the great wailing wall.

[*Enter* BESSIE *with* MR *and* MRS STONE.]

MR STONE: How are you, Sam?

SAM: Not so bad. How are you?

MR STONE: Mustn't grumble.

SAM: Why not? [*There is a shaking of hands all round and the guests sit down.*] How are you, Mrs Stone?

MRS STONE: All right, thank you. How are you, Bessie?

BESSIE: Don't ask me; what with one thing and another, I don't know if I'm coming or going. [*She exits into the house.* MRS STONE *nods continuously like a Chinese mandarin.*]

MRS STONE: Well, Sam, how are you feeling? Bessie tells me you have a chill.

SAM: The chill is gone, thank God; I'm going to follow it.

MRS STONE: Good, good. How are you, David? Working?

DAVID: I'm fine. I've got a job circumsizing yiddisher mice.

MRS STONE: Sounds an interesting job.

MR STONE: He's having you on.

[BESSIE *returns with a tray of tea-things.*]

BESSIE: Take no notice of him, Mrs Stone – what a life I have with that boy, no tongue can tell; there's no house like this, not another house in the world like this; all we do is argue. Oh – come on, let's all have a nice cup of tea. [*They are all seated around the small garden table that has a striped coloured umbrella above it. They sip tea and talk.*]

MR STONE: What do you think of the political situation, Sam?

SAM: What about it? [*He shrugs.*]

MRS STONE: How's Lottie, Mrs Levy?

BESSIE: She's very well, when I heard last; she's living in Leeds – of course you know. He's a school teacher up there; so I mustn't grumble. He looks after her even if he isn't a yiddisher feller. Beautiful weather we are having. How's business, Mr Stone?

MR STONE: Mustn't grumble.

SAM: Why not?

MR STONE: The taxi game never changes; too many new boys taking it up; they all think it a cushy life; they'll learn soon enough. I also stand down the Lane on Sundays now and again. I'm what you might call a purveyor of bad taste; anything that I can get my hands on I sell; you know, those horrible plaster dogs and boys eating cherries, balloons, little men running up sticks, nonsense. Give the British public something to waste money on and they cry for the opportunity. Alabaster saints and plaster ducks, oh, horrible. Mustn't grumble. Did you hear that fight the other night, Sam? Gerry Freed, the yiddisher boy from Brooklyn, got knocked out in the first round by the coloured boy. I told you so.

SAM: I don't listen to boxing any more.

SEGAL: He reads the Bible instead. Nearly all day, nearly all night.

MR STONE: And how are you, Mr Segal?

SEGAL: Why should I complain? I've got such good children: my son sends me fifty dollars a month from the States and my girl looks after me like a little mother. Have a cigar? [*He hands one to* MR STONE *and one to* SAM.] He sends these to me from America; I feel like a millionaire; still, why not? Didn't I slave long enough for them?

MRS STONE: I wish I had some children to appreciate me. I would appreciate that.

[*She looks at* MR STONE *and he pinches her cheek.*]

MR STONE [*sings*]: When your hair has turned to silver
                 I will love you just the same;
                 I will always call you sweetheart,
                 It will always be your name ...

DAVID: Oh, Christ!

MR STONE: What's the matter, David? Don't you like my voice? I had a good voice when I was younger; I once won an amateur competition at the Troxy. Anyway, Sam, what's all this about you reading the Bible in your old age?

SAM: There are a couple of reasons why I started to re-read the Bible; first, I wanted to get what you may call a little spiritual comfort; I wanted to understand life a bit more.

MRS STONE: Anyway, Alf [to her husband], what's wrong with the Bible? Intelligent men read it, educated men, I can tell you that; more people should read it; there wouldn't be so many blackguards about.

DAVID: I am a blackguard and I read the Bible.

SEGAL: What's this? What's this? Sam, do you hear that? Your own son said he was a blackshirt. You should be ashamed of yourself.

[BESSIE hands him some cake.]

SAM: Shut up, Davey, take no notice of him everyone, he's trying to assert himself. Well, where was I? Oh, yes. I wanted to clear up a few points that worried me since I was a child. Now, Adam and Eve had only two sons: Cain and Abel; as you know Cain killed Abel. Well, how did future generations come about? Who did Cain sleep with, I ask you. Incest, you might think. I looked it up yesterday and found that Cain went out into the land of Nod, and knew his wife.

ALL: Land of Nod?

SAM: Yes, the land of Nod.

[They all look at MRS STONE who has been nodding all the time.]

MRS STONE: Why are you looking at me? What have I got to do with it?

SAM: You see, it's allegorical.

MR STONE: Sounds like a sweet.

SAM: That's paragorical. Listen, don't interrupt; well, who was this wife that he suddenly started to know, who wasn't even created? Where did she come from? Was she a monkey? So what can you believe? Then there's the Talmud, the Apocrypha, the story of

Lilith, Susanna, and the Elders; you see, none of you have heard of these things. This is the age of the specialist; you've got to specialize, otherwise where are you? Has anyone here heard of the Tarot cards? The Kaballa?

[*They all shake their heads.*]

MRS STONE: Kaballa, Smaballa, leave us alone. What's the matter, Bessie? Is he delirious? Bessie, I bought a lovely halibut for tomorrow's dinner – Well, Bessie, how are you keeping?

BESSIE: I've got a bit of fibrositis as usual, the same as yesterday.

MR STONE: Yes, Sam, the world's in a terrible state.

DAVID: Well – Halibuts are in a terrible state – and the world's suffering from fibrositis – my old man's dying to die – my mother's got a Kaballa in the oven – all right with the world – please nod by you – The world's turning and I'm yearning to sing through the streets about my sadness and joy – Good-bye – so nice to have met you – don't call again. Charming nice son you have – tata – What a world! – What a crazy, beautiful world!

[*He goes off humming and* BESSIE *chases off after him.*]

BESSIE [*off*]: Davey – wrap up warm – it's getting chilly.

[MR *and* MRS STONE *get up and make ready to go.* BESSIE *comes on again.*]

MR STONE: Well, Sam, take it easy; I wish you better.

MRS STONE: So long, Sammy, see you some more. Good-bye, Mr Segal, take care of yourself.

BESSIE: Wheel him back into the house, Mr Segal. Don't listen to him.

[BESSIE *exits with* MR *and* MRS STONE.]

SAM: Good-bye – good-bye. Thank God for that.

[*It is getting very dark now.*]

SEGAL: Shall I wheel it in now; you heard what she said?

SAM: Segal, never be intimidated by a woman; leave me here for another half an hour. I want to see the first star in the sky. Thank you, go on now, go inside, leave me alone; we'll play cards later.

SEGAL: You know what I miss? A good game of chess; there are no chess players left in the East End. Mr Solomans and me were the champion players; I haven't played since he died last year. Where has Bessie gone?

SAM: To the spiritualist meeting with the others; they want to talk to the dead; they are fed up with the living.

SEGAL [*puffing on his cigar*]: Madam Blavatsky was an intelligent woman; I saw her once.

SAM: So was Ouspensky.

SEGAL: Rasputin was a terrible man; evil and hypnotic.

SAM: So was Ivan.

SEGAL: So was Stalin.

SAM: So they say.

SEGAL: So was Bakunin.

SAM: So was Trotsky.

SEGAL: Oh, no, Trotsky was a wonderful man.

SAM: Lenin was a wonderful man.

SEGAL: Kropotkin was a wonderful man.

SAM: My father was a wonderful man.

SEGAL: Gorki was a wonderful man, my father knew him.

SAM: Tolstoi was a wonderful man, my father never knew him. Mr Segal, do you think that there's going to be a war?

SEGAL: What do you mean? The war never finishes; the independent struggle of the individual to break his chains; the Workers themselves – and the distribution of property. In the words of our greatest comrade, 'Comrades, down with politics'.

SAM: What's the name of this greatest comrade?

SEGAL: Izzy Cohen; you know him. He's a furrier, lives in Commercial Street.

[SEGAL *exits and* HAVA *enters.*]

HAVA: Hello, Mr Levy, have you seen my father?

SAM: He's gone inside for a moment. Is it urgent?

HAVA: No. I've just come to take him home. How are you feeling?

SAM: Not too good, but I'll be better presently.

[*He seems to be in pain.*]

HAVA: You rest. It'll do you the world of good.

SAM: Do me a favour, Hava. Try to get to know my son.

HAVA: I would love to. We used to play together, but since I came back he looks right through me. I think he's a very nice boy and I wish he would speak to me; he probably thinks I'm still a child.

SAM: Maybe it's a natural reaction against women; after all, he hasn't exactly a good impression of married life. Listen, I'm going to die –

HAVA: Going to die? Please, Mr Levy, don't speak that way; you scare me. It's a lovely day, all the flowers are out –

SAM: Listen, be a good, sensible girl – I've had my time and I'm going to die – what's more natural than that? Face facts – you're a woman now.

HAVA: What will happen to David?

SAM: Try to get to know him – he's my big worry.

HAVA: If only he'd let me – I don't want to push myself – he's too busy with worrying about his voice.

SAM: But I thought you liked his voice.

HAVA: I do – I love it – but he doesn't like me. What can I do?

SAM: Take your time – there isn't a woman yet been born who let her quarry slip through her fingers – encourage him to sing if you want to – my part – but bring him down to earth – tempt him – you're just the girl he needs.

HAVA: Do you think so?

SAM: Sure – you're such a lovely girl – so attractive and good-natured – ideals are very fine but they don't keep you warm in bed – he'll fall – be patient.

HAVA: Do you really think so? Anyway – I'm not that hard up – plenty more fish in the sea.

SAM: Yes, but not such a lovely red herring like my Davey – anyway – do your best.

HAVA: I'll try.

SAM: Promise? For my sake – his sake – your sake?

HAVA: I promise. You sleep now, Mr Levy – you'll feel much better tomorrow, you'll see. I must go now and find my daddy – Are you comfortable? Can I get you something?

SAM: No, no, no. There's a good girl – Go now – you're an angel.

HAVA: Are you sure you don't need anything?

[SAM *shakes his head.* HAVA *goes off into the house.*]

SAM: Little girls are so lovely – so gentle and kind. Lots of things I need, darling, but it's too late to think about them now.

[*The* CHILDREN *start to sing again: their voices are much slower and slightly off key.*]

CHILDREN [*off*]: On the hill there stands a lady,
          Who she is I do not know.
          All she wants is gold and silver,
          All she wants is a fine young man –

[DAVID *jumps over the garden fence and stands inconspicuously among some flowers.*]

DAVID [*sings*]: On the hill there stands a lady,
          Who she is I do not know.
          All she wants is gold and silver,
          All she wants is a fine young man.
          On the hill there stands a lady
          Who she is I do not know,
          I have seen her often lately,
          In the sun and in the snow,
          All she wants is golden rings and silver,
          So I heard the little children sing,
          She must know that I am not a Rockefeller,
          I am skint and haven't got a thing.
          All she wants are diamonds, and all she wants are sables,
          All she wants are all the things that I could never
          Hope to give her –
          When I stretch my hands to reach her,
          Stretch my longing hands to reach her,
          The city throws its lonely streets at me.

SAM: It got dark suddenly, as if the sun fell like a stone; I thought I heard someone singing. The world would be very dark if there wasn't any light; that goes without saying. Ah, there it is, the evening star. Starlight. Starbright, first star I've seen tonight, wish I may, wish I might, grant this wish. [*He closes his eyes and makes a wish and then he opens them again and fumbles in the bedclothes for a cigarette; he lights the cigarette, puffs at it for a few moments and then throws it away.* DAVID *picks up the cigarette and smokes it.*] A funny thing has happened to me, I know it. I've been poisoned.

DAVID: Poisoned?

SAM: My heart is jumping, all the bitterness of years I can taste in my throat. I've been poisoned by someone or something. What's the odds? By my life or my wife. But my wife was my life; so my life poisoned me, so my wife poisoned me.

DAVID: She? Poisoned him? My mother?

SAM: What do I care? I don't want to live another day; die quietly, Sam, let no shame come on the name of Levy.

DAVID: He knows all about it, but is not going to reveal the truth. I will. I will. She'll see.

SAM: Who'll miss me, anyway? Caruso is dead and Chaliapin is dead; Melba is dead; Stepney Green is dead; Whitechapel is dead. What am I waiting for? Whatever became of Whitechapel? Teeming with people, so gay, so alive . . . where are they? Where are the old men with the long white beards, where are the women selling beigels? Where are the young fellers following the young ladies along the waste? Everyone I ever loved is dead, everything that was any good is dead, has been murdered.

[DAVID *hurriedly walks across the back of the garden and goes into the house.*]

SAM: Our standards are lowering; everything is dead and being put into tins, smaller and smaller, good-bye cabbages, good-bye oranges, good-bye silver fishes; everything is in tins and compressed, frozen and chopped up. We are being dried and turned inside out and we are watching ourselves in this process on little silver screens; I may as well be dead.

[DAVID *returns to the garden and is about to go over to his father when he decides against this and takes his previous position.*]

Mumma? Yes, I can hear you. Speak louder. How are you? [*He is sitting up and staring at the air.*] I am cold. Oh, rock me, Mumma, I am tired. Oh Mumma, Mumma, hold me. Where are you? Let me

see, oh there you are. Come closer, closer, stand by the candles.
You haven't changed. There is a long river that flows from the
Minories, under Tower Bridge; it flows into the sea, but it doesn't
lose itself; it flows all over the long ocean and I am swimming so
easily along it – to you. To Russia, where you are standing, smiling
at me; oh, Mumma, how lovely you look!

[*He climbs out of bed.*]

What's up with you, Sam? Your mind's wandering. You should
be ashamed of yourself, calling for your mother.

[*He walks about the stage deliriously and by the time the next speech
ends he is slumped across the bed.*]

Oy, Mumma, I remember how you used to swing me, right up
into the sky, and then – down to the ground . . . I remember you
singing . . . [*He sings.*]

[*Note: Song will be sung in Russian or Yiddish.*]

[*singing*]: Go to sleep, mine baby, go to sleep.

Whilst the stars above begin to peep,

Through the window of heaven, angels watch over you.

Roshenkers mit munderlun, sluft mein kinderla, sluft . . .

Oh, Mumma, look. I am crying on your apron. Let me sleep
against you. I love the smell of your clothing. Oy, what can you
do when you die alone?

[*He is lying spreadeagled across the bed looking upwards.* DAVID
rushes to him.]

DAVID: Dad, listen to me; you are not alone.

SAM: If you die alone, wherever you are, what can you do?

DAVID [*shakes him*]: I tell you, Dad, you are not alone. Oh, can't you
hear me?

SAM: Even if fifty people surround your bed, you die alone.

DAVID: Dad, Dad, you are not alone. This is David. I'm with you.

SAM: For when the eyes close – no one can go into that total darkness
with you.

DAVID: I'm with you. Listen, Dad, I love you.

SAM: So here – goes – Sam – Lev-y poisoned by his wife or his life;
a smaltz herring dealer of Wentworth Street – mourned by his

d-ial-ect-ical daughter and by his crazy crooning son. Oy, oy, Shema Yisroel – Dead Mother keep me warm.

[*He dies.*]

DAVID [*rushing around the stage*]: Hi, there, everyone; come out, come out, my father is dead; he is dead; he's been poisoned; for God's sake let's have some light, lights – lights . . .

[*All the lights go full on.* SEGAL *and* HAVA *rush on to the stage.* DAVID *weeps into his father's body.* SEGAL *rushes to* DAVID *and pulls him away.* HAVA *clutches at* DAVID'S *sleeve.*]

DAVID: Who are you? What do you want?

[HAVA *runs off the stage crying.* SEGAL *and* DAVID *stand together looking at* SAM'S *body, unable to move. The* CHILDREN *are heard singing quietly.*]

CHILDREN: Sky, sky the children cry,
        Where do we go to when we die?
        What are we doing in this dream?
        Sky, sky, the children scream.
        SKY: SKY: SKY: SKY: SKY: SKY: SKY: SKY.

[*The word becomes louder and louder until it becomes metallic and unbearable.*]

SLOW CURTAIN

ACT TWO

SCENE I

It is a few days later.

Late evening and the stage is almost in darkness. Only a little of the garden is seen now. Action mainly takes place in the living-room.

When the curtain rises a figure is seen walking slowly into the house from the garden. It walks slowly around the room, looking at things, but is not discernible; the figure then sighs audibly and slumps into an armchair.

DAVID enters. He is dressed in a casual dark grey suit. He puts on the light and sings. The figure (SAM) joins in the chorus but DAVID at first does not notice anything.

DAVID: Quiet and still was the garden of Eden,
  Oh woe – woe is me –

TOGETHER: Oh woe – woe is me –

DAVID: God said I'll start humanity breathing,
  wake my baby son Adam,
  under the tree the serpent lay scheming,
  Oh – woe is me.
  Eve gave Adam the apple of bitterness,
  Oh woe – woe is me –

TOGETHER: Oh woe – woe is me –

DAVID: Guilty and sad they covered their nakedness,
  out of Eden they ran,
  far from that place they fled into nothingness,
  Oh woe – is me.

  Quiet and still is the garden of Eden,
  Oh woe – woe is me –

TOGETHER: Oh woe – woe is me –

DAVID: There sits the Lord alone and grieving,
    weeping over his son –
    Under the tree the serpent lies sleeping –
    [DAVID *is choked and stops singing;* SAM *continues.*]

SAM: Oh – woe is me.
    [DAVID *turns around and gasps; rushes quickly to the door and switches the light off.*]

SAM: Come on, Davey boy, don't be scared of your own father.

DAVID: I must be going out of my mind. I don't believe it. [*He switches on the light.*] But – b–b–b–but – you're dead . . .

SAM [*looking slightly better in health than he did in the previous Act and still in pyjamas*]: Believe me, I should be as scared as you, after all, it's my funeral you've just come from.

DAVID [*approaches* SAM *slowly and cautiously*]: I must be dreaming all this. That's right, I'm dreaming. I'm dreaming I'm awake. I'm dreaming that we buried you. [*He touches* SAM'*s face, then shakes his head several times.*] No! I'm not dreaming.

SAM: Who knows who's dreaming?

DAVID: Are you – a ghost?

SAM: What's in a name?

DAVID: But you are dead.

SAM: Yes, I'm dead. It's as if I just walked in from that garden because I was cold; came in to sit down and think.

DAVID: I must be going crazy, of course he's dead. I've just come from the grounds. I threw earth on his coffin. Oh, that terrible sound of earth falling on wood.

SAM: Don't be morbid. Where are the others?

DAVID: They'll be here soon. We washed our hands and strangers filled up the hole. Daimlers brought us back. Those same cars will be fluttering with white ribbons on Sunday, carrying brides instead of corpses.

SAM: Shut up, you give me the willies.

DAVID: The shiva is starting soon. Oh, those seven days of mourning. The weeping and wailing.

SAM: Arh! Weeping will do them good – let them get it all out of their systems. When I came in just now I went to look at myself, and when I saw the mirror was covered I knew definitely that I was dead.

DAVID: Why do we cover mirrors?

SAM: So that we shouldn't see our own grief.

DAVID: Why shouldn't we see our own grief?

SAM: How should I know?

[*Pause.*]

DAVID: Why did you come back?

SAM: To help you.

DAVID [*annoyed and surprised*]: What do you mean?

SAM: I only mean and know one thing: you need me.

DAVID: Don't make me laugh. [*He laughs.*]

SAM: You're unhappy – that's why I came; you're holding on to me.

DAVID: I'm not doing anything of the kind. Don't give me that – there's another reason – a deeper reason – you're fooling yourself.

SAM: Davey – you're all mixed up – I've come to help you settle down – I'm at your disposal.

DAVID: Help me? How can you? Besides, you can't even help yourself. Everyone knows that ghosts are displaced persons. You made a mess of your life and now you're making a mess of your death – if you want to hang around the house don't use me as an excuse. You came back because you were killed and not because I'm unhappy.

SAM: So – you admit you're unhappy – why?

DAVID: Oh! Well, because – you died too soon.

SAM: But I kept warning you.

DAVID: Yes, but I never listened and I argued with you and never amounted to anything – oh, go away.

SAM: You called me, so I'm here – everything's turning out fine.

DAVID: No, it's not. You died in very strange circumstances.

SAM: Stop depressing me. Listen, Davey – life is a very strange circumstance; for years I told you I was going to die. Well, here I am, or rather, here I am not.

DAVID: You're hedging – poor ghost.

SAM: 'Ere, cut that out. Don't you poor ghost me. And don't sulk. Incidentally you've got a lovely voice.

DAVID: But only the other day you were saying exactly the opposite.

SAM: Only the other day *I* was exactly the opposite.

DAVID: What's it like being dead?

SAM: I can't answer that question. It's without meaning. You may as well ask a blind man to describe the colour green.

DAVID: It's going to be just fine, I know – apart from all my other worries, I now have a ghost on my hands – another father would have the decency to die and to stay dead – trust you.

SAM: Davey, don't you see – I live only in your mind and heart. No one else will see me; nobody else will want to.

DAVID: Tell me, Dad – do you believe in God?

SAM: Do I believe in God? Davey, do I believe in ghosts? Well, not really, yet I am a ghost. Only certain people see ghosts, only certain people want to see ghosts. You don't look into the gutter for flying birds. Only certain people see God, only certain people want to see Him. I want to find God and I'm still looking for Him, that's why I believe in Him.

DAVID [*recites*]: I fled Him down the years and down the days –
  I fled Him down the arches of the years –

SAM: Come on, Davey – don't mope – you're only young once – let's be gay.

DAVID: Look – how can I? Especially now – don't you see you were killed – we've got to avenge your murder.

[DAVID *wanders around the room wrapped in thought.*]

SAM: Murder? Oh, what's he on about now? Oh, well – listen – even if I was killed, I don't want revenge for that, whether I was poisoned, gassed, burned, or struck by lightning. I want revenge for the way I lived – for the self-deception, the petty lies and silly quarrels. Anyway, what do you mean murdered?

DAVID: Come off it – you know perfectly well that you were poisoned.

SAM: Oh, Davey – you've got it all –

DAVID: I heard you on your death-bed.

SAM: Oh – listen – I meant –

[*There is a ring on the bell.* SAM *is about to go quickly to the door when he realizes his ghostly position. He beckons* DAVID *to go.* DAVID *returns with a well-dressed young man; dressed in the manner of a City gentleman. He is wearing a bowler hat.*]

MAN: So terribly sorry to disturb you, especially at a time like this. Could I speak with Mrs Levy, please?

DAVID: My mother hasn't come back yet. Can I help you?

MAN: I'm Mr Green of the Jewish Memorial Company. I would like to wish you a long life.

[*They shake hands and* DAVID *finds in his hand a visiting-card.*]

GREEN: Excuse the slight indiscretion of coming so soon, but facts have to be faced. Your poor father will be needing a stone. We have the finest stones in the country.

SAM: He sounds like a kidney doctor.

[GREEN *takes out a book of photos and shows them to* DAVID.]

GREEN: Italian marble. Lovely green with black streaks; hard as iron. Same as Lyons Corner House.

DAVID: Look, just leave me alone. I don't think we want any today.

SAM: Oh, cheer up, Davey, you're a long time dead.

GREEN: Well, I'll just wait for your mother – she'll be more practical, more down to earth, about your poor father. [*Muses through his catalogue.*] Yes, we've got the lot – here's a nice inexpensive job – contemporary design, you know, all the rage. I've ordered one for my own mother.

SAM [*looking at the catalogue*]: Arh, it's flashy.

DAVID: Did you meet anybody on the other side?

[GREEN *looks at him strangely.*]

SAM: Not a soul – it was even somehow lonelier than my life.

DAVID: How long do you think you're going to stay?

GREEN: Until she comes.

SAM: Until you become a happy boy.

DAVID: Looks as if we're going to have you around until I'm dead also.

[*There is another ring at the door.* DAVID *shrugs and goes and returns with another man. He is wearing glasses and dressed similarly to the first man. The new man remembers that he is wearing a carnation in his buttonhole. He discards this promptly and* SAM *picks it up, smells it, and puts it into a small jug on the mantelpiece. The new man and* GREEN *frown at each other.*]

MAN: May I have a word with Mrs Levy?

DAVID: Are you a door-to-door salesman?

MAN: Indeed not.

SAM: He is, in a way.

DAVID: She's not home just yet. I'm her son.

MAN [*shakes* DAVID'S *hand violently and leaves within it a visiting-card*]: I wish you long life. I'm Mr Black of the Hebrew Remembrance Company. I want to sell your mother a beautiful memorial stone; one that would be worthy of your dear dead father. Such a fine, kind man, wouldn't harm a fly. I knew him well.

SAM: A feller of infinite jest. Never saw him before in my life, and I used to swat flies all day.

BLACK: Forgive me for coming so soon, but in the words of our motto: GET THE STONE SETTLED AND LEARN TO SMILE AGAIN.

[*He sits down near* GREEN. *They ignore each other.*]

DAVID: Look at them, how similar they are.

SAM: And look how much they hate each other.

DAVID: And you wanted me to become something like this. A nice respectable job with prospects.

SAM: God forbid. I must have been mad.

DAVID: That's what you accused me of being.

SAM: All right – don't go on, and stop arguing. That's what I seemed to do all my life. That's how I wasted it away.

DAVID: You admit, then, that I'm on the right track?

SAM: The trouble is you're not on any track – running wildly nowhere.

DAVID: What do I do? What can I do?

[GREEN *nods to* BLACK: *points a finger to his temple, suggesting that* DAVID *is mad.*]

BLACK: Don't upset yourself, have a rest. You've gone through a hard time.

DAVID: Please don't tell me that everyone lives for ever.

GREEN: All right, we won't tell you that.

SAM: I should say that it's extremely unlikely. How many people would want to live for ever? Some want only to die. These two, for instance. How tired of life they must be! Already they are connected with the paraphernalia of death. They even smell of death.

[SAM *sniffs at them and* DAVID *follows suit.*]

DAVID: Yes, you're right, they do.

[*The men feel most uncomfortable.*]

SAM: When these two die, they'll swallow their own kishkers and will be dead for ever.

DAVID: Thank God for that.

GREEN: Thank God for everything. Look, son, what's your name?

DAVID: David. Why?

GREEN: Davey, listen, I'm your age, by my life. Here's my birth certificate to prove it. [*He shows* DAVID *the certificate.*] Please, you can help me; I'm not really a tombstone salesman, God forbid. I'm a feller like yourself really.

[SAM *is blowing on* BLACK'S *neck, who moves to the back of the stage and has a quiet smoke.*]

DAVID: How did you find out so soon that there'd been a death in the family?

GREEN: You're a bright boy. That's a very interesting question and I'm glad that you asked me. [*He puts his arm around* DAVID'S *shoulder.*] This is where the job is really interesting. We follow Coroners' reports, tip the porters at hospitals, make friends with mortuary keepers; check casualty lists for yiddisher names, scan obituary columns. Oh, it's a very subtle and interesting profession. Ever thought of trying it? There's a good living to be made if you're bright.

SAM: How sordid!

DAVID: I find all this very distasteful – excuse me, you see I'm not really myself. [*Turns to* SAM.] Well, what are we going to do?

GREEN [*whispers to* BLACK]: He's mad, you know – stone bonkers. I've often seen him around the streets talking to himself, everyone knows him. You may as well leave – it's a waste of time.

BLACK [*now approaches* DAVID *and takes him to one side*]: Dave, listen boy, I want to speak to you openly. Now, I don't know what that other geezer told you, but I can guess. He said his prices were more reasonable – well – it's a lie. My stone is the cheapest.

SAM: It's becoming like Hatton Garden. I should have been cremated.

BLACK [*his voice has disintegrated into Cockney*]: Look, give us a break with our unbreakable stone. Do me a favour, by my life – I should drop dead on this spot if our stone ain't the best. By my mother's life, by my father's life, by my life – I need the order – put in a good word with your mother. Look, Dave – [*He takes a photo out of his pocket and kisses it.*] Here's my wife and my baby daughter – her name's Angela – a real angel – help me earn an honest coin – I'm not really a traveller in tombstones – I'm just a yiddisher boy, like yourself, forced by circumstances to take up this vocation.

[*There is another ring at the door and* DAVID *goes. He returns, followed by a third man.*]

DAVID: I know, don't tell me – you're not really selling tombstones.

MAN: That's right – how did you guess? I'm not selling anything; as a matter of fact, I've come to give you something. Two hundred pounds for you and two hundred and fifty pounds for your mother.

DAVID: Well – please sit down.

[SAM *and* DAVID *bow him into a chair near to the other two.*]

DAVID: Well – isn't this marvellous? – I'm really mixed up now. Suddenly I've got two hundred pounds to play with. What shall I do with it?

SAM: Remember if you keep on talking to me, they'll think you're out of your mind.

DAVID: Who cares what they think?

GREEN [*to the new man, whose name is* WHITE]: Don't be afraid of him – he's quite harmless.

BLACK: Just a bit touched in the head. Nice boy; pity.

WHITE: I've been coming to the house long enough. He hasn't changed one bit. That reminds me – [*He consults a little notebook.*] In the case of insanity I don't think we are liable to pay out on an endowment, but I can't see anything here. I'll check back to the office later. Meanwhile, I'll hold on to the money.

DAVID: I'm going to do something to really make them sit up. [*He stands on a table.*] I'll recite and wake up the world.

SAM: Don't be a bloody fool; come down here. You must grow up. You must become yourself.

DAVID: I've got it! At last! There's someone I will become.

SAM: What do you mean?

DAVID [*excited*]: Everything fits together. Why didn't I think of it before? I'm the boy with a ghost of his own. Isn't that terrific? You're my own special ghost. Before, you were only my father – now! Nothing can stop us – we're going to have a marvellous time. I've got it all worked out.

SAM: Davey – Davey – calm down – take it easy. What can I do with him?

DAVID: Don't worry, Dad – I'm doing this for you. To avenge your death – your murder.

SAM: Where do you keep on getting that idea from – I wasn't –

DAVID [*very excited*]: Listen – Shush! No time for argument – you're right – I must become myself – I must become a crazy prince to the bitter end. I can hardly wait for all that murder and chaos at the end.

SAM: Davey – just explain – what you mean.

DAVID: I'll wait until I have all the evidence and I'll strike! When everyone is dead I'll live here all alone – just crooning to the cobwebs.

[DAVID *stands in characteristic 'Hamlet' pose and* SAM *nods his head.*]

SAM: Oh – I see – Oy-vay – smir – I'll have to go along with him – otherwise – Please, Davey – I must hand it to you – a wonderful scheme – but please – take your time – and let me arrange the killings – after all, they can't hang a ghost.

DAVID: Oh – all right – but I must decide – who – when and where.

SAM: Besides, if you are the prince then I am the king.

DAVID: That's right – the king of my imagination. One minute – my mind's playing tricks on me – oh – anyway, who cares? – as long as there's a way forward into tomorrow – I wish I really knew what you really wanted of me.

SAM [*shrugs*]: I wish you knew what you wanted of yourself. Anyway, your guess is as good as mine.

[*The men are still looking at* DAVID *with astonishment.*]

DAVID: All right, my poor father – my condolences, for, for some reason, you can't rest in peace.

SAM: We make a fine pair.

DAVID: What do we do first?

SAM: First we dance and sing.

[*They chant and move together to a Jewish melody. They clap hands and dance around the rather terrified salesmen.*]

SAM: ⎫ They are not really themselves,
DAVID: ⎬ Oy, yoy, yoy, yoy, yoy.
⎭ They are doing it for their girls,
And their little boys.
Tombstone selling is a job,
Like anything else to earn a bob;
They are not selling themselves,
Oy, yoy, yoy, yoy, yoy.

They don't know who they are,
Oy, yoy, yoy, yoy, yoy,
On this mad demented star,
Oy, yoy, yoy, yoy, yoy.
A policy will pay the rent,
Will buy the bread and his wife's scent.
They are not really bent,
Oy, yoy, yoy, yoy, yoy.

SAM: Have a good time – don't worry – well, how do you want to begin?

DAVID: I want to stay and wait for the fireworks. I want to make them and throw them. I know! I'll dress up. I'll be unique. I'll get a great mad gimmick. I'll dye my hair red or maybe light blue.

SAM: Don't be such a silly fool. That would spoil everything.

DAVID: I'll make and break the rules just as I feel like it. I'll shock them out of their lives. There'll be no more rest for anyone from now on.

[DAVID *rushes off in a maniac state and the three men continue with the card game they have been engrossed in.*]

GREEN: Stick!

BLACK: Twist . . . oh, bust!

SAM: Schmeral.

[BESSIE *comes on, dressed in black, followed by* MR *and* MRS STONE, SEGAL, *and* HAVA, *who also are dressed in mourning.*]

SAM [*goes to* HAVA *and forgets that he is a ghost*]: Hello, sad eyes – why are you looking so sad? Oh, I forgot – is it on account of me? Don't worry, I'm all right.

HAVA: My, it's chilly in here. The nights are drawing in. Where's Davey?

SAM: Do have a word with my boy; try to help him. He needs a nice girl like you.

HAVA: Daddy, I'll be glad when we move from Stepney Green. It's only full of memories now. All my friends are gone. It's full of bomb-sites and ghosts. It was the first funeral I ever went to.

WHITE: Mrs Levy, I would like to speak with you for a moment.

[*They go to one corner of the room, where they whisper.*]

SAM [*goes to* BESSIE]: Suddenly I'm dead – and buried. Why didn't we make a go of it? Where did our love go to? Oh, I'm not blaming you – I'm only asking.

MRS STONE: Are you feeling all right, dear?

HAVA: Yes, not too bad. Wonder where Davey is? I'd like to talk to him. Maybe he'll take me for a walk and everything will be different now.

SEGAL: Don't you worry about him. You worry about your poor

old father. So, here we are back at the house, everyone here except poor old Sam.

SAM: Don't be too sure.

STONE [*goes close to his wife and places his arm around her*]: It's funny how a person you know suddenly just dies – they go into a room, a hospital, and never come out. My own mother, the last time I saw her, was in a narrow bed surrounded by flowers and fast asleep. She looked just like marble. I left the ward and five minutes later she died. She went into that place and never came out again. They wheeled the body out. A shell, a husk that resembled my mother. Where did she go to?

SEGAL: Ask me.

HAVA: I'm sure Mr Levy wouldn't want us to be morbid.

SAM: Oh darling, you're so right.

STONE: Millie, be a good girl, go and make a nice cup of tea. Come on, everyone, we mustn't get the miseries. That's what shivas are for. For friends and relations to come and try to make the family forget.

BESSIE: I'll never forget him. Never. He was such a good man. I tried. Didn't I try? Ask anyone.

SEGAL: When you've finished whispering, Bessie, remember this is a house of mourning.

[HAVA *and* MRS STONE *go off to make tea, and* BESSIE *sits on a low chair.*]

SAM: What a bloody hypocrite you are, Mr Segal. You can't wait to get your hands on my Bessie.

STONE: Where's David, Bessie?

BESSIE: Yes, where is he? Where's my Daverler? Am I the only mourner?

SEGAL: Don't upset yourself. He'll be here soon. He's probably very upset.

STONE: And why didn't Lottie come?

BESSIE: Oh, why didn't she come? Am I the only mourner for my poor dear husband, God rest his soul? Lottie didn't come. Her own father and not a word.

[HAVA *and* MRS STONE *return with tea, which they pour and hand round.*]

HAVA: I wonder why she didn't come? He was such a nice, kind man.

MRS STONE: Don't cry, Bessie. Don't waste your tears. The younger generation are not worth it. I'm glad I didn't have any kids. For what? What for? Do they appreciate you?

SEGAL: I tell you my son shows respect for me; he sends me fifty dollars a month; is that bad?

BESSIE: What can you expect? Lottie's husband is a school-teacher and, apart from being Communists, I think they are also vegetarian.

STONE: That explains it; blood is thicker than water.

BESSIE: Yes, I am the only mourner. No one ever cared for my poor husband like I did.

SAM: Why didn't you show it now and again? Still, it's easy to see things when you're not so mixed up in them. Don't cry, Bessie. Once I didn't know that everything was wrong, now I know but I don't know how to put things right.

HAVA [*to* BESSIE]: Don't cry, because your husband is sleeping now.

SAM: Yes, but dreaming heavy – no rest for the wicked.

HAVA: He is at rest and better off than the lot of us.

SAM: No – one minute of life is better than a million years of sleep.

HAVA: You're not the only mourner – all Stepney Green misses him.

SAM: Thank you, Hava, but real grief is very personal – Stepney Green will carry on as if nothing happened. Yes, Bessie, you are the only mourner, I think. Let me see. There was brother Harry who died in Warsaw thirty-five years ago. Izzy who deserted in the Great War and was never seen again. Jack who came to England with me and died of home-sickness and Betty who went to America and died drinking highballs in a low dive. Lottie is in Leeds and Davey is upstairs. There you are – Bessie with all her faults is the only mourner.

[*The* THREE MEN *approach* BESSIE *and surround her with photos and catalogues.*]

SAM: Like dirty postcards.

SEGAL: Have a heart, gentlemen, this is a house of mourning.

[*Chastised, the* MEN *make ready to go, but* SEGAL *stops them.*]

SEGAL: No, no – don't go. We need you here for prayers.

[SAM *stands facing the audience; the stage gets darker; all the men stand up and face the appropriate way. They know their lines perfectly and they chant in chorus. The women sway and weep softly in the background.*]

ALL MEN: We think of those dear to us . . .

Who are no longer with us in the body . . .

[*Their voices get softer and softer, until it is just above a whisper, and they continue with the Kaddush. Meanwhile* SAM *interpolates his own chant.*]

SAM: Hear this, all you people. Listen, children of the world, both high and low, rich and poor; I shall speak the truth.

ALL: Death does not sever the bonds of devotion which unite loving hearts.

Oh God, we ever accept your goodness and greatness.

[*They all start davening in unison until they are a swaying wave of bodies; the stage is getting darker and darker.*]

Praise be His great name for ever and ever.

SAM: God will redeem my soul from the grasp of the grave.

ALL: Let Him be glorified and exalted –

[*All move together, softly and loudly; up and down goes the chant of voices. The women weep.*]

He will grant peace unto Israel and all mankind.

SAM: For He alone can grant peace.

May He who is the source of strength grant comfort to those in sorrow and peace to the heart of all His children.

[DAVID *enters. He is dressed in a white shirt, black tapering trousers, and a bootlace for a tie; he is now what is termed a* TEDDY BOY *but the similarity to Hamlet must be stressed. He jumps upon a sideboard. They all gasp and are shocked.*]

DAVID [*sings*]: Yiddisher father,

I bet he misses Matzo Bry,

Cheesecake and Smoked Salmon,
I hope he finds some in the sky,
Will you look at them here,
As they stand and pray.
When they're all very glad that he's out of the way.
Oh my wonderful yiddisher father –
Somebody will have to pay.

[*He points dramatically at his mother as* THE LIGHTS FADE.]

CURTAIN

SCENE 2

When the lights come up a week has apparently passed.

All the characters are placed exactly as before, except SAM, *who is lying on the floor. The mirrors are uncovered and the three* MEN *are playing cards.*

BESSIE *and* DAVID *get up from their low chairs.* DAVID *is obviously in a very agitated state but is very excited and manic still. Everyone seems completely tired out – as if he had been driving them right out of their wits.*

DAVID: Well – I'm glad that ritual's over – now my little drama can begin.

MRS STONE: David – do me a favour – do us all a favour – don't go on any more. I can't stand it. What's the matter? Aren't you happy? Don't you sleep well?

BESSIE: You've been driving us mad for a week; now take off those ridiculous clothes and put something decent on. What am I going to do with him?

SOLLY: What's he going to do with us?

DAVID: You'll find out. No – I'm sticking to these clothes.

BESSIE: But why?

DAVID: They make me feel good.

MRS STONE: I don't like saying this, Bessie, but your boy is meshuga. Why do you let him go on like this?

BESSIE [*sings to tune* Tum Balaloyka]:

> Listen, Davey, listen to me,
> What a bad boy you turned out to be,
> Driving me crazy, fast to my grave,
> Killing me, darling, can't you behave?

> Other mothers see joy from their child,
> You are thoughtless, hopeless and wild,
> Didn't I bring you into this life?
> Do me a favour – go get a wife.

> Oy-yoy-yoy-yoy – what have I done
> To deserve such a terrible son?
> Driving me frantic, driving me mad,
> Oh my dear Dave – you're just like your dad.

[*She slaps him lightly upon the face, and makes a gesture as if she could kill him.*]

BESSIE: Davey – you're killing me.

DAVID: Leave me alone.

BESSIE: I'll be dead and you'll be sorry.

DAVID: You talk too much.

BESSIE: You only have one mother – one mother!

DAVID: Thank God for that.

BESSIE: You'll cry – you'll see – when I'm gone – you don't know when you've got it good. Didn't I give you everything you wanted?

DAVID: You gave me everything you thought I wanted.

BESSIE: Tell me what you want now – I'll give it to you – if it's not too dear – don't you love your mother?

DAVID: What's love? How can I recognize it? I never saw any in this house.

BESSIE: There he goes again – clever dick. Didn't I give you enough food? [*She pinches his face.*] Come on, darling –

DAVID [*embarrassed*]: Oh – get away from me.

BESSIE [*she pinches him harder*]: I could kill him. [*She turns to* MRS STONE.] What can I do with him?

MRS STONE: He'll grow out of it – anyway, who cares what he's like as long as he's a nice boy?

[DAVID *sweeps around the stage and booms out; they all look at him.*]

DAVID: To be or not to bloody well be, believe me, that is the question! Whether it is besser to ne a bisle meshuga –

WHITE: Twist.

DAVID: Or to take alms for the love of Allah. To kick the bucket or to take forty winks.

[*All look entranced at the boy.* SAM *wakes up.*]

STONE: He should have been an Hector.

BLACK: BUST!

GREEN: Pay twenty-ones – five cards and pontoons only.

WHITE: Pay me, then.

DAVID: To take forty vinks no more and by Ali Abracadabra to end the sourous and the hire purchase, please God by you.

[BESSIE *and* SEGAL *are flirting in a corner.*]

DAVID: These are the consumer goods for the frum yids. To kick the bucket, to take a nap at the race-track – ah! there's the snag, for on that slip of paper what names were written – blown away by the wind – blown away, etcetera, you should live so long.

STONE: Davey! I've got it all worked out. You team up with Prince Monologue and together you sell tips and sing your philosophy to the boys down the lane.

DAVID: Oh, pipe down! [*He turns to* SEGAL.] And you watch yourself.

SEGAL: What do you mean?

DAVID: If you must carry on like that with my mother – at least wait until my father is cold.

SEGAL: You must have more respect for older people.

DAVID: Respect! What a dirty word that is. Look, we haven't even taken the memorial light from the mantelpiece – when's the wedding?

SEGAL: What are you talking about? I was being sympathetic.

BESSIE: Darling! Davey! How could you? Please, shut up. Do me a favour – be a nice boy. LEAVE HOME.

DAVID: Look – you drove him to the grave and there he is!

[DAVID *points to* SAM, *who laughs, and all the others look incredulously on.*]

DAVID: No, I'm staying – staying here.

BESSIE: As a matter of fact, we were discussing the details of getting rid of your father's business.

DAVID: Getting rid of it? Oh no, you're not. That herring stall is the kingdom I've inherited. I am THE PRINCE OF HERRINGS. I'm starting work there next Monday. The smell of those little silver fishes will follow me wherever I go. I've seen millions of them one way and another and I'll see millions more. I've brushed those sticky scales from my suits a thousand times. I've watched you cut their heads off and gut them – I've seen you souse them and smaltz them, pickle them and grill them. I've dreamed of them – had nightmares about them. Millions and millions of herrings, all with the same face; kippers, bucklings, bristlings – all my loyal subjects.

SAM: Don't work down the market – plenty of time – don't rush into things. Get that two hundred pounds and go to auditions. I've got faith in you. But I must say herrings are delicious – try one, one day. I even used to eat them now and again. They have a very high vitamin yield.

BESSIE: And what's wrong with herrings? Everything in this house has been bought by them. This table – that pack of cards – your bed upstairs – your clothes – the holidays at Cliftonville.

HAVA: David didn't mean – you see, he's got other fish to fry.

[MR STONE *laughs.*]

DAVID [*to* SAM]: Honestly! If you had your time over again, which way would you choose to earn a living?

STONE: Well – er – let me see.

SAM: I would probably do exactly the same. I make no excuses. A ghost can't afford to.

HAVA: I would like to have married – a great man – a great singer –
like someone I know.

STONE: I would have liked to have been a lawyer.

SEGAL: I would have liked to have been the leader of the greatest
political party in the world and a diamond merchant in my spare
time.

MRS STONE: I would like to have been a ballet dancer.

BESSIE: I would have liked to have married a Rothschild.

WHITE: Stick. I would have liked to be Joe Lyons.

BLACK: I would have liked to have been an Epstein. Bust.

GREEN: Pay pontoons only. I would have liked to be a Rabbi; you see
this is not my real work.

ALL [except SAM]: And you? What would you like to be?

DAVID: The same as I am. Prince of the Herrings. Prince Hamlet . . .
[They all laugh.]

HAVA: I would like to go to the cinema. Coming, anyone?
[She quickly kisses her father and hurriedly exits.]

SAM: Listen, Boychick. Hamlet wasn't an important man. Where
would he have been if Shakespeare didn't rescue him from
obscurity? Now Shakespeare was a different kettle of fish.

DAVID: You know everything! First I must sell herrings and then I
mustn't sell herrings – then I had a terrible voice and now I've a
lovely voice – make up your mind.

SAM: Why shouldn't I change my mind? Why should ghosts be
different from people?

DAVID: Arh, you're not a very successful ghost – you don't bother
anyone – except me.

SAM: I'm doing my work properly – if you've any complaints –
you'd better get in touch with my union.

DAVID: It's all very well for you to be frivolous.
[The telephone rings; several rush to lift the receiver but BESSIE beats
all of them.]

BESSIE: Hello! Yes! Speaking! Who's that? Lottie? Is that you,
Lottie? Darling! [She talks now to the room.] Mrs Stone, my Lottie's
on the phone – all the way from Leeds – Hello, Dolly – speak

louder – [*to* DAVID *now*] Davey – your sister's on the line – come
and say hello.

DAVID: Oh – do me a favour.

BESSIE: He won't even say hello to his own sister – what do you
think of that? The trouble I have with that boy – what's that,
darling? – no, he hasn't changed –

DAVID: Stop talking about me and carry on talking about nothing –

BESSIE: He's mad – he's mad – his own sister – believe me, Lottie
– you're better off in Leeds.

[DAVID *stomps off into the kitchen.*]

BESSIE: He's gone out of the room now – into the kitchen – how do
I know? Well, how are you, darling? Good – you should be
ashamed of yourself. What? No! Where? Yes – listen. Lottie – you
should be ashamed of yourself – your own father – your own flesh
and blood and you never came – after all the years he slaved for
you – what? I can't hear! You want to speak to Davey? [*Shouts
towards kitchen.*] Davey – Lottie wants a word with you.

DAVID [*off*]: I'm busy.

BESSIE [*into phone*]: He's busy – always busy – he's driving us mad –
no tongue can tell what I have to put up with – there's no other
house like this house – you bad girl – Lottie – why didn't you even
come to the shiva? What? Going to have another one? When?
That husband of yours – oh, such bad news – it always comes
together –– Mazeltoff, darling – kiss the babies for me – wrap up
warm – take care – there are the pips – you should be ashamed –
good-bye, Dolly – teta! Take care – I'm all right – there're the pips –
the pips – I'm all right – I'll survive somehow – Teta, Lottie! [*She
puts the phone down.*] She's going to have another baby. Davey!
You're going to be an uncle again!

DAVID [*off*]: Hurray!

MRS STONE: How many will this make?

BESSIE [*proudly*]: This will be my fifth grandchild.

MRS STONE: Hasn't she heard of them new clinics? Nobody goes in
for big families any more.

BESSIE: Her husband is a Catholic.

SEGAL: Not long ago – you said he was a Communist.

BESSIE: He is a Communist and a Catholic.

MRS STONE [*sings suddenly*]: To sigh for you – to cry for you – yes –
even die for you – that's what God made mothers for –

BESSIE: Believe me – you're right.

[DAVID *comes on, drinking*.]

SAM: What are you drinking?

DAVID: Chocolate.

SAM: Good – it was the magical drink of the Aztec gods – anyway,
it won't do you any harm.

DAVID: No more smoozing me – something has got to happen soon –
I must get revenge – they killed you and you won't directly admit
it. WHY? You're getting cold feet – you can't rely on your own
father – not even when he's a ghost. LOOK AT THEM! Just
look at them!

BESSIE: We ruined him – he's feeling like this because he's got to
face up to reality. He hasn't worked properly for years. He read
too many books. We gave him everything he wanted. The boy
with the ever-open hand. Money for jazz records – money for
clothes – money for jam. He used to bring back stray dogs and
mangy cats.

MRS STONE: Mangy cats?

BESSIE: I put up with a lot to stop him being a low-life. He even kept
lizards as pets.

MRS STONE: LIZARDS! Oh, Bessie – how you must have suffered!

BESSIE: It was all Sam's fault. He was too soft with him.

SAM: Go on, blame the dead – how convenient a corpse can be! Why
did I marry such a woman?

DAVID: But Dad – surely you loved her once.

SAM: Yes – once. [BESSIE *is eating and stuffing herself with chocolates*.]

DAVID [*to* BESSIE]: Why didn't you love Dad? He was such a good
man.

[BESSIE *nearly chokes with a chocolate*.]

SAM: SHUT UP, DAVEY! I had my faults. Things happen
between husband and wife that no one else can know about.

BESSIE: Listen to who's talking. The pot calls the kettle black. I'm going to tell you a few things about Sam –

SAM: Change the subject quick. Otherwise you'll end up by sympathizing with her.

DAVID: Mind your own business. You're no help to me. I want revenge and I want it NOW!

SAM: Davey – calm down.

DAVID: Calm! Calm, he says. You were murdered by some people in this room – and they're going to pay. I've got to avenge the injustice and the scandal.

SAM: Who in this room? What are you talking about?

DAVID: When you died you said she poisoned you – I heard you –

SAM: Oh, don't be so silly.

DAVID: It's no good backing out of it now – with my own ears I heard your last words.

SAM: Oh! I didn't really mean that she poisoned me – what I meant to say was that my life poisoned me and because once she was my life – well –

DAVID: You just said 'She poisoned me' and that's good enough for me. I know why she did – they planned it together – she and that little Soppy Segal [points at the frightened SOLLY].

SAM: You only heard what you wanted to. What was in your mind to pick out.

DAVID: You're a liar! You were telling the truth then, but now you're covering up for them – for some reason.

SAM: Davey – don't be dramatic – settle down like a good boy and learn from my mistakes. Listen, before I didn't know just how much of a mess I made of my life – now I know – but how can I get through to you? – please listen to me.

DAVID: There's only one thing I know or want to know – you were poisoned whether you admit it or not and my sole aim is to avenge your murder – I'm going to do this with or without your help – they've got to pay – anyway, before you promised to help me – well – you'd better make up your mind once and for all.

[He goes into the garden.]

SAM [*reluctantly*]: Very well – I have no choice. I'll have to play along with him.

[DAVID *sulks in the garden*.]

BESSIE: I did love Sam. Yes, I did – I know we didn't get on, but he was a good man and I'm going to miss him so much.

SAM: Poor Bessie – argument was the only way we could stay close. She wasn't a bad girl and if I wasn't a ghost I could get quite carried away and forgive her for everything. ALMOST.

[SAM *follows* DAVID *into the garden; he goes through wall.* SOLLY *goes into garden*.]

CHILDREN: Silly Solly Segal, nose like an eagle,
Eyes like two jelly-fish, teeth like a weasel.

[SEGAL *sits down near* SAM *and* DAVID. *The lights in the house go dim*.]

SAM: Davey – please, what's the matter with you?

DAVID: To tell you the truth – I'm unhappy.

SOLLY: Oh, cheer up, my boy – growing up is hard.

SAM: Why? I know that most of the past was undesirable, but now we must look forward.

DAVID: I wanted so much to please you.

SOLLY: Well, that's very nice of you.

DAVID: It looks like we have permanent guests.

SEGAL: Yes.

DAVID: I wasn't speaking to you.

SEGAL: I wish you would sometimes. I might be able to give you some advice.

DAVID: I wanted you to be proud of me.

SAM: There's still time.

DAVID [*mood changes*]: Now that my dad's out of the way I suppose you'll marry my mother.

SEGAL: I'm lonely. Don't think too badly of me. You're too young to understand loneliness.

DAVID: Am I? Yes, ever since you died the house has been full of people.

SEGAL [*jumps up*]: Ever since I died? [*Feels his face.*] What do you mean?

SAM: Poor old boy. Don't be too hard on him.

DAVID: Every time you talk I get the feeling that it's myself thinking. My other self.

SEGAL: That's a good thing. I could teach you a lot. Politics and economics. Syndicalism. The theories of capital and labour . . .

DAVID: I was with you when you died.

SEGAL: When I died! Oh, you're driving me mad.

SAM: I'm happy to know I didn't die alone. Was it difficult seeing me die?

DAVID: Yes.

SEGAL: What do you mean? Yes?

SAM: Did I call for Bessie?

DAVID: No.

SEGAL: What do you mean? Yes! No!

DAVID: I told you – you said you'd been poisoned.

SEGAL: Poisoned? [*He staggers for a moment and splutters.*]

DAVID: Not you – not yet. [*to* SAM] I can't get over it: your best friend and your wife, glad to get you out of the way.

SAM: The real motives in people's minds are terrible things to discover; yours for instance. Don't look too deeply.

SEGAL: Poor Sam – what a responsibility being your father – is it worth it?

DAVID: Coming in? I'm feeling cold.

SEGAL: No – I want to think.

SAM: No – I want to stop thinking. When I'm with you I think too much.

[DAVID *goes inside house and sits alone.*]

SAM [*looks at* SOLLY]: Poor Solly.

SEGAL [*looks up*]: Poor Sammy.

SAM: Bloody hypocrite. Still, Solly wasn't a bad man – sometimes.

SEGAL [*a reprise of the duologue in Act I*]: Sammy was a wonderful man; I never really knew him.

SAM: The boy's restless and it's up to me. There must be a solution. Anyway, that's what I'm here for.

SEGAL: He was so kind.

SAM: I can't leave until I help him see straight.

SEGAL: Poor David. His mother will kill him, if they live alone. He needs a man – a great man – someone to look up to – what am I saying? He needs someone like me; I'll be a real father to him.

SAM: Bloody cheek. One minute. You're right. You're right! I hate to say this but you're right. That's the answer.

SEGAL: It's getting windy. Think I'll go in and maybe talk to Bessie.

[*As he moves to go in, the* CHILDREN *come and call after him again.*]

CHILDREN: Soppy Solly Seagull, nose like an eagle,
　　　　　Eyes like two jelly-fish –

[*With a gesture of dismay he chases them and then goes into the house.*]

SAM: Mr Segal, I could k – iss you. [*Pause.*] All right, if you and Bessie get married, but I know what will happen: you'll discuss it for years, you'll argue – you'll say not enough time has passed since my burial – I've got to think of some way to get you married as soon as possible –

[*He goes through the wall again into the house and the lights go up.*]

DAVID [*rushing to* SAM *and pointing to* SOLLY *and* BESSIE, *who are now whispering together*]: You know, of course, what they're planning.

SAM [*joking*]: Are they planning more horrible murders?

DAVID: Not yet. Now they're planning to get married.

SAM: Do you think I'm blind? This is a wonderful idea; you must encourage their romance if you want revenge.

DAVID: What do you mean?

SAM: Their marriage would prove they wanted me out of the way – it would prove your theories correct.

DAVID: Yeah! You're right. You're dead right.

SAM: You said it.

WHITE [*from card table*]: Listen, young man – I'm staying round to check your sanity – well, my report won't be very favourable. Our company need not pay your endowment if you're stone bonkers.

DAVID [*to* SAM]: You signed this policy knowing this clause?

SAM: Who reads policies when they sign them? Who has that much time to waste? Anyway, I signed when you were one year old – I didn't know you'd grow up to be a madman.

[MR STONE *suddenly stands up*.]

MR STONE: Well, isn't that a coincidence? Listen, everybody, their names are not really White, Black, and Green! This is really Mr Blackstone, this is really Mr Whitestone, and this is really Mr Greenstone, and I changed my name by deed poll from Goldstone to Stone.

DAVID: They dropped the stone and you picked it up.

[MR STONE *sits down and the three* MEN *stand up*.]

WHITE: In business it's better –

BLACK: It's brief and to the point.

GREEN: It pays to have a simple name.

[*The three* MEN *get into line and sing a smart clipped song; the tune is a variant of the post-horn gallop*.]

MEN: Mr White, Mr Black, Mr Green,
    Our tombstones are simply serene,
    Our companies never look back,
    Mr White, Mr Green, Mr Black.
    Mr Green, Mr Black, Mr White,
    Our companies soon set it right,
    And they're guaranteed not to crack,
    Mr Green, Mr White, Mr Black.
    Mr Black, Mr Green, Mr White,
    Insurance and tombstones are right;
    Buy British and always fight clean,
    Mr Black, Mr White, Mr Green.

[*They sit down again and play cards*.]

MRS STONE [*suddenly sings*]: You die if you worry, you die if you don't – so why worry at all? It's only worry that killed the cat, anybody can tell you that – That's funny – I feel like singing tonight. My mother used to sing that song, and do you know what? She died worrying just the same.

[SEGAL, MRS STONE, *and* BESSIE *are seated around the table.* DAVID *and* SAM *are talking quietly*.]

BESSIE: Shall we begin? Have you got the letters ready?

[MRS STONE *starts arranging letters around the table.* BESSIE *returns to the table with a tumbler.*]

MRS STONE: Come on, Alf, we're ready to begin.

[*She almost has to pull him away from the card game.*]

SEGAL: What's the matter? What's everyone gone quiet for?

BESSIE: Why, the seance, of course.

SEGAL: Who do you want to talk with?

BESSIE: Anyone who's interested in talking to us!

SEGAL: Sounds like a Summit Conference. I hope you don't pick up Sam on the high frequency.

SAM: Oh – he's sensitive.

SEGAL: Oy – the spirits – what they say is sacred – leave them alone.

[SEGAL *is about to place his arm around* BESSIE *when he has a change of heart.*]

SEGAL [*looking at the ceiling*]: Sam – oy – Sam, forgive me, my thoughts are not nice – but my intentions are pure.

SAM: At last! I've got it. The answer.

DAVID: Look at that little hypocrite – I could kill him now.

SAM: Be patient and wait a little while. They'll kill each other.

DAVID: I want them to die – like you. No, not like you. Oh, I don't care how they die.

SAM: I'll help you kill them in such a way that they won't affect you any more. You'll be free and no one will charge you with anything. Just be patient. It's all clicked into place – this is how we get them married. [*He whispers to* DAVID, *who laughs.*]

DAVID: And once they're married, Bob's your uncle.

SEGAL: I'm filled with remorse. He was right – for once that madman, my stepson-in-law, please God, was right – my thoughts are not becoming to a citizen of the world.

BESSIE: What are you muttering about, Mr Segal?

SEGAL: Bessie, how many years have you known me?

BESSIE: About thirty or forty years.

SEGAL: Isn't it time you called me Solly?

SAM: Here we go, Davey.

[BESSIE *smiles and places* SEGAL'S *finger on the tumbler, as the others have done.*]

BESSIE [*whispers*]: Solly, boy, are you comfortable?

STONE: Is there anyone there who wants to speak with anyone here?

[SAM *is laughing his head off, nods, and begins to move the tumbler to various letters. Everyone follows with great concentration the journey of the glass. The* MEN *at the table continue playing cards, totally unaware of the things going on.*]

SAM [*saying the word that he is spelling out*]: HITLER.

[*There is great confusion in the room as the women scream and rush as far from the table as possible.*]

MRS STONE: Oy, what do we do now? Send him back? Send him back, Alf.

BESSIE [*creeps back to the table*]: Let's ignore him and try to get somewhere else.

STONE: You never know what will turn up.

SEGAL: Maybe he just wants to apologize.

DAVID [*who pretends that he didn't see the message*]: What was the message?

STONE: It just said HITLER. Come on, let's try again. Maybe we didn't write the letters clearly enough or they're short-sighted over there.

[*They repeat the process, and* SAM, *who has been reading the sporting page of the newspaper, begins to move the glass again.*]

DAVID: What does it say now?

BESSIE: Hush.

MRS STONE: Shush.

SEGAL: Hush? Shush? What does that mean? It goes too fast. I can't read upside down.

[SAM *spells out the words again.*]

SAM: RED CLOUD . . . TWO-THIRTY . . . TOMORROW . . .

[*They all repeat this as they read the message.*]

SEGAL: Red cloud? Sounds like a Communist pirate.

BESSIE: Look, there it goes again. Red, cloud, tomorrow, two-thirty.

It must be the spirit guide. You know what I mean? White cloud!
Red cloud! They're always Red Indians.

MRS STONE: Why?

BESSIE: How should I know?

SEGAL [*sings*]: Red cloud in the sunset . . .

DAVID [*sings*]: Mushrooms on the sea . . .

STONE: One moment: did it say Red Cloud? [*he looks at the back
page of the newspaper*] Here it is: Red Cloud running in the big
race, two-thirty tomorrow: 100 to 1.

[*He rushes to the phone and dials.*]

MRS STONE: Izzy Posner won't be there at this hour.

STONE: Izzy never leaves the office; that's his motto. Hello? Is that
you, Izzy? This is me: Alf Stone. Five pounds each way, Red
Cloud, two-thirty – never mind, do what I tell you.

[*At this moment the three* MEN *quickly leave the card game and rush
for the telephone. One snatches it from* MR STONE *and each in turn
pulls it from the others; each retains it long enough only to speak his
name.*]

MEN: MR WHITE. MR BLACK. MR GREEN. MR BLACK.
MR WHITE. GREEN. WHITE. BLACK. WHITE.
BLACK. GREEN.

[*The names coagulate into a jumble of sound. At the telephone the* MEN
*continue at the action, only the sound has faded and they play in dumb
show.* SAM *starts spelling out again, and they follow the glass with rapt
attention.*]

SAM [*spelling out the letters he is moving the glass to*]: This is – Sam –
Levy . . . I forgive you, Mr Segal – take care of – my Bessie . . .

[*Everyone cheers.* SEGAL *is ecstatic and kisses* BESSIE, *and* DAVID
and SAM *shake hands.* DAVID *looks at* BESSIE *and* SEGAL, *and rubs
his hands.*]

CURTAIN

ACT THREE

Eight months later.

It is a fine afternoon in early spring; in the house there is a festive tone, that completely contrasts with the previous scene. There are flowers everywhere and the table is set with a large white tablecloth; there are bottles of wine and dishes of fruit everywhere.

DAVID *is sitting on a chair in the garden, looking more like Hamlet and very morose; dressed in teddy boy's clothing;* SAM *is lying on the grass looking up at the sky.* CHILDREN *are playing nearby and are singing.*

CHILDREN: Poor Jenny is a-weeping, a-weeping, a-weeping.

Poor Jenny is a-weeping on a bright summer's day.

Stand up, stand up, on your heels,

Choose the one you like the best, a lady or a gentleman;

Now you're married we wish you joy,

First a girl and then a boy.

Kiss her once, kiss her twice,

Kiss her three times over.

[SAM *gets up and does some gardening, digging, and the scene fades slightly. The* THREE SALESMEN *enter and immediately go to the table where they start helping themselves to sandwiches.*]

WHITE: You'll be happy to know that I sold her a stone; clinched the deal just before she got married.

BLACK: But you're an insurance man.

WHITE: I was an insurance man; I've now started my own little monumental stone company. By the way, why not work for me, the two of you?

BLACK: I'm afraid that's impossible. You see, I've been an insurance agent for several months.

GREEN: So am I. That's strange. I came here today to sell her an insurance policy for her husband.

BLACK: So did I and at the same time to try and get that son of hers to take out a life insurance.

GREEN: There seems to be a close parallel in our lives.

BLACK: There certainly does. Where were you educated?

GREEN: Jews' Free School. Where were you?

BLACK: Why, at the same school. Who was your teacher?

GREEN: Mr Rosen. Yours?

BLACK: Rosen also. What year?

GREEN: About 1940 I left.

BLACK: So did I. We must have been there at the same time.

GREEN: Do you like football?

BLACK: No. Do you like cricket?

GREEN: Yes.

BLACK: So do I. What a coincidence!

GREEN: Do you like me?

BLACK: No. Do you like me?

GREEN: No. How wonderful! [*They shake hands and are all smiles.*]

GREEN [*to* WHITE]: Could you get your company to settle the David Levy claim? That is to say, your old company.

WHITE: I believe that they're doing it today. I sold Mrs Levy a stone on that understanding. I'll call in there and get the money for him.

BLACK: Tell me, what company do you represent?

GREEN: The Providential Life of Mile End.

BLACK [*excited and thrilled*]: How do you do? So do I. [*They shake hands excitedly.*]

WHITE: Did you say the Providential Life of Mile End?
    [*They nod.*]
Why, that's the company I used to work for; this calls for a drink. [*Opens a bottle and they all have a drink.*]

GREEN: Tell me, aren't you a little off your territory?

BLACK: I don't think so. My zone starts at Silvertown, extends all along Commercial Road, Watney Street, Hessle Street, Cable Street, Jubilee Street, Redmans Road, and all the area of Stepney Green, southern side.

GREEN: Let me see, my area begins at Bishopsgate, Houndsditch, Commercial Street, Brady Street Buildings, Old Montague Street, and Stepney Green, northern side. Bow Road right up to Stratford.

BLACK: There you are, you said northern side. Sorry old chap, this is the southern side. You're on my territory; David Levy is mine.

GREEN: I'm so terribly sorry, no hard feelings?

BLACK: Certainly not. Let's all have a drink.

[*They all drink and then* WHITE *and* GREEN *make to exit.*]

GREEN: See you at the office one day. So long.

BLACK: Yes, rather. Who knows, we may see each other quite often. Bye-bye.

[GREEN *exits.* WHITE *is about to leave also.*]

Don't forget to bring him the money today.

WHITE: I shan't. So long, old boy. [*He exits.*]

[BLACK *walks smugly around the stage and starts drinking at the table. He sits down and drinks quite a lot.*]

SAM: Oh, I'm so tired; I feel like I could just sleep and sleep.

DAVID: Why don't you? You always said you deserved a rest – well, here it is.

SAM: I'm worried about you. It's about time you made up your mind? Are you going to look after the barrow or not?

DAVID: I've been in for about ten auditions in the past couple of months. You've got to have a gimmick or influence or both. I've borrowed almost the whole of that two hundred pounds from Mum; it's coming today, but I shan't get any of it. What is going to be the outcome of all this? I mean, what are you going to do? You can't stay here all your life.

SAM: All my life?

DAVID: I mean all your death. It's getting to the state where I'm beginning to think that I'm your father. What are you waiting for now?

SAM: There was the question of revenge and your future that brought me here. I think the two are really the same problem. You must really make up your mind. Do you know that ever since I've been dead I haven't seen anyone over there.

DAVID: You know, of course, what happened today? Today is the big day. The day we've been waiting for.

SAM: I haven't been around so much recently.

DAVID: That's right. Where have you been going? A fine ghost you turned out to be. Why, I've almost got to like Segal in your absence. And when you're here you sleep all the time. Today is my day. I'm free either way. I'll kill myself along with the rest.

SAM [*who hasn't been listening*]: Oh, I've been wandering here and there. I went down the Lane to see all the boys. Solly Segal was there selling herrings at my stall. Then I took a boat trip to Putney and I went to the Tower of London. I walked through the front entrance of Buckingham Palace and strolled right through the place. I didn't see not one member of the Royal Family. I also went on a conducted tour with some wealthy Yanks. Hampton Court, Kew, Greenwich, Ken Wood. Davey, why didn't you tell me that London was so beautiful? What a wonderful history it has. It's like a wonderful woman you can live with your whole life and miss the entire point. It's not so bad being dead after all. I saw the city in the early morning, before anyone gets up to go to work. I walked along the riverside: it's very lovely with the sun rising with the mist, rising over the office blocks and the warehouses. I saw the swans wake up and preen themselves in the mud.

DAVID: You know, of course, what happened today. You're evading the issue. You don't want to leave here.

SAM: Being dead has great advantages. Why I even got the best seat in the Festival Hall for nothing, but I suppose it's **no use**; being dead like this is so impermanent. There's no future in it, don't you agree?

DAVID: You do know what happened today?

SAM: Yes, my Bessie got married.

DAVID: Does that let you out?

SAM: I suppose it must do. Segal is my exit visa.

DAVID: You're still going to help me play it out to the end?

SAM: If you're determined, I suppose so. How do you want them to die?

DAVID: The same way that you died. By poison.

SAM: Fine. Presently I'll give you a list of various ingredients needed. I want you to go out and buy them at the chemist and greengrocer.

I want you to mix the concoction to my specification and then you administer it in your own time. Oh well, this is it. Everything is resolved today.

DAVID: What is the purpose in life? It seems senseless to me.

SAM: The purpose in life is to be aware that that question exists. What is the purpose in life? I wonder. I was borrowed from the darkness by your desire. I've been allowed to slip away for a few moments. I never had roots anywhere, Davey, and I'm still wandering. I love London so much that I hate leaving it, for ever and ever. If being a ghost means having a real pain in the heart then I am the biggest and most successful ghost that ever was. But I have the even greater desire to look for some other light; a light brighter than earth, a light I heard about in symphonies and poetry. I am dead and buried and live only in the imagination of a neurotic young man; you are fickle, you'll forget all about this, then I'll be really dead.

DAVID: Never.

SAM: Yes you will, and quite right too. I, Samuel Levy, of no fixed abode am being charged with loitering and soon I must leave London for ever.

DAVID: In spite of your words I'm happy. In a strange way you make me feel wonderful. I don't seem to want revenge so much.

SAM: Oh yes, you do. When you get revenge in this house, everything will turn out all right, just as it should be. But don't be too confident; you'll be hurt over and over again, and always about the same things.

DAVID: I feel I can face everything. As if I'd been taken by the ankles and battered against a wall; bashed to pulp and yet I can stand up and sing.

SAM: You still haven't grown out of that?

DAVID: I want to sing. I've got to. When I stop I'll lay down and die.

SAM: Where will you go when all this revenge business is settled?

DAVID: I'm not sure. It's been nice of you to help me.

SAM: I'm glad that I could help you, because now instead of only being your father, we are close friends. It's so easy to make a child and so hard to make a friend. Where will you go?

DAVID: Anywhere – everywhere! A grand tour – New York, Mexico, Peru, New Guinea, Siam, China, India. Come on, Dad, let me have that prescription.

SAM: Don't be in too much of a hurry. I haven't finished talking yet.

DAVID: What do you mean?

SAM: Some people never leave home; even when they put a thousand miles between them and the street door; when you leave, really leave.

DAVID: Don't start lecturing me again. We've been having a wonderful time. Don't start getting stuffy now.

SAM: Forgive me, but I think that my time is drawing near; I'm beginning to feel like a ghost should; restless and forgetful. I feel guilty and uncomfortable like a bird that should migrate somewhere; a bird that lost its memory. Don't mind me, though. I will disappear soon and then all our troubles will be over. I shan't bother you. I might, though, sort of vanish inside you; wouldn't that be nice? [*He has been writing and hands* DAVID *the piece of paper.*] There you are, my son. Here is your revenge.

DAVID [*reads it and has difficulty*]: By the sound of it it should be very effective. Where did you learn about it?

SAM: Picked it up since I was buried. It's effective, don't you worry. Now go on, off with you; they're returning soon.

[DAVID *goes off into the house reading it.*]

He'll drink some, too; so will I. I hate unhappy endings. It'll work but not in the way that he expects.

[DAVID *is about to leave the house when* BLACK *stops him.*]

BLACK: Excuse me, sir, could I interest you in a very good life insurance policy?

DAVID: But I thought you sold tombstones?

BLACK: I used to, but you see I was never really . . . I'm a student of life.

DAVID: We must have a drink when I get back. I'm going to something very special; I'm sure after that you'll never be yourself again. [*Exits.*]

BLACK: Wonderful. What a charming boy! He's really turning out a decent sort.

[*There is a great commotion and the crowd of people come in the door. *BESSIE* and *SEGAL* come in arm in arm and dancing; they are already quite drunk. *MR* and *MRS STONE* follow. Then *HAVA*, who looks sad; *GREEN* and *WHITE* also enter. *MR STONE* starts the gramophone and plays a typical Hebrew melody and when *SAM* comes in it all seems to go a little quieter. There is much eating and drinking.*]

HAVA: It seems brighter here now.

BLACK [*to *WHITE* and *GREEN*]: Hello, you two back?

GREEN: Yes, we bumped into them. [*He is quite tipsy and takes hold of *BLACK* and guides him around the stage in a dreamy love attitude, to the music.*]

WHITE [*follows them around*]: I've got the money! [*He is cuddling a brown paper parcel.*]

[*BESSIE* is talking seriously to *MRS STONE*. The *MEN* are now drinking around the table; *HAVA* is looking around the house.*]

BESSIE: I still can't help thinking that I got married too soon. I don't know – I feel it wasn't right.

[*SAM* is also drinking.*]

MRS STONE: Don't worry yourself. It wasn't too soon. Enjoy yourself while there is still time. You're still a young girl. Years ago it might have been different but this is the age of the jet; everything is getting faster and faster.

HAVA: I don't think I've been in this house for a month.

[*SEGAL*, who is very drunk, now stands on a chair.*]

SEGAL: Tonight, everyone, we are going to have a wonderful party. All Stepney Green is invited. A real old-fashioned party; dancing and singing. Forget wars, forget politics, and enjoy yourself.

HAVA [*goes to him*]: I'm so happy for you, Daddy. You've been such a worry to me.

SEGAL: I've got a beautiful wife and a beautiful daughter. [*He kisses both of them.*]

HAVA: I still don't like the idea of moving here.

MRS STONE: What a man he is; how romantic! Why can't you be like that?

STONE: I will be, when I get married again.

HAVA: I wonder where Davey is?

SEGAL: Maybe right now, dear old Sam is getting married to my Sarah; God rest her soul; isn't that a lovely thought?

[SAM *looks round uncomfortably as if he is being pursued.*]

SAM: God forgive you, Mr Segal, don't do me any favours. Bessie is an angel compared to your Sarah. If they gave me a choice of everlasting darkness or your Sarah, I would choose the darkness.

SEGAL [*sings*]: The second time is always nicer,
    And this is my second time.
    For many years I've been a miser,
    That has been my crime.
    Oy, Yoy, wish me joy,
    Tonight I am a lucky boy.
    The second time is so much nicer;
    This is my second time.

BESSIE: They'll say I didn't wait for long
    But a girl must take her chance.
    Solly is so nice and strong
    And Sam led me a dance;
    Well, well, I'm in a spell,
    Tonight I am a lucky girl.
    The second time is so much nicer;
    This is my second time.

THREE MEN: The second hand is whizzing round;
    Soon we'll be on our way.
    Our policies are really sound;
    Sign one with us today.
    Dance, sing, love, and laugh,
    We'll make up your epitaph.
    The second time is so much nicer;
    I DIED OF LOVE TODAY.

MRS STONE: Well, well, Bessie girl, Solly's got you in his spell . . .

ALL [*sing*]: The second time is so much nicer;
>   This is their second time.

> [*They all return to little groups;* DAVID *returns and one can see him busy mixing the ingredients over by a side table;* HAVA *stands close to him but he does not see her.*]

SAM: All right, Bessie, I wish you joy. Mr Segal, er – may I call you Solly now? Solly, Bessie, I wish you both joy. Drive each other mad; here's to your good health and please God by you. [*He raises a glass to them and then he turns and looks in a mirror at himself.*]

HAVA [*to* BESSIE]: Please, er – Mrs – what can I call you?

BESSIE: Call me Aunty Bessie.

HAVA: Please Aunty, help me to know Davey. We can't go on like this.

BESSIE: Leave him alone; don't have much to do with him. He'll drive you mad.

SEGAL: That's all right. They're all a little mad where she came from; working out in the hot sun all day for no pay. Who in his right mind would do that?

> [HAVA *goes into the garden sadly;* DAVID *is pouring out the drinks. The* MEN *sit down to play cards and it becomes very quiet in the room; everybody seems moody and only* SAM *is happy.* BLACK *suddenly sees* DAVID; *he leaves the game.*]

BLACK: Oh, there you are. Now what about that insurance policy? Our company believe that . . .

> [DAVID *snubs him and* BLACK *moodily returns to the card game.*]

BESSIE: There you are. Come on, darling. Davey, come on. Kiss me and shake your Uncle Solly by the hand.

DAVID: Leave me alone. [*Turns his back.*]

> [SAM *goes over to him and reasons with him.*]

SAM: Go on, Davey, play their game. It's nearly over. Wait and see what I've got in store for you.

DAVID: What?

BESSIE: There he goes, talking to himself again.

SAM: Just be patient. Kiss your mother, wish them joy. Give them all a drink [*he winks*] and Bob's your uncle.

[HAVA *has heard* DAVID *talking and she comes into the doorway and stands there watching.*]

DAVID [*goes over to* BESSIE *and* SEGAL]: Mother, I wish you joy and happiness. [*Kisses her.*] Mr Segal, I hope that you'll be very happy. I would like you all to have a little drink with me; I would like to toast your health.

[DAVID *hands around the drinks to everyone. He is about to by-pass* SAM, *but* SAM *takes one.* DAVID *shrugs. He does not give* HAVA *a drink.*]

SEGAL: Thank you, thank you, thank God. Have you decided what you want to do yet?

DAVID: I'll talk to you about it tomorrow.

SEGAL: You mean you'll take over the herring stall? At last? [*to himself*] I can't stand those herrings any longer.

DAVID: No, I'm not. Tomorrow I'm going to leave home.

[*Everyone is despondent and* DAVID *raises his glass.*]

Here's to tomorrow. I wish you both joy. May this be the last of your worries, Lochiam. [*He raises the glass to his lips and is about to drink when he sees* HAVA; *lowers his glass and does not drink.*]

[*Everyone else drinks and as soon as they do they immediately start singing and dancing like mad. Everyone is in love with everyone else.* SAM *is trying to dance with* DAVID – MR *and* MRS STONE *are cuddling and kissing.*]

SAM [*thinking that* DAVID *has had a drink*]: Eh, Davey, what do you think of my love potion? Cabella, Smaballah, hahahhhah.

[*Everyone is dancing around in a ring and* WHITE *hands* DAVID *the parcel of money.*]

DAVID: What's this? Money? I don't want money, I want revenge. Here, take your money – confetti for the wedding.

[*He showers it over the stage and the others dance through it. The* THREE MEN *throw coloured streamers.* DAVID *looks at* HAVA, *who has been standing outside all this.*]

Oh? What's this? Oh, love, love, what a beautiful girl. I never

realized how beautiful she is. Why haven't I seen her before? Who
does she belong to?

SAM: She's yours.

[HAVA *goes into the garden.* DAVID *is very happy and now dances
with* SAM.]

DAVID: Mine? What do you mean? Sam, oh my darling dear dead
Sam. Life is a great time. [*sings*]:

> Life is the gayest time, life is the grandest time,
> Life is the greatest time to be together,
> So sing for all your worth, and learn to love your life,
> And dance upon the earth, and be my lover.
> Life is a dream of sight, life is a blessing bright,
> Life is the time of light, that's not for ever,
> It happens only once, so while we have a chance,
> Come on, let's sing and dance and be my lover.

[BESSIE *is collecting the money together. She hands it to* DAVID.]

DAVID: But I owe it to you – almost the whole of it.

BESSIE: I know, but take it with you – I don't need it.

DAVID: Thank you very much.

[*He looks at her for a while, then she returns to* SEGAL. DAVID *leads*
SAM *to the garden where* HAVA *is sitting nearby.*]

DAVID [*to* SAM]: Is she really mine?

SAM: Exchange is no robbery.

DAVID: But who is she?

SAM: Solly Segal's daughter.

DAVID: I know, but apart from that? [*Calls into house.*] Hold everything! I've changed my mind about a lot of things. Do nothing
until you hear from me.

SAM [*seeing the way* DAVID *is looking at* HAVA]: Well, Davey, did my
potion work or didn't it?

DAVID: I didn't drink any of that stuff [*goes right into the garden and
approaches* HAVA].

SAM [*to the audience*]: So, exchange is no robbery. A Levy becomes a
Segal and a Segal becomes a Levy.

[SAM *now hovers at the back of the garden. All noise and movement in the house stops. The garden scene becomes idyllic.*]

DAVID: There's so much that I want to tell you.

HAVA: There'll be a lot of time.

DAVID: All our lives. [*He kisses her.*] Isn't life wonderful? This is the happiest day of my life. What's your name?

HAVA: Hava.

DAVID: I daren't say it.

HAVA: Why not?

DAVID: If I say it I marry you.

HAVA: Well, say it then – you're the only boy for me. You always were and always will be.

DAVID: Hava! Hava! [*They kiss.*] I love you – why are you so different from any other girl?

HAVA: Why have you been so nasty . . .? If you knew how long I waited just for a kind word.

DAVID: Sorry, Sweetheart, I've been too busy with myself – a very busy time I've had, but now I'm waking up.

HAVA: We used to play with each other when we were kids – then I went to Israel to get away from you but when I found you weren't there I came back again.

DAVID: I've been so mad – so crazy – how could I have missed someone so lovely as you – you're lovelier than my voice even.

HAVA: I wouldn't go as far as to say that.

DAVID: Why not – it's true – incredibly true.

HAVA: Oh, we'll get married and have lots of children – beautiful children with lovely voices – life will be wonderful . . .

DAVID: Life will be wonderful and life is wonderful – here we are on this little atlas – the world is a topical island in space – a bit of dust in time – and I own it and I give it to you – it doesn't matter where we are as long as we're happy.

HAVA: Oh, Davey – Davey – come down to earth a moment. How will we live? Your voice might enchant the gods, but we can't live on those kind of notes.

DAVID: But everything is all right – I've had a brainwave – I'll sell herrings and croon at the same time. Later I'll open a shop to be on the safe side – then I'll open another shop on the other side. What a gimmick! I'll be a sensation. I'll be the first singing herring salesman in history – I'll be terrific – I am terrific – A great success – the happiest crooner with the heart of gold.

[*sings*]: A singer I must be, for all the world to see,

There's no one else like me, the whole world over.

I want to be a king – a great fantastic thing,

The boy with everything,

I love you, Hava.

[HAVA *smiles and hugs* DAVID *for joy.*]

DAVID [*to* SAM]: Well, Dad, what did you think of that? Don't you think it's a marvellous idea? Me in the market: you can visit me there. Why didn't I think of it sooner?

[SAM *looks at the audience and shrugs.*]

SAM: Bravo, Davey boy, I'm pleased you're coming to your senses.

HAVA: Oh, dear, are you still talking to yourself?

DAVID: Oh, I'm not talking to myself; I'm talking to my father. I hope you don't mind?

HAVA: Will you be speaking to him for long? This father of yours?

DAVID: No, not for long.

HAVA: Oh, Davey, I'm so happy, all my dreams are coming true.

SAM: What a lucky boy you are, Davey. I envy you.

HAVA [*to* DAVID]: I will not share you with anyone else.

DAVID: May I just have a few last words with him?

HAVA: Of course. I loved your father almost as much as my own.

SAM: Well, Davey, it's all over. Hamlet is dead and may flights of angels sing him down the stairs. He died two hours ago, when Mrs Levy became Mrs Segal; and I can go back whence I came.

DAVID: Are you revenged?

SAM: Certainly. You are the only Levy left in the world, but you are facing the right way. Segal is all right, moody and stingy; they will make an ideal couple. How subtle revenge can be! One last word of advice. I think you will be very happy, but try and remember me, commit arson every day in your imagination, burn

down the previous day's lies, have a little revolution now and
again in your heart; try and help lonely people. People are lonely
all over the world; lonely and lovely because they are animals with
souls and memories.

HAVA: Come on, Davey, let's get away from here.

DAVID: Are you saying good-bye to your father?

HAVA: No, not now.

[*She cries softly, but everything else is silent.*]

DAVID: Good-bye, father of mine. This, then, is your exorcism.
Good-bye – I'll take the memory of you everywhere that I go.

[*He tries to embrace* SAM, *but* HAVA *is tugging at him.*]

SAM: That's what you think!

DAVID: Good-bye, Dad, go in peace. So long.

[DAVID *leans upon the fence, head in his hands.* HAVA *comforts him.*
SAM *dances towards the house, he is very gay.*

SAM: Good-bye, my boy; take care of your lovely girl. I'm going
from Stepney Green and so are you. Your mother will move out
from here and others will move in; they will cover the walls and
floorboards and ceilings and then call it security. There will be
nothing left of the places I knew. I will soar away from Whitechapel, and follow all my dear dead friends. Look out for me now
and again, even if I am not there. Whitechapel is curling up and going
to sleep, and the Thames looks like a little trail of water running
along the stones. All the names and faces I know are fading.

[*He is in the house and he dances among the people. As he does so they
become animated again and dance round.* SAM *withdraws to the street
door and he stands there.* BLACK *rushes to the garden.*]

Hava, David, Solly, Bessie. I'm so glad that there is going to be a
happy ending. [*He stands in the open doorway.*]

[BLACK *touches* DAVID *on the shoulder.*]

DAVID: Didn't you see him? Didn't you hear him?

HAVA: Yes, I almost saw him. I think I heard him.

BLACK [*gives card to him*]: David Levy, I think you have an excep-
tional voice. With your gimmick, you'll go a long way. Come to
my office Monday. I have a proposition for you.

DAVID: But you're not an agent?

BLACK: No, but I'm going to be. I'll start with you. We'll work out something. I'm a student of life. If we put our heads together, plus a little money, the world will hear you.

[BLACK *returns into the house.*]

HAVA: Wonderful, marvellous; come, let's go. Where shall we go to?

DAVID: Let's go to a dance.

HAVA: Life is going to be one long dance; you've got two hundred pounds, let's go and find a place to live.

DAVID: Why do you love me?

HAVA: Because I have no choice. Why do you love me?

DAVID: Because I love you.

[*They kiss, laugh heartily and exit ecstatically, laughing and kissing.*]

SAM: They are not really themselves. I'm going now, my children, to regions unknown – enjoy yourselves. Make the most of your youth – because youth is a wreath of roses – make the most of your life – because life is a holiday from the dark – make the most of the world – because it is *YOUR WORLD* – because the world is a wedding – so– Let the wedding continue –

[*He shrugs and smiles and as the room animates again and the people dance, he holds out his arms to the audience and then turns and quickly goes.*]

[*The* CHILDREN *are heard singing.*]

CHILDREN [*off*]: Now you're married I wish you joy,
    First a girl, then a boy,
    Kiss her once, kiss her twice,
    Kiss her three times over . . .

[*There is a great gust of laughter as the curtain falls.*]

THE END OF THE PLAY

[*After curtain falls the cast line up and sing.*]

DAVID: I am the boy who wanted to be king – see me on the tele – please God by me – please God by you.

HAVA: I am the girl who owns the boy – who wanted to be king –
does anyone know of a flat in Golders Green – please God by me –
please God by you.

SAM: I am the ghost who was haunted by my life, wasn't lucky
enough to love someone like this girl – who owns my only son –
who wanted to be king – I'll be seeing you all – please God by me –
please God by you.

BESSIE: I am the wife who drove her husband mad so he became the
ghost who wants to pinch the girl who owns my little boy who
wanted to be king – God bless him – it's enough to give you heart-
burn – still – please God by me – please God by you.

SEGAL: I am the friend who jumped into the bed to comfort poor
Bessie who drove Sam to his grave – so he became a ghost with
designs on my daughter – why the dirty dog – I'm glad she's out of
danger – and now she owns the boy who wanted to be king – my
mad step-son – still I wish them joy – Comrades, down with
religion – please God by me – please God by you.

MR STONE: I am the cabbie – believe me, business ain't so good – I
drove the Prime Minister the other day – he didn't give me a tip –
please God by me – please God by you.

MRS STONE: I am his wife – enough has been said – by my life – by
your life – the children of today – please God by your daughter –
please God by your son – please God by God – please God by me –
please God by you.

THREE: We are the salesmen, the backbone of the nation – may we
press our stones upon you in our never-never fashion – Hip, Hip,
Hooray, we haven't got a clue – please God – for he's a jolly good
fellow – please God by you.

ARNOLD WESKER

Chicken Soup with Barley

AUTHOR'S NOTE

CHICKEN SOUP WITH BARLEY was not written
as an anti-Soviet play and the author insists that no
theatrical, film, television, or broadcasting company
should present it as such. He would further remind
all concerned that an indictment against the In-
quisition is no more an attack on Christianity than
the indictment based on recent Soviet admissions is
an attack upon socialism. Let no mud be thrown;
few people's hands are clean. Just let us think again.

CHICKEN SOUP WITH BARLEY

First presented at the Belgrade Theatre, Coventry, on 7 July 1958, and subsequently at the Royal Court Theatre, London, on 14 July 1958, with the following cast:

SARAH KAHN	Charmian Eyre
HARRY KAHN	Frank Finlay
MONTY BLATT	Alfred Lynch
DAVE SIMMONDS	Richard Martin
PRINCE SILVER	Patrick Carter
HYMIE KOSSOP	Henry Manning
CISSIE	Cherry Morris
ADA KAHN	Jacqueline Wilson
RONNIE KAHN	Anthony Valentine
BESSIE BLATT	Patsy Byrne

Directed by John Dexter

THE SOLO GAME

	Clubs	*Hearts*	*Diamonds*	*Spades*
CISSIE:	K,4,3,2	3	K,2	A,K,J,6,4,2
SARAH:	A,Q,6	10,5,4	A,6,5,4	9,8,3
PRINCE:	J,10,8	K,7,J	J,10,9,8,7	Q,5
HYMIE:	9,7,5	A,Q,9,8,6,2	Q,3	10,7

1st Hand: CISSIE: 3 Hearts – 10 – K – A
             HYMIE: 3 Diamonds – 2 – 4 – J
             PRINCE: Q Spades – 10 – J – 9
             PRINCE: 5 Spades – 7 – 6 – 8
             SARAH: 5 Hearts – 7 – 6 – K Diamonds
             PRINCE: 7 Diamonds – Q – K Clubs – A
             SARAH: 3 Spades – J Clubs – 9 Clubs – 2 Spades

[CISSIE *shows Hand*]

ACT ONE

The date is 4 October 1936.

SCENE I

*The place is the basement of the Kahns'
house in an East End street.*

*The room is warm and lived in. A fire is burning. One door, at the back
and left of the room, leads to a bedroom. A window, left, looks up to the
street. To the right is another door which leads to a kitchen which is seen.
At rear of stage are the stairs leading up into the street.*

SARAH KAHN *is in the kitchen washing up, humming to herself. She is a
small, fiery woman, aged 37, Jewish and of European origin. Her movements indicate great energy and vitality. She is a very warm person.*

HARRY KAHN, *her husband, comes down the stairs, walks past her and into
the front room. He is 35 and also a European Jew. He is dark, slight,
rather pleasant looking and the antithesis of Sarah. He is amiable but weak.
From outside we hear a band playing a revolutionary song.*

SARAH [*from the kitchen*]: You took the children to Lottie's?

HARRY [*taking up book to read*]: I took them.

SARAH: They didn't mind?

HARRY: No, they didn't mind.

SARAH: Is Hymie coming?

HARRY: I don't know.

SARAH [*to herself*] Nothing he knows! You didn't ask him? He
didn't say? He knows about the demonstration, doesn't he?

HARRY: I don't know whether he knows or he doesn't know. I didn't
discuss it with him – I took the kids, that's all. Hey, Sarah – you
should read Upton Sinclair's book about the meat-canning industry
– it's an eye-opener . . .

SARAH: Books! Nothing else interests him, only books. Did you see
anything outside? What's happening?

175

HARRY: The streets are packed with people, I never seen so many people. They've got barricades at Gardner's Corner.

SARAH: There'll be such trouble.

HARRY: Sure there'll be trouble. You ever known a demonstration where there wasn't trouble?

SARAH: And the police?

HARRY: There'll be more police than blackshirts.

SARAH: What time they marching?

HARRY: I don't know.

SARAH: Harry, you know where your cigarettes are, don't you?
[*This is her well-meaning but maddening attempt to point out to a weak man his weakness.*]

HARRY: I know where they are.

SARAH: And you know what's on at the cinema?

HARRY: So?

SARAH: And also you know what time it opens? [*He grins.*] So why don't you know what time they plan to march? [*Touché.*]

HARRY: Leave me alone, Sarah, will you? Two o'clock they plan to march – nah!

SARAH: So you do know. Why didn't you tell me straight away? Shouldn't you tell me something when I ask you?

HARRY: I didn't know what time they marched, so what do you want of me?

SARAH: But you did know when I nagged you.

HARRY: So I suddenly remembered. Is there anything terrible in that?
[*She shakes a disbelieving fist at him and goes out to see where the loud-speaker cries are coming from. The slogan* MADRID TODAY – LONDON TOMORROW *is being repeated. As she is out* HARRY *looks for her handbag, and on finding it proceeds to take some money from it.*]

SARAH [*she is hot*]: Air! I must have air – this basement will kill me. God knows what I'll do without air when I'm dead. Who else was at Lottie's?

HARRY [*still preoccupied*]: All of them.

SARAH: Who's all of them?

HARRY: All of them! You know. Lottie and Hymie and the boys, Solly and Martin.

[*He finds a ten-shilling note, pockets it and resumes his seat by the fire, taking up a book to read.* SARAH *returns to front room with some cups and saucers.*]

SARAH: Here, lay these out, the boys will be coming soon.

HARRY: Good woman! I could just do with a cup of tea.

SARAH: What's the matter, you didn't have any tea by Lottie's?

HARRY: No.

SARAH: Liar!

HARRY: I didn't have any tea by Lottie's, I tell you. [*injured tone*] Good God, woman, why don't you believe me when I tell you things?

SARAH: *You* tell *me* why. Why don't I believe him when he tells me things! As if he's such an angel and never tells lies. What's the matter, you never told lies before I don't think?

HARRY: All right, so I had tea at Lottie's. There, you satisfied now?

SARAH [*preparing things as she talks*]: Well, of course you had tea at Lottie's. Don't I know you had tea at Lottie's? You think I'm going to think that Lottie wouldn't make you a cup of tea?

HARRY: Oh, leave off, Sarah.

SARAH: No! This time I won't leave off. [*her logic again*] I want to know why you told me you didn't have tea at Lottie's when you know perfectly well you did. I want to know.

[HARRY *raises his hands in despair.*]

I know you had tea there and you know you had tea there – so what harm is it if you tell me? You think I care whether you had a cup of tea there or not? You can drink tea there till it comes out of your eyes and I wouldn't care only as long as you tell me.

HARRY: Sarah, will you please stop nagging me, will you? What difference if I had tea there or I didn't have tea there?

SARAH: That's just what I'm saying. All I want to know is whether you're all of a liar or half a liar!

HARRY [*together with her*]: . . . all of a liar or half a liar!

[*A young man,* MONTY BLATT, *comes down the stairs. He is about 19, Jewish, working-class, and Cockney. His voice is heard before he is seen, shouting:* Mrs Kahn! Sarah! Mrs Kahn! *He has interrupted the row as he dashes into the room without knocking.*]

MONTY: Ah, good! You're here! [*moves to window and, looking out, shouts up*] It's O.K. They're here. Here! [*Offering parcel.*] Mother sent you over some of her strudel. C'mon down. [*to* HARRY] Hello, Harry boy, how you going? All fighting fit for the demo?

HARRY: I'm fit, like a Trojan I'm fit!

SARAH: You won't see him at any demo. In the pictures you'll find him. [*Goes to landing to make tea.*]

MONTY: The pictures? Don't be bloody mad. You won't hear a thing! You seen the streets today? Sarah, you seen the streets yet? Mobbed! Mo-obbed! The lads have been there since seven this morning.

[*Two other young men in their early twenties come down the stairs* DAVE SIMMONDS *and* PRINCE SILVER. *They are heatedly discussing something.*]

PRINCE: But Dave, there's so much work here to do. Hello, Sarah.

DAVE: I know all about the work here, but there are plenty of party members to do it. Hello, Sarah. Spain is the battle-front. Spain is a real issue at last.

SARAH: Spain? Spain, Dave?

HARRY: Spain?

PRINCE: Dave is joining the International Brigade. He's leaving for Spain tomorrow morning. [*to* DAVE] But Spain is only one issue brought to a head. You're too young to . . .

HARRY: Dave, don't go mad all of a sudden. It's not all glory, you know.

DAVE: Harry, you look as though you didn't sleep last night.

MONTY: He didn't – the old cossack. [*to the tune of* All the nice girls love a sailor] For you know what cossacks are . . . Am I right, Harry?

PRINCE: I saw your sister Cissie at Aldgate, Harry. She was waving your mother's walking-stick in the air.

HARRY: She's mad.

MONTY [*loudly calling*]: Where's this cup of tea, Sarah?

SARAH [*bringing in tea*]: Do your fly-buttons up, Monty, you tramp you. Now then, Dave, tell me what's happening and what the plans are.

[*Everyone draws up a chair by the table.*]

DAVE: It's like this. The Party loudspeaker vans have been out all morning – you heard them? The Fascists are gathering at Royal Mint Street near the bridge. They plan to march up to Aldgate, down Commercial Road to Salmon Lane in Limehouse – you know Salmon Lane? – where they think they're going to hold a meeting. Then they plan to go on to Victoria Park and hold another meeting.

SARAH: *Two* meetings? What do they want to hold two meetings for?

HARRY: Why shouldn't they hold two meetings?

SARAH: What, *you* think they should hold two meetings?

HARRY: It's not what I think – she's such a funny woman – it's not what I think, but they want to hold two meetings – so what's so strange about that?

SARAH: But it costs so much money.

HARRY: Perhaps you want we should have a collection for them?

DAVE: Now. They could go along the Highway by the docks and then up Cable Street, but Mosley won't take the Highway because that's the back way, though the police will suggest he does.

SARAH: I bet the police cause trouble.

PRINCE: They've had to call in forces from outside London.

SARAH: You won't make it a real fight, boys, will you? I mean you won't get hurt.

MONTY: Sarah, you remember they threw a seven-year-old girl through a glass window? So don't fight the bastards?

PRINCE: Now Monty, there's to be discipline, remember. There's to be no attack or bottle-throwing. It's a test, you know that, don't you, it's a test for us. We're to stop them passing, that's all.

MONTY: Sure we'll stop them passing. If I see a blackshirt come by I'll tap his shoulder and I'll say: 'Excuse me, but you can't come this way today, we're digging up the road.' And he'll look at my hammer and sickle and he'll doff his cap and he'll say: 'I beg your pardon, comrade, I'll take the underground.'

DAVE: Comrades! You want to know what the plans are or you don't want to know? Again. As we don't know what's going to happen we've done this: some of the workers are rallying at Royal Mint Street – so if the Fascists want to go through the Highway they'll have to fight for it. But we guess they'll want to stick to the main route so as not to lose face – you follow? We've therefore called the main rally at Gardner's Corner. If, on the other hand, they do attempt to pass up Cable Street –

SARAH: Everything happens in Cable Street.

HARRY: What else happened in Cable Street?

SARAH: Peter the painter had a fight with Churchill there, didn't he?

MONTY: You're thinking of Sidney Street, sweetheart.

HARRY: You know, she gets everything mixed up.

SARAH: You're very wonderful I suppose, yes? You're the clever one!

HARRY: I don't get my facts mixed up, anyway.

SARAH: Per, per, per, per, per! Listen to him! My politician!

MONTY: Sarah, do me a favour, perhaps you should leave the fists till later?

DAVE: If, on the other hand, they do try to come up Cable Street then they'll meet some dockers and more barricades. And if any get through that lot then they still can't hold their meetings either in Salmon Lane or Victoria Park Square.

SARAH: Why not?

PRINCE: Because since seven this morning there's been some of our comrades standing there with our platforms.

MONTY: Bloody wonderful, isn't it? Makes you feel proud, eh Sarah? Every section of this working-class area that we've approached has responded. The dockers at Limehouse have come out to the man. The lot!

PRINCE: The unions, the co-ops, Labour Party members and the Jewish People's Council –

SARAH: The board of deputies?

HARRY: There she goes again. Not the Jewish Board of Deputies – *they* asked the Jewish population to keep away. No, the Jewish People's Council – the one that organized that mass demo against Hitler some years back.

[SARAH *pulls face at him.*]

MONTY: There's been nothing like it since the General Strike.

HARRY: Christ! The General Strike! That was a time, Sarah, eh?

SARAH: What you asking me for? You want I should remember that you were missing for six days when Ada was ill?

HARRY: Yes, I was missing, I'm sure.

SARAH: Well, sure you were missing.

HARRY: Where was I missing?

SARAH: How should I know where you were missing. If I'd have known where you were missing you wouldn't have been missing.
[*There is heard from outside a sound of running feet and voices shouting. Everyone except* HARRY *moves to the window.*]

FIRST VOICE: They're assembling! They're assembling! Out to the barricades – the Fascists are assembling!

SECOND VOICE: Hey, Stan! Where's the best place?

FIRST VOICE: Take your boys to Cable Street. The Fascists are assembling! Come out of your houses! Come out of your houses!

MONTY: What about us, Dave?

SARAH: You haven't suggested to Harry and me where to go yet.

DAVE: There's plenty of time. They won't try to march till two, and it's only twelve-thirty.

SARAH: You eaten? You boys had lunch?

PRINCE: We all had lunch at my place, Sarah; sit down, stop moving a few seconds.

DAVE: Take your pick, Sarah. If you fancy yourself as a nurse then go to Aldgate, we've got a first-aid post there, near Whitechapel Library.

SARAH: Such organization! And you lot?

DAVE: Monty is taking some of the lads to the left flank of Cable Street, Prince is organizing a team of cyclist messengers between the main points and headquarters, I'm going round the streets at the last minute to call everyone out and – and that's the lot.

MONTY [*rubbing his hands*]: All we have to do is wait.

DAVE: Where is Ada?

SARAH: Ada and Ronnie are at Hymie's place. I thought it best they get right out of the way.

DAVE [*guiltily*]: You think she'll stay away? Your precocious daughter is a born fighter, Sarah.

MONTY: 'Corse she is! She'll be round the streets organizing the pioneers – you see.

SARAH: Never! I told her to stay there and she'll stay there.

HARRY: I'm sure!

SARAH: God forbid she should be like you and run wild.

HARRY: All right, so she should be like you then!

SARAH: I'm jolly sure she should be like me! Ronnie isn't enough for him yet. A boy of five running about at nights and swearing at his aunts. [*Smiles at thought.*] Bless him! [*to the others*] He didn't half upset them: they wouldn't let him mess around with the radio so he started effing and blinding and threw their books on the floor. [*turning again to* HARRY] Like you he throws things.

HARRY: Have you ever come across a woman like her before?

MONTY: I'd love another cup of tea.

HARRY [*jumps up and goes to kitchen*]: I'll make it, I'll make it.

SARAH: He's so sweet when anybody else is around. I'll make some sandwiches.

PRINCE: But we've eaten, Sarah.

SARAH: Eat. Always eat. You don't know what time you'll be back. [SARAH *goes to cupboard and cuts up bread ready for cheese sandwiches. A very distant sound of people chanting is heard:* They shall not pass, they shall not pass, they shall not pass.']

MONTY: The boys! Listen. Hear them? You know, Sarah, that's the same cry the people of Madrid were shouting.

PRINCE: And they didn't get past either. Imagine it! All those women and children coming out into the streets and making barricades with their beds and their chairs.

DAVE [*sadly*]: It was a slaughter.

PRINCE: And then came the first International Brigade.

DAVE: The Edgar André from Germany, Commune de Paris from France, and the Dombrovsky from Poland.

MONTY: Wait till our Dave gets over there. You'll give 'em brass balls for breakfast, Dave, eh?

SARAH: You really going, Dave? Does Ada know?

DAVE: Don't tell her, Sarah. You know how dramatic calf-love is.

PRINCE: Calf-love? If you get back alive from Spain she'll marry you at the landing stage – mark me.

SARAH: How are you going?

DAVE: They tell me it's a week-end trip to Paris and then a midnight ramble over the Pyrenees. The back way!

SARAH: It's terrible out there, they say. They say we've lost a lot of good comrades already.

PRINCE: We've lost too many good comrades out there – you hear me, Dave?

MONTY: Sammy Avner and Lorimer Birch at Boadilla, Felicia Brown and Ernst Julius at Aragon.

SARAH: Julius? The tailor who used to work with us at Cantor's? But he was only a young boy.

PRINCE: And Felicia an artist and Lorimer an Oxford undergraduate.

MONTY: And Cornford was killed at Cordova.

PRINCE: And Ronnie Symes at Madrid.

MONTY: And Stevie Yates at Casa del Campo.

SARAH: Casa del Campo! Madrid! Such beautiful names and all that killing.

MONTY: Hey! You know who organized the first British group? Nat Cohen! I used to go to school with him. Him and Sam Masters were on a cycling holiday in France. As soon as they heard of the revolt they cycled over to Barcelona and started the Tom Mann Centuria.

HARRY [*coming to the door*]: He's a real madman, Nat Cohen. He chalks slogans right outside the police station. I used to work with him.

SARAH: God knows if they'll come back alive.

DAVE: When three Fascist deserters were asked how they reached our lines they said they came through the hills of the widows, orphans and sweethearts; they'd lost so many men attacking those hills.

MONTY: And may they lose many more!

DAVE [*angrily*]: The war in Spain is not a game of cards, Monty. You don't pay in pennies when you lose. May they lose many more! What kind of talk is that? Sometimes, Monty, I think you only enjoy the battle, and that one day you'll forget the ideal. You hate too much. You can't have brotherhood when you hate. There's only one difference between them and us – we know what we're fighting for. It's almost an unfair battle.

[HARRY *now returns to kitchen to pour out tea.*]

MONTY: Unfair, he says! When Germany and Italy are supplying them with guns and tanks and aeroplanes and our boys have only got rifles and mortars – is that unfair? You call that unfair, I don't think?

DAVE: When you fight men who are blind it's always unfair. You think I'm going to enjoy shooting a man because he calls himself a Fascist? I feel so sick at the thought of firing a rifle that I think I'll board that boat with a blindfold over my eyes. Sometimes I think that's the only way to do things. I'm not even sure that I want to go, only I know if I don't then – then – well, what sense can a man make of his life?

SARAH: You're really a pacifist, aren't you, Dave?

DAVE: I'm a terribly sad pacifist, Sarah.

HARRY: I understand you, Dave – I know what you mean, boy. What do you want we should say? You go – we're proud of you. You stay behind – we love you. Sometimes you live in a way you don't know why – you just do a thing. So you don't have to shout – you're shouting at yourself! But a pacifist, Dave? There's going to be a big war soon, a Fascist war: you think it's time for pacifism?

SARAH: He's right, Dave.

DAVE: I know it's not time yet. I know that. I know there is still some fighting to be done. But it'll come. It will come, you know – when there'll be a sort of long pause, and people will just be frightened of each other and still think they *have* to fight. That'll be the time to be a pacifist. When people can't see beyond fear. But now – well, I feel like an old gardener who knows he won't live through to the spring to plant his seeds.

[HARRY *comes in with the teas and at the same time a voice from the streets is heard frantically shouting:* Man your posts! Men and women of the East End, come out of your houses! The black-shirts are marching! Come out! Come out! *There is a hurried movement from the people in the room.* DAVE *and* MONTY *rush to the window.* PRINCE *rushes upstairs and knocks a cup of tea out of* HARRY'S *hand.*]

MONTY: Christ! They've started before time.

DAVE: It might be a false alarm.

PRINCE [*from the stairs*]: We can't take the risk. Let's get going.

[MONTY *moves off quickly, taking a poker from the fireplace on his way out and concealing it in his clothes.*]

MONTY: I'll clean it and bring it back later.

HARRY: But I've made your tea.

DAVE: Stick it back in the pot. We'll drink it later. Now you two, you know where the posts are – Cable Street, Royal Mint Street and Gardner's Corner.

HARRY [*at the window*]: The street is mobbed. Jesus! Look at them, everybody is coming out, everybody.

SARAH [*putting on her coat in general rush*]: Where's the first-aid post?

DAVE [*having helped* SARAH *with coat, moves off*]: Whitechapel Library. Harry, you coming?

HARRY [*still at window*]: I'm coming, I'm coming. You go on. Good God, there's Alf Bosky and his wife. She's got the baby with her. [*shouts down*] Hey Alf – good luck, comrade – we're coming. Sarah, there's Alf Bosky and his wife.

SARAH [*looking for something in kitchen*]: I heard, I heard! [*She finds a rolling pin and, waving it in the air, dashes into the front room.*] Are you coming now, Harry? I'm going to Gardner's Corner – come on, we'll be late.

HARRY [*backing away from rolling pin*]: Don't hit anybody with that thing, Sarah, it hurts.

SARAH: Fool!

[SARAH *dashes to the stairs but stops and, remembering something, returns to front room. From a corner of the room she finds a red*

flag with a hammer and sickle on it and thrusts it in HARRY'S
hand.]

SARAH: Here, wave this! Do something useful!

[EXITS *upstairs*]

HARRY [*grabbing his coat*]: Hey, Sarah, wait for me – Sarah! Hey, wait
for me!

[*He follows her, banner streaming. The voices outside grow to a
crescendo:* They shall not pass, they shall not pass, THEY SHALL
NOT PASS!]

CURTAIN

SCENE 2

Same room, later that evening

There is commotion and some singing from the streets outside. MONTY *and* PRINCE *are coming down the stairs leading* HYMIE KOSSOP. *He has blood all over his face. He is a short, rotund man with a homely appearance.*

MONTY [*leaving* PRINCE *and* HYMIE *to go into the room*]: I'll get some water on the stove. Sit him in a chair. [*shouts upstairs*] Cissie! Don't come down yet, go and get some first-aid kit from somewhere. [*Fills kettle.*]

PRINCE: Now don't talk too much and don't move, Hymie. Jesus! What a state you're in. Sarah'll go mad.

HYMIE: Well, clean me up quickly then.

MONTY [*rushing from kitchen to window*]: Cissie! CISSIE! Try that sweet shop near Toynbee Hall. I saw a first-aid group there. They might still be there. [*comes away but remembering something else sticks his head out again*] ASPROS! Try and get hold of some aspros.

SARAH [*from the top of the stairs – off*]: Monty! Is Hymie down there?

HYMIE: Oh, my goodness, she's here. If there is one thing Sarah loves it's someone who's ill to fuss over. Why didn't I go home?

MONTY: Because you know Lottie would say serves you right!

[SARAH *appears;* MONTY *rushes to her.*]

Now don't panic, Sarah, he's all right, he's all right.

SARAH [*entering*]: Hymie!

HYMIE: Sarah Nightingale!

MONTY: Now don't frighten him, I tell you.

SARAH [*taking over towel and wiping him*]: Fool you! They told me you were hurt – I nearly died.

HYMIE: So did I!

SARAH: Fool! *You* had to go straight into it.

HYMIE: I was only hit by a truncheon. Now do me a favour, Sarah, and just make some tea, there's a good girl.

SARAH: Nobody else got hurt. Only him. The brave one!

MONTY [*significantly handling the poker*]: Plenty got hurt! Oh, he's all right. Aren't you all right, Hymie?

HYMIE: I'm here, aren't I?

SARAH [*taking off her coat*]: Well, why hasn't anybody done something?

PRINCE: Cissie has gone to get some first aid.

SARAH: Cissie? Harry's sister?

PRINCE: Yes. Where is Harry, by the way? Anybody seen him?

SARAH [*ominously*]: Wait till I see him. I'll give him. You expected him to stay there?

MONTY: I saw him at Cable Street; he was waving the old red flag, but he didn't stay long. He took one look at the artillery and guns and said he was going to find us some sandwiches.

SARAH: They had guns at Cable Street? Did they use them?

MONTY: Nah! It was only brought out to frighten us. *Frighten* us, mark. If they'd have dropped a bomb today we wouldn't have been frightened. Christ! What a day!

HYMIE: I mean, did you ever see anything like it? We threw stones and bottles at them, Sarah. They were on horseback with batons and they kept charging us, so we threw stones. And you should have seen Monty when one policeman surrendered. Surrendered! A policeman! It's never happened before. He didn't know what to do, Monty didn't. None of us knew. I mean, who's ever heard of policemen surrendering? And after the first came others – half a dozen of them. My goodness, we made such a fuss of them. Gave them cigarettes and mugs of tea and called them comrade policemen.

PRINCE: There's no turning back now – nothing can stop the workers now.

MONTY: I bet we have a revolution soon. Hitler won't stop at Spain, you know. You watch him go and you watch the British Government lick his arse until he spits in their eye. Then *we'll* move in.

HYMIE: I'm not so sure, Monty. We won today but the same taste doesn't stay long. Mosley was turned back at Aldgate pump and everyone shouted hurrah. But I wonder how many of the people at Gardner's Corner were just sightseers. You know, in every political movement there are just sightseers.

MONTY: Ten thousand bloody sightseers? Do me a favour, it wasn't a bank holiday.

[SARAH *goes to kitchen to pour the water into the bowl.* CISSIE *appears.*]

HYMIE: Any big excitement can be a bank holiday for a worker, believe me.

[*Enter* CISSIE. *Woman of about 33. She is a trade-union organizer – precise in her manner, dry sense of humour.*]

CISSIE: Ointment, lint, bandage and plaster. Let's have a look at him.

SARAH [*entering with bowl of water*]: I'm coming, it's all right, I'm here.

[CISSIE *makes way and* SARAH *begins to sponge her brother's face and then puts bandage round his head.*]

PRINCE: Where were *you*, Cis?

CISSIE: Gardner's Corner holding a banner. The union banner. And you?

MONTY: Digging up the paving stones in Cable Street.

CISSIE: Paving stones? [*She hoists the back of her skirt to warm her behind in front of the fire.*]

MONTY: We pulled out the railings from a nearby church and the stones from the gutter. I'll get some more coal for the fire. [*Goes to kitchen, pinching* CISSIE'S *behind on the way.*] We turned over a lorry.

SARAH: A lorry?

HYMIE: But it was the wrong one. The lorry we'd laid on was in a nearby yard and when the call went up to bring the lorry the boys, if you don't mind, grabbed one at the top of the street. I ask you!

SARAH: Keep still. There, you look more respectable now.

[MONTY *re-enters with coal and on his way to fire takes a feather from a hat nearby and plants it among* HYMIE'S *bandages.*]

HYMIE: Anyone get hurt your way, Cissie?

CISSIE: Some of the boys from my union got arrested.

SARAH: I'll go and make some tea now.

CISSIE: Mick and Sammy and Dave Goldman – and that bloody fool, if you'll excuse the expression, Sonny Becks. Everybody is standing behind the barricades waiting for the blackshirts to appear. The place is swarming with policemen waiting, just waiting, for an opportunity to lay their hands on some of us. So look what he does: not content with just standing there – and Sonny knew perfectly well that the orders were for the strictest discipline – not content with just standing he chose that moment to get up on Mrs O'Laoghaire's vegetable barrow and make a political speech. 'Let us now remember the lessons of the Russian revolution', he starts like he was quoting Genesis, the nitwit. And then he finds that the barrow isn't safe so he steps over to an iron bedstead and put his foot through the springs just as he was quoting Lenin's letter to the toiling masses!

MONTY: You can never stop Sonny making a speech.

CISSIE: But not in bed! Anyway, you know Sonny – a mouth like a cesspool and no shame – so he lets out a torrent of abuse at the capitalist bed-makers and the police just make a dive at him. Mick and Sammy tried to argue with the police so they were hauled off and then Dave Goldman tried to explain – that was when he was hauled off, poor bastard, if you'll excuse the expression!

HYMIE: What'll happen?

CISSIE: The union'll have to find the lawyers and probably pay their fine – what else? Which reminds me – Monty and Prince. Get all the boys and girls you can find and bring them to that social next Saturday, the one for Sally Oaks.

HYMIE: Wasn't it her husband caught his bicycle in a tram-line and was killed?

CISSIE: That's right. She's a Catholic. The local priest is trying to raise some money to keep her going for a bit and we promised we'd support it. Well, I'm going.

SARAH [*entering with tea*]: Cissie, have you seen Harry?

CISSIE: Harry? No!

SARAH: He's not at your place, I suppose?

CISSIE: How should I know? I haven't been there all day.

SARAH: He always is at your place.

CISSIE: Sarah, I'm not responsible for my brother's actions. None of us have ever been able to control him, the eldest brother! We warned you what you were taking on – you wanted to change him! She wanted to change him.

SARAH: It's your mother who spoils him, you know that?

CISSIE: Spoils him! Do me a favour – the woman's been bed-ridden for the last ten years. Spoils him!

SARAH: He knows he can go to her – she'll feed him.

CISSIE: He's her son, for God's sake.

SARAH: Don't I know it. He's her son all right – and he wants to be looked after like everyone looks after her. Only it's such a pity – he can walk!

CISSIE: Yes, yes – so I know all this already. Good night, everyone.

[CISSIE *exits amid varied good-byes and* I'll be seeing you.]

SARAH: I hate her!

HYMIE: Don't be a silly girl. Cissie is a good trade-union organizer.

SARAH: She's a cow! Not a bit of warmth, not a bit! What's the good of being a Socialist if you're not warm.

HYMIE: But Cissie has *never* liked Harry.

SARAH: Not a bit of warmth. Everything cold and calculated. People like that can't teach love and brotherhood.

PRINCE: Love comes later, Sarah.

SARAH: Love comes now. You have to start with love. How can you talk about socialism otherwise?

MONTY: Hear, hear, Comrade Kahn. Come on now, what is this? We've just won one of the biggest fights in working-class history and all we do is quarrel.

[MONTY *settles down and all is quiet. Suddenly, softly, he starts to sing.*]

   England arise, the long long night is over.

[*others join in*]

   Faint in the East behold the dawn appears.
   Out of your evil sleep of toil and sorrow,

England arise, the long long day is here.

England arise . . .

SARAH [*suddenly*]: Hymie! The children! God in heaven, I've forgotten the children.

HYMIE: They're at my place. What's the matter with you?

SARAH [*putting on her coat*]: But I can't leave them there. How could I forget them like that; what am I thinking of? Won't be long. [*Exits.*]

HYMIE [*calling up to her*]: But Ronnie'll be asleep. Don't tell Lottie I got hit. Tell her I'm coming home soon. [*returning to front room*] Impetuous woman!

[*They all settle themselves comfortably round the fire.* SARAH *is heard calling from the street.*]

SARAH [*off*]: Make yourself some food! And there's tea in the pot.

HYMIE [*coming away from window*]: Make yourself some food! With her it's food all the time. Food and tea. No sooner you finished one cup than you got another.

MONTY: She's a sweetheart.

HYMIE: God forbid you should ever say you're not hungry. She starts singing that song: As man is only human he must eat before he can think.

MONTY [*picking up the song and singing it*]:
As man is only human
He must eat before he can think,
Fine words are only empty air
But not his meat or his drink.

[*others join in chorus*]
Then left right left, then left right left,
There's a place, comrade, for you.
March with us in the ranks of the working class
For you are a worker too.

[HARRY *enters. As they finish the song he stands in the doorway and, waving the banner, cries*]

HARRY: We won! Boys, we won the day !

MONTY: Harry! Welcome home the hero! Where are those bloody sandwiches?

HYMIE: Your wife's looking for you.

HARRY: What, she's gone *out* for me? [*Places banner in corner and looks concerned.*]

MONTY: Yes! Just this minute.

HARRY: Did she have a rolling pin in her hand?

HYMIE: No, no. She's gone to my place to collect the children.

HARRY: Blimey, Hymie! What happened to you? You all right, Hymie?

HYMIE: Now don't you fuss, Harry; drink your tea.

MONTY: That's it, Harry, swill up, mate.

HARRY: Sure, sure. [*goes to kitchen*] The children, you say? But I saw Ada in the streets.

PRINCE [*looking to* MONTY]: She was helping me, Harry, but don't tell Sarah. She was taking messages from Cable Street to head-quarters. I knew she wouldn't stay in on such a day. Marched with us on the victory march, then went to look for Dave.

MONTY: She'll break her little heart when she hears he's going to Spain.

[ADA *comes tearing down the stairs at this point – she is the* KAHNS' *daughter, aged* 14.]

ADA: Mother! Mother! Hello everyone – Dad, where's Mother?

HARRY: Hello, Ada – you haven't seen her yet? You'll cop it. She's gone to look for Ronnie.

ADA [*going off again*]: Be back in quarter of an hour – excuse me.

HARRY: Where you going now?

ADA: Must check up on the last few posts, see that all the other pioneers are safe. [*She calls back through the window.*] It was a proud day, wasn't it, comrades? [*Exits.*]

HARRY: And *we* didn't force her to be in the pioneers. Wasn't necessary. I tell you, show a young person what socialism means and he can't do anything else but accept it. It's a life! A future! But it won't be pure in our lifetime, you know that, don't you, boys? Not even in hers, maybe – but in her children's lifetime – then they'll begin to feel it, all the benefits, despite our mistakes – you'll see, despite our mistakes. Now boys, tell me everything that happened.

PRINCE: Don't you know? Sir Philip Game, the police commissioner, got the wind up and banned the march. He told Mosley to fight it out with the Home Secretary. He wasn't going to have any trouble. And what happened to you?

HARRY (*proudly*): I was nearly arrested.

MONTY: You?

HARRY: I was running through the streets waving a red banner Sarah gave me and a policeman told me to drop it.

PRINCE: So?

HARRY: I dropped it! And then I turned into Flower and Dean Street and raised it again. He must have guessed what I was going to do. Christ! I never saw so many policemen appear so quickly. They seemed to pour out of all the windows when they heard that pennyfarthing whistle. I only just had time to hop into my mother's place.

MONTY: And you stayed there?

HARRY: I had a cup of tea and at about four o'clock I came out. I got to Gardner's Corner and police were charging the barricades. I didn't see no Fascists. Any get there?

PRINCE: They stayed in the back streets. The police did all the attacking. So?

HARRY: So I saw the police were picking our boys off like flies and then I saw my policeman – his hat was missing by this time. Oooh! There was a vicious look came into his eye when he saw me. I didn't stop to ask him where he'd lost it. I just ran back to my mother's and read a book.

HYMIE [*ominously*]: So you *were* at your mother's. [*to the others*] I think we'd better go before Sarah comes back. Harry, we're going.

HARRY: You're not staying for something to eat?

HYMIE: Lottie's waiting for me, Harry. Come on, you two.

HARRY: Hey, Hymie. You won't tell her I was at my mother's all the time, will you? No?

[*The boys assure him with pats and shakes of the head.* HARRY *pours himself out a cup of tea and, taking it into the front room, he settles down to a book by the fire. After some seconds* SARAH *comes down the stairs with* RONNIE, *a boy of about five. He is asleep in her arms. She takes him straight into the other bedroom.* HARRY *tries to appear very absorbed.* SARAH *comes out of the room, takes off her coat and hangs it up. She is eyeing* HARRY *most of the time with a gaze to kill while he does his best to avoid it. She clears a few things from the table, then goes out to get herself a cup of tea. As she watches* HARRY *she seats herself at the table and slowly stirs her drink. He shrinks under her gaze as her head begins to nod. It is an 'I-know-you-don't-I nod'.*]

SARAH: You think I'm a fool, don't you?

[HARRY *shifts uncomfortably, doesn't answer.* SARAH *watches him.*] Think I can't see, that I don't know what's going on. [*Pause.*] Look at him! The man of the house! Nothing matters to him! [*Pause.*] Well, Harry, why don't you look at me? Why don't you talk to me? I'm your wife, aren't I? A man is supposed to discuss things with his wife.

HARRY [*at last*]: What do you want me to say?

SARAH: Must I tell you what to say? Don't you know? Don't you *just* know! [*Pause.*] Artful! Oh, you're so artful!

HARRY: Yes, yes. I'm artful.

SARAH: Aren't you artful, then? You think because you sit there pretending to read that I won't say anything? That's what you'd like – that I should just come in and carry on and not say anything. You'd like that, wouldn't you? That you should carry on your life just the same as always and no one should say anything.

HARRY: Oh, leave me alone, Sarah.

SARAH: Oh, leave me alone, Sarah! I'll leave you alone all right. There'll be blue murder, Harry, you hear me? There'll be blue murder if it carries on like this. All our life is it going to be like this? I can't leave a handbag in the room. You remember what happened last time? You left me! Remember?

[HARRY *tries to turn away out of it all and* SARAH *shakes him back again.*]

Remember? And you wanted to come back? And you came back –
full of promises. What's happened to them now?

HARRY: Nothing's happened! Now stop nagging! Good God, you
don't let a man live in peace.

SARAH: You can still pretend? After you took ten shillings from my
bag and you know that I know you took it and you can still be
righteous? Say you don't know anything about it, go on. Say you
don't know what I'm talking about.

HARRY: No, I *don't* know what you're talking about.

SARAH [*finally unable to control herself, cursing him*]: Fire on your
head! May you live so sure if you don't know what I'm talking
about. The money fell out of my purse, I suppose. I dropped it in
the street. [*screaming at him*] Fire on your head!

HARRY [*rising and facing her in a rage*]: I'll throw this book at you – so
help me I'll throw this book at you.

[*At this point* ADA *rushes in.*]

ADA: Harry, stop it. [*she cries*] Oh, stop it!

HARRY [*shouting*]: Tell your mother to stop it, she's the cause, it's her
row. Don't you know your mother by now? [*He has moved away
to the door.*]

SARAH: I'm the cause? Me? You hear him, Ada, you hear him?
I'm the cause! [*throws a saucer at him*] Swine, you!

HARRY [*in speechless rage, throws his book to the ground*]: She's mad,
your mother, she's stark raving mad!

[HARRY *rushes out of the room up the stairs.* SARAH *follows him
to bottom of stairs and, picking up a basin in her hands, brandishes it.*
ADA *goes to look out of the window.*]

SARAH: That's it, run away. Go to your mother! She'll give you
peace! She'll do everything for you! Weakling, you! WEAK-
LING!

ADA [*crying*]: Everybody's outside, Mummy. Everybody is looking
down at us.

SARAH [*turning to comfort her*]: There, there, Boobola. There, there,
meine kindt. Shuh! Shuh! I'm sorry. [*bends over her and strokes her*]
Shuh! Shuh! It's finished, I'm sorry, it's over.

HARRY [*from the street*]: She's mad, she's gone mad, she has.

SARAH: Shuh! shuh! Ada, don't listen. It'll pass. Shuh – loolinka, shuh! [*cooing*] Ada, Ada, Ada.

[*As she comforts* ADA, RONNIE *comes out and stands watching them – listening and bewildered . . .*]

CURTAIN

ACT TWO

It is June 1946 – the war has come and gone.

SCENE I

The scene is now changed. The Kahns have moved to an L.C.C. block of flats in Hackney – the 1930 kind, with railings. The working class is a little more respectable now, they have not long since voted in a Labour Government.

The part of the flat we can see is: the front room from which lead off three rooms; the passage to the front door – and a door leading from the passage to the kitchen (off); and part of the balcony with its iron railings.

It is a late afternoon one Friday. HARRY *is lying down on the sofa.* SARAH *walks along the balcony, puts her hand through the letter box, withdraws the key and enters the front room – energetic as ever.*

SARAH: What! you here already? [*accepting the fact*] You haven't been working?

HARRY: The place closed down.

SARAH [*takes off coat and unpacks shopping bag*]: The place closed down! But you only started there on Monday.

HARRY: Well! So the place closed down! Is it my fault?

SARAH: It always happens where *he* works. You can't bring luck anywhere, can you! When it's a slump you always manage to be the first one sacked and when the season starts again you're the last one to find work. Ah, Harry, you couldn't even make money during the war. The war! When *everybody* made money.

HARRY [*laying pay packet on table*]: Nah!

SARAH [*reading it*]: What's this? Seven pounds thirteen? Why only seven pounds thirteen?

HARRY: Four days' work.

SARAH: You haven't worked *all* day today? So what you been doing?

198

HARRY: I felt tired.

SARAH: Sleep! That's all he can do. You didn't peel potatoes or anything? [*no answer*] Oh, what am I standing here talking to you for? Don't I know you by now?

HARRY: I got a headache.

SARAH [*going to kitchen and talking from there*]: Yes, yes – headache! Ronnie not home yet?

HARRY: He's distributing leaflets.

SARAH: What leaflets?

HARRY: I don't know what leaflets. What leaflets! Leaflets!

SARAH: Come and make some tea. Ada will be here soon.

HARRY: Leave me alone, Sarah.

SARAH [*ordering from the kitchen*]: Make some tea when I ask you!
[HARRY *rises and* ADA *is seen coming along the balcony. She enters through the front door in the same manner as Sarah. She is 25 years of age, well-spoken, a beautiful Jewess and weary of spirit.*]

HARRY [*kissing her*]: Hello, Ada.

SARAH: Ada? Ada? You here? Go inside, Daddy'll make some tea. Supper will soon be ready. [*Appears cheerfully from kitchen with all the signs of a cook about her. Kisses* ADA.] Got a nice supper.

ADA: What nice supper?

SARAH: Barley soup. I left it on a small light all day while I was at work [*returns to kitchen*].

ADA: Do you know if Ronnie has gone to my place to see if there is mail from Dave?

SARAH: Suppose so. He usually does when he knows you're coming here straight from work.
[RONNIE *appears on the balcony and lets himself in. Aged 15, enthusiastic, lively, well-spoken like his sister.*]
[*hearing the noise at the door*] Ronnie?

RONNIE: I'm here.

SARAH: He's here.

RONNIE [*to* ADA *as he enters*]: Two hundred and fifty leaflets in an hour and a half!

ADA: Very good. What for?

RONNIE: The May Day demo. Are you coming?

ADA: I doubt it.

RONNIE [*mocking her*]: I doubt it! Don't you find the march exciting any longer?

ADA: I do *not* find the march exciting any longer.

RONNIE: Can't understand it. You and Dave were such pioneers in the early days. I get all my ideas from you two – and now –

ADA: And now the letters, please.

RONNIE: Letters? Letters? What letters?

ADA: Oh, come on, Ronnie – Dave's letters.

RONNIE [*innocently*]: But I've been distributing leaflets!

ADA: You didn't go to my home to find . . .?

RONNIE: Miles away – other direction.

ADA [*sourly*]: Thank you.

[*While* ADA *sits down to read a newspaper* RONNIE *withdraws three letters from his pocket and reads some initials on the back.*]

RONNIE: I.L.T. Now what could that mean – I love thee?

ADA: Give me those letters, please.

RONNIE [*teasing*]: Oh, I love thee, sister.

ADA: You've been reading them.

RONNIE [*reading front of envelope*]: Letter number 218 – Christ! he's prolific. And here's number 215 – lousy service, isn't it? And number 219. This one says I.L.T.T., I love thee terribly, I suppose. And if I loved you I'd also love you terribly [*bends over and kisses her*].

ADA: Idiot! [*reads*].

RONNIE: Isn't it time that husband of yours was demobbed? The war's been over a year already. Imagine! I was only nine when he left. I've still kept all his letters, Ada, all of them [*ambles round the room to wall and tears off a little piece of wall-paper which he hurriedly crumples and stuffs into his pocket, making sure no one has seen him*]. We've been living here for five years – he hasn't even seen this place, God help him! [*shouting to kitchen*] Harry! Harry! Where's Harry?

[HARRY *comes in with some tea and* RONNIE *goes to take a cup.*]

Good old pops. Dad, I saw Monty Blatt. He says you must attend the meeting tonight.

HARRY: Ach! Do me a favour!

RONNIE: Listen to him! Party member! Won't attend branch meetings! How can you know what's going *on* in the world? That's where Ada gets her apathy from. She's you! And you're a lazy old sod – whoopee!

[RONNIE *hoists* HARRY *over his shoulder, fireman fashion, and dances round the room.*]

RONNIE: Are you going to the meeting?

HARRY: Let me down, you fool! Let me down!

RONNIE: The meeting?

HARRY: Stop it, you idiot – I've got a headache.

ADA: Do be quiet, you two.

RONNIE [*lowering his father*]: I'll fight you. Come on, fists up, show your mettle; I just feel in the mood [*assumes quixotic boxing stance*].

HARRY [*grinning*]: Bloody fool! Leave off!

RONNIE: Windy! [*playfully jabs* HARRY].

HARRY [*raising his fists*]: I'll knock your block off.

[*They follow each other round – fists raised. First* RONNIE *moves forward, then he backs away and* HARRY *moves forward. Thus they move – to and fro, without touching each other, until* SARAH *comes in with some soup in plates.*]

SARAH: The table! the table! Lay the table someone.

RONNIE: The table, the table – oh, oh, the table!

[*Everyone moves to lay the table;* RONNIE *in haste,* ADA *while reading, and* HARRY *clumsily. Then they all sit down.*]

ADA: Lovely soup, Mummy.

RONNIE: Magnificent!

SARAH: You like it?

HARRY: They just said they did.

SARAH: I wasn't talking to you.

RONNIE: She wasn't talking to you.

HARRY: Your mother never talks *to* me.

RONNIE: You're so ugly, that's why. I wouldn't talk to you either only you wouldn't give me any spending money.

SARAH: He won't give you any spending money this week anyway.

RONNIE: Don't tell me. He's out of work.

HARRY [*pathetically*]: The shop closed down.

ADA: Oh, Daddy, why does it always happen to you?

HARRY: It doesn't always happen to me.

ADA: Always! All my life that's all I can remember, just one succession of jobs which have fallen through.

HARRY: Is it my fault if the garment industry is so unstable?

ADA: It's not the industry – it's you.

HARRY: Yes, me.

ADA: Well, isn't it you?

HARRY: Oh, Ada, leave off. I have enough with your mother. I've got a headache.

ADA: I don't wonder you have a headache, you spend most of your time sleeping.

HARRY: Yes, sleeping.

ADA: What are you going to do now?

HARRY: I'll look for another job on Monday.

ADA: What's wrong with Sunday – on the Whitechapel Road? There's always governors looking for machinists.

HARRY: Those people aren't there for work. They go to gossip. Gossip, that's all! Monday I'll find a job and start straight away. It's busy now, you know.

SARAH [*collecting the soup dishes and taking them out*]: Morgen morgen nor nischt heite, sagen alle faule leite.

ADA: Daddy – you are the world's biggest procrastinator.

RONNIE: Give the boy a break, Addy, that's a big word.

ADA: He ought to be ashamed of himself. The industry's booming with work and he's out of a job. You probably got the sack, didn't you?

HARRY [*offended*]: I did not get the sack.

ADA: All her life Mummy's had to put up with this. I shall be glad to get away.

[SARAH, *entering with the next course, hears this remark and glares with hatred at* HARRY.]

RONNIE: Get away where?

ADA: Anywhere. When Dave comes back we shall leave London and live in the country. That'll be our socialism. Remember this, Ronnie: the family should be a unit, and your work and your life should be part of one existence, not something hacked about by a bus queue and office hours. A man should see, know, and love his job. Don't you want to feel your life? Savour it gently? In the country we shall be somewhere where the air doesn't smell of bricks and the kids can grow up without seeing grandparents who are continually shouting at each other.

SARAH: Ada, Ada.

RONNIE: And no more political activity?

ADA: No more political activity.

RONNIE: I bet Dave won't agree to that. Dave fought in Spain. He won't desert humanity like that.

ADA: Humanity! Ach!

RONNIE: Listen to her! With a Labour majority in the House? And two of our own Party members? It's only just beginning.

ADA: It's always only just beginning for the Party. Every defeat is victory and every victory is the beginning.

RONNIE: But it is, it is the beginning. Plans for town and country planning. New cities and schools and hospitals. Nationalization! National health! Think of it, the whole country is going to be organized to co-operate instead of tear at each other's throat. That's what I said to them in a public speech at school and all the boys cheered and whistled and stamped their feet – and blew raspberries.

ADA: I do not believe in the right to organize people. And anyway I'm not so sure that I love them enough to *want* to organize them.

SARAH [*sadly*]: This – from *you*, Ada? You used to be such an organizer.

ADA: I'm tired, mother. I spent eighteen months waiting for Dave to return from Spain and now I've waited six years for him to come home from a war against Fascism and I'm tired. Six years in and out of offices, auditing books and working with young girls who are morons – lipsticked, giggling morons. And Dave's experience is the same – fighting with men whom he says did not know what the war was about. Away from their wives they behaved like animals. In fact they wanted to get away from their wives in order to behave like animals. Give them another war and they'd run back again. Oh yes! the service killed any illusions Dave may have once had about the splendid and heroic working class.

HARRY [*pedantically*]: This is the talk of an intellectual, Ada.

ADA: God in heaven save me from the claptrap of a threepenny pamphlet. How many friends has the Party lost because of lousy, meaningless titles they gave to people. *He* was a bourgeois intellectual, *he* was a Trotskyist, *he* was a reactionary Social Democrat. Whisht! Gone!

HARRY: But wasn't it true? Didn't these people help to bolster a rotten society?

ADA: The only rotten society is an industrial society. It makes a man stand on his head and then convinces him he is good-looking. I'll tell you something. It wasn't the Trotskyist or the Social Democrat who did the damage. It was progress! There! Progress! And nobody dared fight progress.

SARAH: But that's no reason to run away. Life still carries on. A man gets married, doesn't he? He still has children, he laughs, he finds things to make him laugh. A man can always laugh, can't he?

ADA: As if that meant he lived? Even a flower can grow in the jungle, can't it? Because there is always some earth and water and sun. But there's still the jungle, still the mad disorder of trees and fern, struggling for its own existence, and the sick screeching of animals terrified of each other. As if laughter were proof!

HARRY: And we and the Party don't want to do away with the jungle, I suppose?

ADA: No, you do not want to do away with the jungle, I suppose. You have *never* cried against the jungle of an industrial society. You've never wanted to destroy its *values* – simply to own them yourselves. It only seemed a crime to you that a man spent all his working hours in front of a machine because he did not own that machine. Heavens! the glory of owning a machine!

SARAH: So what, we shouldn't care any more? We must all run away?

ADA: Care! Care! What right have we to care? How can we care for a world outside ourselves when the world inside is in disorder? Care! Haven't you ever stopped, Mother – I mean stopped–and seen yourself standing with your arms open, and suddenly paused? Come to my bosom. Everyone come to my bosom. How can you possibly imagine that your arms are long enough, for God's sake? What audacity tells you you can harbour a billion people in a theory? What great, big, stupendous, egotistical audacity, tell me?

RONNIE: Whoa, whoa!

HARRY: But it *is* an industrial age, you silly girl. Let's face facts –

ADA [*mocking*]: Don't let us kid ourselves.

HARRY [*with her*]: Don't let us kid ourselves – it's a challenge of our time.

ADA: Balls!

HARRY: You can't run away from it.

ADA: Stop me!

HARRY: Then you're a coward – that's all I can say – you're a coward.

SARAH: She had a fine example from her father, didn't she?

HARRY [*to this stab in the back*]: What do you mean – a fine example from her father?

SARAH: You don't understand what I'm saying, I suppose?

HARRY [*he is hurt and throws a hand at her in disgust*]: Ach! you make me sick.

SARAH [*mocking*]: Ach, you make me sick. *I* make *him* sick. Him, my fine man! You're the reason why she thinks like that, you know that?

HARRY: Yes, me.

SARAH: Well, of course you. Who else?

RONNIE [*collecting dishes and escaping to the kitchen*]: I'll wash up.

HARRY: I didn't bring her up – she's all your work.

SARAH: That's just it! You didn't bring her up. You weren't concerned, were you? You left it all to me while you went to your mother's or to the pictures or out with your friends.

HARRY: Yes. I went out with my friends. Sure!

SARAH: Well, didn't you? May I have so many pennies for the times you went up West to pictures.

HARRY: Oh, leave off, Sarah.

SARAH: Leave off! That's all he can say – leave off, leave me alone. That was it. I did leave you alone. That's why I had all the trouble.

ADA: I'm going home, Mummy.

SARAH [*caressingly and apologetically*]: Oh no, Ada, stay, it's early yet. Stay. We'll play solo.

ADA: I'm feeling tired and I must write to Dave.

SARAH: Well, stay here and write to Dave. We'll all be quiet. Ronnie's going out. Daddy'll go to bed and I've got some washing to do. Stay, Ada, stay. What do you want to rush home for? A cold, miserable, two-roomed flat, all on your own. Stay. We're a family, aren't we?

ADA [*putting on her coat*]: I've also got washing to do, I must go –

SARAH: I'll do it for you. What's a mother for? Straight from work I'll go to your place and bring it back with me. Stay. You've got company here – perhaps Uncle Hymie and Auntie Lottie 'll come up. What do you want to be on your own for, tell me?

ADA: I'm not *afraid* of being on my own – I must go.

SARAH [*wearily*]: Go then! Will we see you tomorrow?

ADA: Yes, I'll come for supper tomorrow night. Good night. [*calling*] Good night, Ronnie.

RONNIE [*appearing from kitchen*]: 'Night, Addy.

SARAH: You washing up, Ronnie?

RONNIE: I'm washing up.

SARAH: You I don't have to worry about – but your sister runs away. At the first sight of a little bother she runs away. Why does she run away, Ronnie? Before she used to sit and discuss things, now she runs to her home – such a home to run to – two rooms and a shadow!

RONNIE: But, Ma, she's a married woman herself. You think she hasn't her own worries wondering what it'll be like to see Dave after all these years?

SARAH: But you never run away from a discussion. At least I've got you around to help me solve problems.

RONNIE: Mother, my one virtue – if I got any at all – is that I always imagine you can solve things by talking about them – ask my form master! [*Returns to kitchen.*]

SARAH [*to HARRY*]: You see what you do? That's your daughter. Not a word from her father to ask her to stay. The family doesn't matter to you. All your life you've let the family fall around you, but it doesn't matter to you.

HARRY: I didn't drive her away.

SARAH [*bitterly*]: No – you didn't drive her away. How could you? You were the good, considerate father.

[*HARRY turns away and hunches himself up miserably.*]

Look at you! Did you shave this morning? Look at the cigarette ash on the floor. Your shirt! When did you last change your shirt? He sits. Nothing moves him, nothing worries him. He sits! A father! A husband!

HARRY [*taking out a cigarette to light*]: Leave me alone, please leave me alone, Sarah. You started the row, not me, you!

SARAH [*taking cigarette from his hand*]: Why must you always smoke? – talk with me. Talk, talk, Harry.

HARRY: Sarah! [*he stops, chokes, and then stares wildly around him*] Mamma. Mamma. [*He is having his first stroke.*]

SARAH [*frightened but not hysterical*]: Harry! Harry! What is it?

HARRY [*in Yiddish, gently*]: Vie iss sie – der mamma?

SARAH: Stop it, Harry.

HARRY: Sie iss dorten – der mamma?

SARAH: Ronnie! Ronnie!

[*RONNIE comes in from the kitchen.*]

Doctor Woolfson – quick, quick, get him.

RONNIE: What's happening?

SARAH: I don't know. It's a stroke maybe.

[RONNIE *runs out.*]

Harry, it was only a quarrel, you silly man. None of your tricks now, Harry – Harry, you hear me?

HARRY: Vie iss sie? Mamma, mamma.

CURTAIN

SCENE 2

It is October 1947.

We are in the same room. RONNIE *is making a fire in the grate. When this is done he puts on the radio and goes into the kitchen. The* Egmont *overture comes over the radio.* RONNIE *comes out of the kitchen with a cup of tea. On hearing the music he lays down the cup and picks up a pencil and proceeds to conduct an imaginary orchestra until* CISSIE *is seen moving along the balcony. She lets herself in and surprises* RONNIE. *She is carrying a briefcase.*

RONNIE: Aunt!

CISSIE: Hello, Junior. I've come to see your father.

RONNIE: Not back from work yet. Just in time for a cuppa [*goes off to make one*].

CISSIE: He still has that job, then?

RONNIE [*from kitchen*]: Can't hear you.

CISSIE: Turn this bloody wireless down [*does so*].

RONNIE [*entering with tea*]: Aunty! Please! Beethoven!

CISSIE: I know, I know. Some other time. I'm not feeling so good [*takes cigarette from handbag*].

RONNIE [*entering with tea*]: What price partition in Palestine, aunt?

CISSIE: Russia's backing the plan.

RONNIE: Yers – and haven't the Arabs got upset over that. They're taking it to the high courts. They expected Russia to attack the United Nations plan if only to upset the West. Power politics!

CISSIE: Has your father still got that job?

RONNIE: No, he's a store-keeper in a sweet factory now. Look. [*Shows her a biscuit tin full of sweets.*] Jelly babies. Can't help himself. Doesn't do it on a large scale, mind, just a handful each night. Everyone does it.

CISSIE: How long has he been there?

RONNIE: Three weeks. You know he can't stay long at a job – and now he has got what he has always wanted – a legitimate excuse.

CISSIE: He can *walk*, can't he?

RONNIE: He walks – slowly and stooped – with his head sunk into his shoulders, hands in his pockets [*imitates his father*]. His step isn't sure – frightened to exert himself in case he should suddenly drop dead. You ought to see him in a strong wind – [*moves drunkenly round the room*] – like an autumn leaf. He seems to have given up the fight, as though *thank God* he was no longer responsible for himself. You know, Aunt, I don't suppose there is anything more terrifying to a man than his own sense of failure, and your brother Harry is really a very sensitive man. No one knows more than he does how he's failed. Now that's tragedy for you: having the ability to see what is happening to yourself and yet not being able to do anything about it. Like a long nightmare. God! fancy being born just to live a long nightmare. He gets around. But who knows how sick he is? Now we can't tell his lethargy from his illness.

CISSIE: It sounds just like mother. Mother was bed-ridden for years. He seems to be moving that way –

RONNIE: Almost deliberately. Here! [*goes to a drawer and takes out a notebook*] Did you know he once started to write his autobiography? Listen. [*reads*] 'Of me, the dummy and my family.' How's that for a poetic title! 'Sitting at my work in the shop one day my attention was drawn to the dummy that we all try the work on. The rhythm of the machines and my constant looking at the dummy rocked me off in a kind of sleepy daze. And to my surprise the dummy began to take the shape of a human, it began to speak. Softly at first, so softly I could hardly hear it. And then louder and still louder, and it seemed to raise its eyebrows and with a challenge asked: your life, what of your life? My life? I had never thought, and I began to take my mind back, way back to the time when I was a little boy.' There, a whole notebook full, and then one day he stopped! Just like that! God knows why a man stops doing the one thing that can keep him together.

CISSIE: How's Ada and Dave?

RONNIE: Struggling in a tied cottage in the country. Ada suckles a beautiful baby, Dave lays concrete floors in the day-time and makes furniture by hand in the evening.

CISSIE: Lunatics!

RONNIE: They're happy. Two Jews in the Cotswolds! They had to get a Rabbi from Cheltenham to circumcise the baby. A Rabbi from Cheltenham! Who'd ever think there were Rabbis in Cheltenham?

CISSIE: And you?

RONNIE: A bookshop.

CISSIE: Same one?

RONNIE: Same one.

CISSIE: You're also crazy and mixed up, I suppose?

RONNIE [*highly indignant*]: Don't call me that! God in heaven, don't call me that! I'm a poet.

CISSIE: Another one!

RONNIE: A Socialist poet.

CISSIE: A Socialist poet!

RONNIE: I have all the world at my fingertips. Nothing is mixed up. I have so much life that I don't know who to give it to first. I see beyond the coloured curtains of *my* eyes to a world – say, how do you like that line? Beyond the coloured curtains of *my* eyes, waiting for time and timing nothing but the slow hours, lay the thoughts in the mind. Past the pool of *my* smile . . .

CISSIE: What does that mean?

RONNIE: What, the pool of my smile? It's a metaphor – the pool of my smile – a very lovely metaphor. How's trade-union activity?

CISSIE: We've got a strike on. Dillingers are probably going to lock out its workers.

RONNIE: Ah, Dillingers! 'Dillinger styles gets all the men's smiles, this is the wear for everywhere!' No wonder the workers don't like poetry.

CISSIE: The old boy wants to reduce their wages because they're doing sale work.

RONNIE: What's that?

CISSIE: You know – sale work – especially made-up clothes for the big West End sales.

RONNIE: You mean a sale is not what is left over from the season before?

CISSIE: Oh, grow up, Ronnie. You should know that by now. It's cheaper stuff, inferior quality.

RONNIE: And the union doesn't protest? [*jumping on a chair and waving his arms in the air*] Capitalist exploiters! The bastards – if you'll excuse the expression. I'll write a book about them! I'll expose them in their true light. What a novel, Aunt – set in a clothing factory, the sweat shops, the –

CISSIE: Look, you want to hear about this strike or you don't want to hear about this strike?

[RONNIE *sits down.*]

So because it's sale work Dillinger wants to cut the women's wages by ten per cent and the men's by twelve and a half per cent. So what does he plan to do? I'll tell you what he plans to do – he plans to pay all thirty of them for one full week, sack them, and then re-employ them, which would mean they were new employees and only entitled to Board of Trade rate, which is considerably less.

RONNIE: But can he do that?

CISSIE: He did it! He did it! The girls told me. But this year the shop stewards got together and asked me to go down and negotiate. They didn't all want it, mind you. One wagged his finger at me and cried: 'We're not taking your advice, we're not taking your advice!' I gave them – you know me. First I read the Riot Act to them and then I lashed out. You ought to be ashamed of yourselves, I told them, after the union struggled hard, tooth and nail, for every penny you get and at the first sign of intimidation you want to give in. For shame! I yelled at them – for shame! I tell you, Ronnie – a boss you can always handle because he always wants to bribe you, and that gives you the upper hand – but the worker . . .

[HARRY *has by this time entered through the front door and shuffles down the passage into the front room. He is slightly paralysed down*

one side but is still very able to move around. The first stroke has just
made him age prematurely.]

HARRY: Hello, Cissie, what are you doing here?

CISSIE: I've come to see you. Well, how are you?

HARRY: I'm all right, Cissie, I'm fine.

CISSIE: Can you work all right?

HARRY: I can't move my left hand very well. Lost its grip or something [*clutches and unclutches fist to prove the point*].

RONNIE [*gripping* HARRY'S *hand in a shake*]: Strong as an ox. You're
a sham, Harry boy. Want some tea?

HARRY: Yes please, son.

CISSIE: What do the doctors say is wrong with you?

HARRY: I had a stroke – that's all they know. They don't tell you
anything in the hospitals these days. Sarah's gone to the doctor's
now to find out if I can go back again for observation.

CISSIE: More observation?

HARRY: Ach! Don't talk to me about them, they make me sick.

CISSIE: All those blood tests they took and they still don't know –
after a year. I'm surprised you had that much blood. Well, I'm
going. Here, smoke yourself to death [*hands him forty cigarettes*].

RONNIE [*bringing in tea*]: Going?

CISSIE: I've got a strike meeting.

RONNIE: In the evening?

CISSIE: Anytime. So long, Junior.

[*She kisses* HARRY *and* RONNIE *and goes out. On the landing she
meets* SARAH.]

Hello, Sarah. I just come to see Harry. Sorry I must go. How are
you?

SARAH: I'm all right. Why don't you stay for supper?

CISSIE [*out of sight by now*]: I've got a strike meeting. I'll be seeing you.

HARRY [*to* SARAH *as she comes in*]: Did you go to the doctor's?

SARAH [*wearily*]: I've been, I've been. Oh, those stairs will kill me.

HARRY: What does he say?

SARAH [*taking out a letter from her bag and placing it on the mantelpiece*]:
He gave me a letter: you should take it to the hospital.

HARRY: What does it say; show me.

SARAH: It's sealed; you mustn't open it.

HARRY: Show me it.

SARAH: What can you see? It's sealed.

HARRY [*irritably*]: Oh, I want to see who it's addressed to.

[*Too tired to cope with him she hands him the letter and then goes to the kitchen.*]

SARAH [*from the kitchen*]: Did anybody make supper?

RONNIE: We've not long come in. [*to* HARRY, *taking away the envelope he is trying to open*] Uh-uh. Mustn't open. It's for the hospital.

SARAH [*entering with a cup of tea and sitting down*]: I've got a branch meeting tonight. Ronnie, you can take your own supper. It's fried fish from yesterday. You want to come with Harry?

HARRY: I don't feel like going to any branch meeting.

SARAH: You want to get well, don't you? You don't want to become an invalid, do you? So come to a meeting tonight. Mix with people. They're your comrades, aren't they?

HARRY: Yes, my comrades.

SARAH: Nothing is sacred for him. Ach! Why should I worry whether you come or not. What are you doing, Ronnie?

RONNIE: An evening in. I want to write a novel tonight.

SARAH: What, all in one night? Ronnie, do you think you'll ever publish anything? I mean, don't you have to be famous or be able to write or something? There must be such a lot of people writing novels.

RONNIE: Not Socialist novels. Faith, Mother, faith! I am one of the sons of the working class, one of its own artists.

HARRY: You mean a political writer like Winston Churchill?

SARAH: What, does he write novels as well? I thought he was only a politician.

RONNIE: Well, he's both – *and* he paints pictures.

SARAH: A painter? He paints pictures? Landscapes and things?

RONNIE: Of course! And in his spare time he –

SARAH: What, he has spare time also?

RONNIE: In his spare time he builds walls at the bottom of his garden.

SARAH [*in admiration*]: A bricklayer! Ronnie, I told you you should take up a trade! Why don't you? Go to evening classes. Why should you waste your time in a bookshop? If I were young, oh, what wouldn't I study! All the world I would study. How properly to talk and to write and make sentences. You'll be sorry – don't be like your father, don't be unsettled. Learn a good trade and then you have something to fall back on. You can always write – and when you work then you'll have something to write about.

RONNIE: Give me a chance, Ma. I only left school a year ago.

SARAH: That's what he kept on saying. Give me a chance! Everybody had to give him a chance: now look at him. Harry – you're not working in the sweet factory any more, are you?

HARRY: Who said I'm not?

RONNIE: Well, isn't he?

SARAH: Well, ask him, he knows.

[RONNIE *inclines his head inquiringly.*]

HARRY: Of course I'm still working there.

SARAH [*wearily, for the time has gone for violent rows*]: Harry, answer me. What do you gain by telling me this lie? Tell me, I want to know. All my life I've wanted to know what you've gained by a lie. *I* know you're not working because I saw the foreman. You're not even a good liar. I've always known when you've lied. For twenty-five years it's been the same and all the time I've not known what it's about. But *you* know – no one else knows, but you do. I'm asking you, Harry – let me be your doctor, let me try and help you. What is it that makes you what you are? Tell me – only tell me. Don't sit there and say nothing. I'm entitled to know – after all, this time I'm entitled to know. Well, aren't I, Ronnie?

[*Nobody answers her.* HARRY *avoids her gaze,* RONNIE *waits till it's all over.*]

So look at him. He sits and he sits and he sits and all his life goes away from him. [*to* RONNIE] You won't be like that, will you?

RONNIE: I shall never take up a trade I hate as he did – if that's what you mean; and I shall never marry – at least not until I'm real and healthy. [*cheerfully*] But what's there to grumble about, little Sarah? You have two splendid children, a fine son-in-law and a grandson.

SARAH: I haven't seen my grandson yet. My daughter lives two hundred miles away from me and my husband is a sick man. That's my family. Well, it's a family, I suppose. [*She rises to go.*]

RONNIE: What about me? [*He regards himself in a mirror.*] Young, good-looking, hopeful, talented . . . hopeful, anyway.

SARAH [*sadly*]: You? I'll wait and see what happens to you. Please God you don't make a mess of your life, please God. Did you ask for that rise?

RONNIE: I did ask for that rise. 'Mr Randolph,' I said – he's the manager of that branch – 'Mr Randolph, I know that the less wages you pay us bookshop assistants the more you get in your salary. But don't you think I've sold enough books for long enough time to warrant you forgoing some of your commission?'

SARAH: So what did he say, you liar?

RONNIE: 'You're our best salesman,' he said, 'but I've got to keep head office happy.'

SARAH: So what did you say, you liar?

RONNIE: So I said, 'It's not head office, it's your wife'.

SARAH: So what did he say, you liar?

RONNIE: He said, 'Kahn,' he said, 'as you're so frank and you know too much I'll give you a two pound rise.'

SARAH: Ronnie, did you get a rise, I asked you?

RONNIE [*kissing her*]: No.

SARAH: Mad boy, you! I'm going to the meeting.

RONNIE: That's it, Mother. You go to the meeting. At least if you keep on fighting then there's hope for me.

[*He helps her on with a coat as he speaks, then she goes.*]

[*returning to room*] You want supper, Dad? It's the old dead fish again. I'll lay it for you. [*Moves to kitchen.*]

HARRY: Aren't you going to eat?

RONNIE [*from kitchen*]: I'm not hungry. I'll eat later. I must work now. You want me to read the first chapter to you, Dad?

HARRY: Oh, leave me alone, Ronnie – I'm tired.

RONNIE: Tired! You're not tired, Harry – you're just drowning with heritage, mate! [*re-enters with an assortment of plates which he lays on the table*] There, you can wash up after you. I'm going to my room now.

[RONNIE *goes to his room.* HARRY *moves to the table and commences to eat. He eats in silence for a few seconds then stretches out for a newspaper. After glancing through this he turns to the mantelpiece and sees the letter. He looks to Ronnie's room to make sure he is not coming and then moves slowly across to get the letter. First of all he tries to prise it open without tearing anything. Then not succeeding in this he moves to the table to get a knife. As he picks up the knife* RONNIE *enters again.*]

RONNIE: Christ! It's bloody cold in that room: I – now then, Harry – [*as though playfully scolding a child*] – you know you must not read the letter, remember what Mummykins said [*he moves to take it*].

HARRY [*retaining it*]: Let me read the letter, I want to know what's in it.

RONNIE [*making another bid for it*]: Use some will-power, Dad; you know the letter is not for you. Now leave it be, there's a good boy.

HARRY [*retaining it again*]: I want to see it; it's about me, isn't it? Now leave off, Ronnie.

RONNIE [*snatching it from his father's hand*]: No!

HARRY [*banging his hand on the table in rapid succession with the words he cries, like a child in anger, hating to be like a child – he shrieks*]: GIVE ME THAT LETTER. GIMME. S'mine. S'mine. I WAN' THAT ENVELOPE. Now. This instant. I – wan' – that – envelope!

[RONNIE *stands there trembling. He had not meant to provoke such anger and having done so is now upset. He is not quite sure what to do. Almost involuntarily he hands over the envelope and when he has done so he goes to a wall and cries. He is still a boy – he has been frightened.* HARRY *picks up envelope, himself distraught. He does not bother to open it now. Seeing that* RONNIE *is crying he goes over to him and clasps him.*]

HARRY: You shouldn't do these things. I'm a sick man. If I want to open the envelope you shouldn't stop me. You've got no right to stop me. Now you've upset me and yourself – you silly boy.

RONNIE: Can't you see that I can't bear what you are. I don't want to hear your lies all my life. Your weakness frightens me, Harry – did you ever think about that? I watch you and I see myself and I'm terrified.

HARRY [*wandering away from him; he does not know what to say*]: What I am – I am. I will never alter. Neither you nor your mother will change me. It's too late now; I'm an old man and if I've been the same all my life so I will always be. You can't alter people, Ronnie. You can only give them some love and hope they'll take it. I'm sorry. It's too late now. I can't help you. [*He shuffles miserably to his room, perceptibly older.*] Don't forget to have supper. Good night.

CURTAIN

ACT THREE

It is November 1955.

SCENE I

ANNOUNCER: It was further stated by Group Captain Townsend that he was staying at Uckfield until the week-end. After that he was going back to resume his post as air attaché in Brussels. The weather forecast for tomorrow is mainly dry with sunny periods, winds coming mainly from the north-east. That is the end of the nine o'clock news and now until our next programme, which opens in just under two minutes, here is part of Ravel's *La Valse*.

CURTAIN RISES

[HARRY *has had his second stroke, and now paralysis has made him completely unfit for work. He can only just move around, has difficulty in talking and is sometimes senile.* SARAH *retains much of her energy but shows signs of age and her troubles – her tone of speaking is compassionate now.*

It is one evening in the week, in the same L.C.C. *flat.* HARRY *sits in a chair – huddled by the fireplace. He smokes more than ever, it is his one comfort.* SARAH *is sitting by the table struggling to fill out an official Government form – she talks a lot to herself.*]

SARAH [*reading form*]: Have you an insurance policy for life or death? Name of company. Amount insured for. Annual payments. How should I know the annual payments? I pay one and a penny a week – that's fifty-two shillings and fifty-two pennies [*makes mental reckoning*].

[*The music by this time has reached a climax and is too loud.* SARAH *goes to turn it off.*]

Oh, shut that off! Classical music! All of a sudden it starts shouting at you.

HARRY: No, no, no, no, I was – I was listening.

SARAH: You *liked* it?

HARRY: I liked it. It reminds me of – of – of – of, it reminds me of Blackfriar's Bridge in a fog.

SARAH: Blackfriar's Bridge in a fog it reminds you of? Why a fog?

HARRY: Oh, I don't know why a fog. Why a fog?

SARAH: And why Blackfriar's Bridge?

HARRY: Because I said so! Och, you're such a silly woman sometimes, Sarah.

SARAH: But if it's in a fog so what difference whether it's Blackfriar's Bridge or London Bridge? Ach, I must get these forms done before Bessie and Monty arrive. You remember Bessie and Monty are coming tonight? [SARAH *continues to complete forms*] If Ronnie were here I'd get him to fill it in for me . . . as if they don't know how many times I was at work this year. Forms! You tell the National Insurance office that you started work on such and such a day so they tell the National Assistance and the National Assistance tells the Income Tax and then there's forms, forms, forms, forms - Oi – such forms. They can't get enough of them into one envelope. [*writing*] No, I haven't got any property, I haven't got any lodgers, I haven't got a housekeeper. A housekeeper! A housekeeper wouldn't do what I do for you, Harry – washing all those sheets.

[MONTY BLATT *and his wife* BESSIE *appear on the balcony. They knock.* SARAH *jumps up.*]

They're here already. Now Harry, sit up. Do your flies up and brush that cigarette ash off you. And remember – don't let me down – you promised. You want to go now?

[*She takes* HARRY'S *arm but he pushes her away; he doesn't want to go.* SARAH *opens the door to her visitors, both are richly and over-dressed, full of bounce and property.*]

MONTY: Sarah – little Sarah. How are you, sweetheart? You remember Bessie?

[*They all shake hands and enter the front room.*]

Harry boy! How's Harry? You're looking well. You feeling well? They haven't changed a bit. Neither of them.

SARAH: Sit down, both of you; I'll get the kettle on. [*Goes off to kitchen.*]

MONTY [*to* BESSIE]: Always put the kettle on – that was the first thing Sarah always did. Am I right, Harry? I'm right, aren't I? [*shouting to* SARAH] Remember, Sarah? It was always a cup of tea first.

SARAH [*coming in*]: I remember, I remember.

MONTY [*to* BESSIE]: We used to 'live' in their old place in the East End, all the boys. Remember Prince and your brother Hymie? How is Hymie? Since we moved to Manchester I've lost contact with everybody, everyeee-body!

SARAH: Hymie's all right. He's got a business. His children are married and he stays at home all the time. Prince works in a second-hand shop.

MONTY: A second-hand shop? But I thought – and Cissie?

SARAH: The union members have finished with her. She lives on a pension, visits the relatives – you know . . .

MONTY: It's all broken up, then?

SARAH: What's broken up about it? They couldn't keep up with the Party – so? The *fight* still goes on.

MONTY [*hastily changing the subject*]: And Ada and Dave and Ronnie? Where are they all? Tell me everything. Tell me all the news. I haven't seen you for so long, Sarah – it's so good to see you – isn't it good to see them, Bessie?

SARAH: Ada and Dave are still in the country. They've got two children. Dave is still making furniture by hand –

MONTY: He makes a living?

SARAH: They live! They're not prosperous, but they live.

MONTY: And Ronnie? Ronnie had such ambitions; what's he doing?

SARAH: My Ronnie? He's in Paris.

MONTY: There, I told you he'd go far.

SARAH: As a cook.

MONTY [*not so enthusiastically*]: A cook? Ronnie?

BESSIE [*helping them out*]: A cook makes good money.

MONTY [*reviving*]: Sure a cook makes good money. Ronnie is a smart boy, isn't he, Sarah? Didn't I always say Ronnie was a smart boy? Nobody could understand how an East End boy could speak with such a posh accent. But cooking! He likes it? I mean he's happy?

SARAH: I tell you something, Monty. People ask me what is Ronnie doing and, believe me, I don't know what to answer. He used to throw his arms up in the air and say 'I want to do something worth while, I want to create'. Create! So, he's a cook in Paris.

MONTY: Please God he'll be a hotel manager one day.

SARAH: Please God.

MONTY: And Harry? [*He indicates with his head that* HARRY *has dozed off.*]

SARAH: Poor Harry. He's had two strokes. He won't get any better. Paralysed down one side. He can't control his bowels, you know.

BESSIE: Poor man.

SARAH: You think *he* likes it? Its ach a nebish Harry now. It's not easy for him. But he won't do anything to help himself. I don't know, other men get ill but they fight. Harry's never fought. Funny thing. There were three men like this in the flats, all had strokes. And all three of them seemed to look the same. They walked the same, stooped the same and all needing a shave. They used to sit outside together and talk for hours on end and smoke. Sit and talk and smoke. That was their life. Then one day one of them decided he wanted to live so he gets up and finds himself a job – running a small shoe-mender's – and he's earning money now. A miracle! Just like that. But the other one – he wanted to die. I used to see him standing outside in the rain, the pouring rain, getting all wet so that he could catch a cold and die. Well, it happened: last week he died. Influenza! He just didn't want to live. But Harry was not like either of them. He didn't want to die but he doesn't seem to care about living. So! What can you do to help a man like that? I make his food and I buy him cigarettes and he's happy. My only dread is that he will not mess himself. When that happens I go mad – I just don't know what I'm doing.

MONTY: It's like that, is it?

SARAH: It's like that. That's life. But how about you, Monty? You still in the Party?

MONTY: No, Sarah – I'm not still in the Party, and I'll tell you why if you want to know –

BESSIE: Now, Monty, don't get on to politics. Sarah, do me a favour and don't get him on to politics.

MONTY: Don't worry, I won't say much –

SARAH: Politics is living, Bessie. I mean everything that happens in the world has got to do with politics.

BESSIE: Listen, Sarah. Monty's got a nice little greengrocer's business in Manchester, no one knows he was ever a member of the Party and we're all happy. It's better he forgets it.

MONTY: No, no – I'll tell her, let me tell her.

BESSIE: I'm warning you, Monty, if you get involved in a political argument I shan't stay. No political argument, you hear me?

MONTY: Listen, Sarah. Remember Spain? Remember how we were proud of Dave and the other boys who answered the call? But did Dave ever tell you the way some of the Party members refused to fight alongside the Trotskyists? And one or two of the Trotskyists didn't come back and they weren't killed in the fighting either? And remember Itzack Pheffer – the Soviet Yiddish writer? We used to laugh because Itzack Pheffer was a funny name – ha, ha. Where's Itzack Pheffer? everyone used to say. Well, we know now, don't we. The great 'leader' is dead now, and we know. The whole committee of the Jewish Anti-Fascist League were shot! Shot, Sarah! In our land of socialism. That was *our* land – what a land that was for us! We didn't believe the stories then; it wasn't possible that it could happen in our one-sixth of the world.

SARAH: And you believe the stories now, Monty?

MONTY [*incredulously*]: You don't –

BESSIE: Now, Monty –

MONTY: You don't believe it, Sarah? You won't believe it!

SARAH: And supposing it's true, Monty? So? What should we do, bring back the old days? Is that what you want?

MONTY: I don't know, sweetheart. I haven't got any solutions any more. I've got a little shop up North – I'm not a capitalist by any means – I just make a comfortable living and I'm happy. Bessie – bless her – is having a baby [*taps* BESSIE's *belly*]. I'm going to give him all that I can, pay for his education, university if he likes, and then I shall be satisfied. A man can't do anything more, Sarah, believe me. There's nothing more to life than a house, some friends, and a family – take my word.

SARAH: And when someone drops an atom bomb on your family?

MONTY [*pleading*]: So what can I do – tell me? There's nothing I can do any more. I'm too small; who can I trust? It's a big, lousy world of mad politicians – I can't trust them, Sarah.

SARAH: The kettle's boiling – I'll make some tea. [*Goes to kitchen.*]

BESSIE: Enough now, Monty, enough.

MONTY [*he has upset himself*]: All right, all right. I didn't tell her anything she doesn't know. She's a fine woman is Sarah. She's a fighter. All that worry and she's still going strong. But she has one fault. For her the world is black and white. If you're not white so you must be black. She can't see shades in character – know what I mean? She can't see people in the round. 'They' are all the same bunch. The authorities, the Governments, the police, the Post Office – even the shopkeepers. She's never trusted any of them, always fighting them. It was all so simple. The only thing that mattered was to be happy and eat. Anything that made you unhappy or stopped you from eating was the fault of capitalism. Do you think she ever read a book on political economy in her life? Bless her! Someone told her socialism was happiness so she joined the Party. You don't find many left like Sarah Kahn. I wish you'd have known us in the old days. Harry there used to have a lovely tenor voice. All the songs we sang together and the strikes and the rallies. I used to carry Ronnie shoulder high to the May Day demonstrations. Everyone in the East End was going somewhere.

It was a slum, there was misery but we were going somewhere. The East End was a big mother.

[SARAH *comes in with the tea.*]

We'll talk about the good times now, shall we, Sarah? Blimey, sweetheart, it's not often that I come to London for a week-end. Here, remember the stall I used to have in Petticoat Lane? I'll take you there tomorrow, Bessie. And Manny the Corn King? Him and his wife used to go to Norwich, to sell phoney corn cures. His wife used to dress up as a nurse and they'd hang letters round the stall from people who were supposed to have been cured.

SARAH: And what about Barney?

MONTY: And Barney, that's it! He used to sell all the old farmers a lucky charm to bring them fortune. Sixpence each he'd sell them for and you know what they were? Haricot beans! Haricot beans dropped in dye to colour them. You could get them for threepence a pound in a grocer's shop and Barney sold them for sixpence each! Sixpence! A pound of beans used to last him for months.

SARAH: Ach! Horrible times! Horrible times – dirty, unclean, cheating!

MONTY: But friendly.

SARAH: Friendly, you call it? You think it was friendly to swindle people?

MONTY: Sweetheart, you take life too seriously. Believe me, those farmers knew very well what they were buying. Nobody swindled anybody because everyone knew.

SARAH: You think so, Monty?

[HARRY *wakes up with a jerk. Something has happened. He tries hurriedly to rise.*]

HARRY: Sarah, quick, help me.

SARAH: What! It's happened? [*She moves quickly to him.*]

MONTY: What is it, Harry boy?

SARAH: It's happened, Harry? Well, quickly then, quickly.

[HARRY, *crippled by paralysis and this attack of incontinence, shuffles, painfully, towards the toilet with* SARAH *almost dragging him along. He whines and groans pathetically.*]

I told you to go before, didn't I? You said it would be all right. It's always all right. Now look what's happened. In front of Monty and Bessie. I'm so ashamed.

[MONTY *attempts to help* HARRY *move.*]

[*abruptly*] No, leave him. It's all right. I'll manage. Leave him, Monty.

[*They struggle out and into the passage. When they have left the front room,* BESSIE *turns her head away and shudders.*]

BESSIE: Oh, good God!

MONTY: Poor Sarah and Harry. Jesus! It's all come to this?

CURTAIN

SCENE 2

It is December 1956.

The KAHNS' *room. It is late one evening.*

SARAH, PRINCE, HYMIE, *and* CISSIE *are sitting round the table playing*
solo. HARRY *is by the fire, gazing into it, quite oblivious of what is going*
on. The cards have just been dealt for a round. Everyone is evaluating his
cards in silence. After some seconds:

PRINCE [*studying his cards*]: What time you expecting Ronnie,
  Sarah?

SARAH [*studying her cards*]: He's supposed to arrive at nine-thirty
  tonight.

  [*Again silence.*]

HYMIE [*to* CISSIE]: Nu? Call!

CISSIE: Misère.

SARAH: How can you call a misère when I want to call a misère?

CISSIE: Please, Sarah – don't give the game away.

PRINCE: Wait a minute, not everybody has passed.

CISSIE: All right then, call!

SARAH: Pass.

PRINCE: Pass.

HYMIE: Pass.

CISSIE: Thank you. Can I start now?

SARAH: Is it your lead? I thought Prince dealt the cards.

CISSIE: What's the matter with you, Sarah? – Hymie dealt them.

PRINCE: I could have sworn Sarah dealt them.

CISSIE: Hymie, who dealt the cards?

HYMIE: We've been so long deciding what to call that I don't know
  any more. Did I deal them? I don't remember.

  [*There is a general discussion as to who dealt them.*]

CISSIE: Now quiet, everybody. Quiet! Every time I come to this
  house to play solo there's the same confusion. Why don't you pay

attention to the game? Now then, what was laid on the table for trumps?

SARAH: The two of spades.

HYMIE: That was the last round. It was the six of diamonds.

SARAH: But I saw it with my own eyes, it was the –

HYMIE: You aren't wearing your glasses, Sarah.

PRINCE: It was the six of hearts, I remember now.

CISSIE: Ah, thank God! We've got two people to agree. I also saw the six of hearts on the table. Who's got the six of hearts?

HYMIE: I have.

CISSIE: Which means that you dealt and if you dealt that means that I lead. Everybody happy now? There!

[CISSIE *throws down a card. The others follow. It's* HYMIE'S *trick. He lays down a card and the others follow, but* SARAH *realizes she has made a mistake.*]

SARAH: Wait a minute, wait a minute. I didn't mean to play that card.

CISSIE: Too late; you should watch the game.

SARAH: Ach! fool that I am. But you can see I shouldn't have played that card.

CISSIE: Of course I can see, but I'm glad that you did!

SARAH: Now, Hymie, would I normally play that card?

HYMIE: You aren't wearing your glasses, Sarah: I told you. We can still catch her. Now play.

SARAH: A second, a second. Let me get my glasses. [*Finds her bag, takes out her glasses and proceeds to puff on them and clean them.*] I don't know what's happened to my eyes lately. I went to have my glasses changed the other day – the rims were too big for me, kept slipping into my mouth – so I went to have them changed. The man said he couldn't change them because they were National Health glasses. So you know me, I tell him what for and he says, 'Madam,' he says, 'you want your money back?' So I say, 'Sure I want my money back'. And then I go up to the National Health offices – now listen to this – I go up to the National Health offices and I complain about the small allowance they make me for Harry.

So the chap behind the desk – may he wake up dead – he says, 'What do you want, Madam, ten pounds a week?' Did you ever hear? So I said, 'Son,' I said, 'when you were still peeing all over the floor I was on strike for better conditions, and don't you be cheeky.' 'Oh dear, you mustn't talk to me like that per, per, per, per!'

PRINCE: Come on, Sarah, the game.

[*It is* PRINCE'S *lead. The others follow; it is his trick again. Again he leads and the others follow. Now it is for* SARAH *to lead and she does so.*]

What did you play hearts for? Couldn't you see what suit I was showing you?

SARAH: Prince, let me play my own game. Don't I know what I'm doing?

PRINCE: Well, it doesn't look like it, Sarah, so help me it doesn't. You can't be watching the game. Couldn't you guess she was going to throw off on hearts?

CISSIE: What is this! In the middle of the game!

SARAH: Of course I could see, but how do you know that I can't play anything else?

CISSIE: Are you going to play solo or are you not going to play solo? No inquests, please.

HYMIE: Prince, play your game.

CISSIE: It's always the same. You can't even get a good game of solo these days!

[PRINCE *plays his card and they all follow.*]

SARAH: Look at him! Now he comes out diamonds and he wants to teach me how to play solo.

[SARAH *leads next time and after that* CISSIE *lays down her cards and shows that she can't be caught.*]

CISSIE: There! Three-halfpence from everybody, please.

[*Now everybody looks at everybody else's hand to see where everybody else went wrong.*]

SARAH: Well, of course I couldn't catch her, not with my hand.

PRINCE: Why did you come out with hearts when you knew she might be throwing off on them?

SARAH: Because I wanted to give the lead away – *I* couldn't do any-thing.

HYMIE: But why give the lead away with hearts when you knew she might not have any?

SARAH: How was I to know? It was my smallest card.

CISSIE: You never could play a good game of solo, Sarah.

SARAH: But do me a favour –

CISSIE: Spades! That was the suit to play.

SARAH: Spades? Never!

[*Again everybody starts to speak at once until a loud scream brings them to silence. It comes from the playground below and is followed by a young girl's voice crying.*]

GIRL'S VOICE: Philip! Philip! I want my Philip. Leave me alone – go away.

MAN'S VOICE: Go 'ome, I tell you, 'ome, you silly cow. 'Ome!

GIRL'S VOICE: I won't go till I see Philip. I love him! I love him!

CISSIE: They making a film out there or something?

[*They all go out to the balcony and look down.* SARAH *walks along it off-stage to see what the commotion is all about.*]

Can't see a thing. There's always something happening in these flats. Last week a woman tried to gas herself. Come on, let's go in.

[*They return to room.*]

HARRY: What happened?

PRINCE: Your neighbours are having a party. Sarah's gone to see who's dead.

HYMIE: Why did the woman want to commit suicide?

CISSIE [*raising her skirt to warm her behind*]: Who knows why a woman of 32 wants to commit suicide? These flats are a world on their own. You live a whole life-time here and not know your next-door neighbour.

HARRY: I don' – I don' – I don'.

CISSIE: Do you want to write it down?

HARRY: I don' know the woman downstairs yet.

[*Everyone smiles for him and having said his piece he returns to gazing at the fire.* SARAH *re-enters.*]

SARAH: Children! They don't know what to do with themselves. Seems she'd just spent the evening watching television with Philip and it was a horror film or something and he kept frightening her. Frightening her! That's all they can do to each other! She got home late and her father started on her so she ran back and started screaming for Philip. The great lover! He came out in his pyjamas to soothe her.

CISSIE [*going to get her coat*]: Well, Sarah, I had a nice supper, a nice game of solo and I'm going before the washing up. It doesn't look as though Ronnie caught that train anyway.

SARAH: I can't understand it. He wrote he was leaving Paris at eight this morning.

HYMIE: Well, it's nearly ten-thirty and I must be going as well.

PRINCE: Me too, Sarah.

SARAH: Won't you stay for a cup of tea at least? It's so long since we've played a game of solo. Harry and I don't see many people these days.

HYMIE: It's been a nice evening, Sarah. Why don't you come up to *us* sometimes? I'm always at home.

SARAH: What chance do I get to leave Harry now?

CISSIE: Good night, Sarah.

[HYMIE *kisses* SARAH *and* CISSIE *kisses* HARRY *and all leave.* SARAH *waves to them from the balcony and returns to the room. She collects the cards and tidies up.*]

SARAH: Harry, you want a cup of tea?

HARRY [*slowly rising*]: I'm going to bed.

SARAH: You won't wait up for Ronnie?

HARRY: I'll – I'll – I'll –

SARAH: You'll what?

HARRY: See him in the morning.

[SARAH *helps* HARRY *shuffle away to bed and then settles down in the armchair to read. But she is tired now and lets fall the paper to doze.* RONNIE *appears on the balcony with his cases. He gently opens the door and lets himself in. He tiptoes over to* SARAH *and stands looking*] *at her. It is no longer an enthusiastic* RONNIE. *She opens her eyes and after a second of looking at him she jumps up into his arms.*]

SARAH: I fell asleep.

RONNIE: So I saw.

SARAH: I thought you were a dream.

RONNIE: Perhaps I am.

SARAH [*pushing him away to look at him*]: I hope not, Ronnie. Oh God, I hope not. Don't go away again. It's been so lonely without you and your friends. I don't mind not having any money, we can always eat, you know that, but I can't bear being on my own. [*Begins to cry.*]

RONNIE: I've only once ever seen you cry.

SARAH: What's the good of crying?

RONNIE: I wish I could cry sometimes. Perhaps if you'd have cried more often it would have been easier.

SARAH: It's just that I can't cope any longer, that's all. Three times a week Daddy has that accident and it gets too much. I'm an old woman now.

RONNIE: What makes you think I shall be able to cope?

SARAH: You? What are you talking about? Of course you'll be able to cope. You're young, aren't you? You're going to settle down.

RONNIE: I – I'm sick, Sarah.

SARAH: Sick?

RONNIE: Oh, not physically. That's why I came home.

SARAH: Didn't you like the place where you worked? You always wrote how happy you were – what an experience it was.

RONNIE: I hated the kitchen.

SARAH: But –

RONNIE: I-hated-the-kitchen! People coming and going and not staying long enough to understand each other. Do you know what I finally discovered – it's all my eye! This notion of earning an honest penny is all my eye. A man can work a whole lifetime and when he is 65 he considers himself rich if he has saved a thousand pounds. Rich! A whole lifetime of working in a good, steady, settled, enterprising, fascinating job! For every manager in a

232

restaurant there must be twenty chefs terrified of old age. That's all we are – people terrified of old age, hoping for the football pools to come home. It's all my eye, Sarah.

SARAH: I'll make you some tea. Are you hungry?

RONNIE: No, I don't want anything to eat, thank you – I want to talk to you about something.

SARAH: But you must have to eat, you've been travelling all day.

RONNIE [categorically]: I do not want to eat – I want to talk.

SARAH: I'll just make some tea, then; the water's boiled. You sit and relax and then you'll go straight to sleep. You'll see, by the morning you'll feel much better. [Goes to kitchen.]

RONNIE: Still optimistic, Mother. Food and sleep and you can see no reason why a person should be unhappy.

SARAH [from the kitchen]: I'd have looked blue all these years if I hadn't've been optimistic.

RONNIE: How's Harry?

SARAH [entering with two cups of tea]: You'll see him tomorrow; he was too tired to wait up. Want some biscuits? Have a piece of cake. Look, cake I made specially for you – your favourite.

RONNIE [loudly]: Mother, don't fuss. I'm sorry.

SARAH: Is this how you've come home? You start by shouting? Is this a nice homecoming?

RONNIE [something is obviously boiling in him]: Are you still in the Party?

SARAH [quizzically]: Yes.

RONNIE: Active?

SARAH: So?

RONNIE [suddenly]: I don't suppose you've bothered to read what happened in Hungary.

SARAH: Hungary?

RONNIE: Look at me, Mother. Talk to me. Take me by the hand and show me who was right and who was wrong. Point them out. Do it for me. I stand here and a thousand different voices are murdering my mind. Do you know, I couldn't wait to come home and accuse you.

SARAH: Accuse me?

RONNIE: You didn't tell me there were any doubts.

SARAH: What doubts? What are you talking about?

RONNIE: Everything has broken up around you and you can't see it.

SARAH [*shouting*]: What, what, what, you mad boy? Explain what you mean.

RONNIE: What has happened to all the comrades, Sarah? I even blush when I use that word. Comrade! Why do I blush? Why do I feel ashamed to use words like democracy and freedom and brotherhood? They don't have meaning any more. I have nothing to write about any more. Remember all that writing I did? I was going to be a great Socialist writer. I can't make sense of a word, a simple word. You look at me as if I'm talking in a foreign language. Didn't it hurt *you* to read about the murder of the Jewish Anti-Fascist Committee in the Soviet Union?

SARAH: You as well. Monty Blatt came up some months ago and said the same thing. He's also left the Party. He runs a greengrocer shop in Manchester.

RONNIE: And Dave and Ada in the Cotswolds, and Prince working in a second-hand shop, and Uncle Hymie stuck smugly at home and Auntie Cissie once devoted – once involved – wandering from relative to relative. What's happened to us? Were we cheated or did we cheat ourselves? I just don't know, God in heaven, I just do not know! Can you understand what it is suddenly not to know? [*collapses into armchair*] And the terrifying thing is – I don't care either.

[*They sit in silence for some seconds.*]

SARAH: Drink your tea, darling.

[RONNIE *closes his eyes and talks.*]

RONNIE: Do you know what the trouble really is, Mother? Can't you guess?

SARAH: You're tired, Ronnie.

RONNIE: You *do* know what the trouble is. You just won't admit it.

SARAH: In the morning you'll feel better.

RONNIE: Think hard. Look at my face. Look at my nose and my deep-set eyes; even my forehead is receding.

SARAH: Why don't you listen to me? Go to bed and –

RONNIE: Political institutions, society – they don't really affect people that much.

SARAH: Ronnie!

RONNIE: Who else was it who hated the jobs he had, who couldn't bear the discipline imposed by a daily routine, couldn't make sense of himself and gave up?

SARAH [*frightened*]: Are you mad?

RONNIE: I've lost my faith and I've lost my ambition. Now I understand him perfectly. I wish I hadn't shouted at him as I used to.

SARAH: Mad boy!

RONNIE [*rising, opens his eyes and shouts*]: You know that I'm right. *You've* never been right about anything. You wanted everybody to be happy but you wanted them to be happy your way. It was strawberries and cream for everyone – whether they liked it or not. And now look what's happened. The family you always wanted has disintegrated, and the great ideal you always cherished has exploded in front of your eyes. But you won't face it. You just refuse to face it. I don't know how you do it but you do – you just do. [*louder*] You're a pathological case, Mother – do you know that? You're still a *Communist*!

[*He wants to take back his words but he has lost the power to express anything any more. In despair he gives in and turns his face to the wall to cry as he did over* HARRY'S *shouting years ago.*]

SARAH: All right! So I'm still a Communist! Shoot me then! I'm a Communist! I've always been one – since the time when all the world was a Communist. You know that? When you were a baby and there was unemployment and everybody was thinking so – all the world was a Communist. But it's different now. Now the people have forgotten. I sometimes think they're not worth fighting for because they forget so easily. You give them a few shillings in the bank and they can buy a television so they think it's all over, there's nothing more to be got, they don't have to think any more! Is that what you want? A world where people don't think any more? Is that what you want me to be satisfied with – a television set? Look at him! My son! He wants to die!

RONNIE: Don't laugh at me, Sarah.

SARAH: You want me to cry again? We should all sit down and cry?

RONNIE: I don't see things in black and white any more. My thoughts keep going pop, like bubbles. That's my life now – you know? – a lot of little bubbles going pop.

SARAH: And he calls me a pathological case! Pop! Pop, pop, pop, pop – shmop! You think it doesn't hurt me – the news about Hungary? You think I know what happened and what didn't happen? Do any of us know? Who do I know who to trust now – God, who are our friends now? But all my life I've fought. With your father and the rotten system that couldn't help him. All my life I worked with a Party that meant glory and freedom and brotherhood. You want me to give it up now? You want me to move to Hendon and forget who I am? If the electrician who comes to mend my fuse blows it instead so I should stop having electricity? I should cut off my light? Socialism is my light, can you understand that? A way of life. A man *can* be beautiful. I hate ugly people – I can't bear meanness and fighting and jealousy – I've got to have light. I'm a simple person, Ronnie, and I've got to have light and love.

[RONNIE *looks up at her meaningfully.*]

You think I didn't love your father enough, don't you? I'll tell you something. When Ada had diptheria and I was pregnant I asked Daddy to carry her to the hospital. He wouldn't. We didn't have money because he didn't care to work and I didn't know what to do. He disappeared. It was Mrs Bernstein who saved her – you remember Mrs Bernstein? No, of course not, she died before you were born. It was Mrs Bernstein's soup. Ada still has that taste in her mouth – chicken soup with barley. She says it is a friendly taste – ask her. That saved her. Not even my brothers had money in those days and a bit of dry crust with a cup of tea – ah! it was wonderful. But Daddy had the relief money. Someone told me they saw him eating salt-beef sandwiches in Bloom's. He didn't care. Maybe it was his illness *then* – who knows! He was never really a bad man. He never beat us or got drunk or gambled – he wasn't vulgar or coarse and he always had friends. So what was wrong? *I* could never understand him. All I did was fight him because he didn't care. Look at him now. He doesn't care to live. He's never cared to fully undress himself and put on pyjamas; never cared to keep shaved or washed; or be on time or even turn up! And now he walks around with his fly-buttons and his shoe-laces undone because he still doesn't care to fight his illness – and the dirt gathers around him. He doesn't care! And so I fought him because he didn't care. I fought everybody who didn't care. All the authorities, the shopkeepers, even today – those stinking assistance officers – I could buy them with my little finger – even now I'm still fighting them. And you want to be like them, like your father? I'll fight you then.

RONNIE: And lose again.

SARAH: But your father was a weak man. Could you do any of the things he did?

RONNIE: I would not be surprised.

SARAH: Ronnie, your father would never have left his mother to go abroad as you did. I don't tell you all this now to pull you down but on the contrary – so you should know, so you should care. Learn from us, for God's sake learn from us. What does it matter if your father was a weakling, or the man you worked with was an imbecile. They're human beings.

RONNIE: That doesn't mean a thing.

SARAH: There will always be human beings and as long as there are there will always be the idea of brotherhood.

RONNIE: Doesn't mean a thing.

SARAH: Despite the human beings.

RONNIE: Not a thing.

SARAH: Despite them!

RONNIE: It doesn't mean . . .

SARAH [*exasperated*]: All right then! Nothing, then! It all comes down to nothing! People come and people go, wars destroy, accidents

237

kill and plagues starve – it's all nothing, then! Philosophy? You want philosophy? Nothing means anything! There! Philosophy! I know! So? Nothing! Despair – die then! Will that be achievement? To die? [*softly*] You don't want to do that, Ronnie. So what if it all means nothing? When you know that you can start again. Please, Ronnie, don't let me finish this life thinking I lived for nothing. We got through, didn't we? We got scars but we got through. You hear me, Ronnie? [*she clasps him and moans*] You've got to care, you've got to care or you'll die.

[RONNIE *unclasps her and moves away. He tries to say something – to explain. He raises his arms and some jumbled words come from his lips.*]

RONNIE: I – I can't, not now, it's too big, not yet – it's too big to care for it, I – I . . .

[RONNIE *picks up his case and brokenly moves to his room mumbling:* Too big, Sarah – too big, too big.]

SARAH [*shouting after him*]: You'll die, you'll die – if you don't care you'll die. [*He pauses at door*] Ronnie, if you don't care you'll die. [*He turns slowly to face her.*]

CURTAIN